Women World Leaders Presents

BUILDING KINGDOM WEALTH

Aligning Your *Heart*, *Mind*, and *Money* with God's Truth

VISIONARY AUTHORS
MICHELLE TASCOE & JERIBAI TASCOE

Building Kingdom Wealth: Aligning Your Heart, Mind, and Money with God's Truth

Published by World Publishing and Productions, Jupiter, FL
Worldpublishingandproductions.com

ISBN: 978-1-957111-61-2
Library of Congress Control Number: 2026915925

CONTENTS

INTRODUCTION

Are you longing to build kingdom wealth?

For many, striving to build wealth means earning more money, upgrading our lifestyles, and creating a surplus. We figure that if we can get ahead financially, everything else will fall into place. However, there is a difference between building wealth and building *kingdom* wealth.

The world teaches us to chase money, status, and success as fast as we can. It tells us that more is better, faster is smarter, and our possessions define us. But we can gain everything on the outside and still feel empty on the inside. Scripture says, *For what profit is it to a man if he gains the whole world, and loses his own soul?* (Matthew 16:26 NKJV). That question becomes very real when we live it.

The authors of this book want you to do more than gain financial excess; they long for you to experience a transformation that can only come from aligning your heart, mind, and money with God's truth. They have learned that it is impossible to build something that lasts without having God in your corner. As we develop kingdom wealth, we often have to unlearn habits, face worldly patterns, and allow God to reshape the way we think about money, success, and even ourselves. Unless the Lord builds it, we can work as hard as we want and still come up empty in all the ways that really matter.

God has called you to an incredible journey toward kingdom wealth. The path you are about to walk is not random; it's a process. And the process doesn't start with earning more money; it starts with surrender. There comes a moment in our growth when we realize that doing things our way isn't working and we have to release control, trust God beyond what makes sense, and say, "Okay, God… Your way, not mine." Without that surrender, nothing else can truly align.

From that humble stance, everything begins to shift. We start to understand who we really are—not based on our income, our past, or other people's opinions, but based on who God created us to be. And when our identity becomes clear, something powerful happens. The pressure lifts. We stop trying to prove ourselves and start living from a place of security instead of striving.

Then comes healing.

Whether we realize it or not, many of us carry broken beliefs about money, ourselves, and even what we deserve. When we surrender those beliefs, God begins to restore us—changing our perspective and allowing us to see beyond the temporary. As healing takes place, our thinking begins to change. We no longer react the same way or make the same decisions. Fear starts to lose its grip, and we begin to live out faith—building differently as we recognize that it's not just about *what* we build, but *how* we build it. Integrity matters.

As you read and reflect on your own journey, your foundation will get stronger. God will offer you peace as you grow. Together, we will learn that there is a difference between being busy and being led. We will learn to steward our time, money, and responsibilities differently, and we will become intentional, faithful, and aware that what we do with what we have right now matters for eternity.

Growth doesn't come without pressure and challenges. But as you dive into the testimonies in this book, you will witness firsthand how even difficult seasons can refine our character and prepare us for what's ahead. Humility in this process is essential as God works. As you read and process, staying grounded in the truth that protects, something powerful will begin to happen.

Prayerfully reading the testimonies and teachings in this book and allowing God to lead you will put you on the path toward your purpose. Wealth is a tool that has eternal impact, and God has prepared blessings for you that will impact generations.

Hold on tight! Your journey to kingdom wealth won't happen overnight, and it won't always be easy. Allow the stories in this book to lead you toward growth, obedience, and breakthrough. The voices you will hear are not here by accident; each one carries a piece of what God wants to show you.

A lot of people want financial freedom, but not everyone is prepared for the responsibility that comes with it. Without the right foundation, wealth will not last. Without discipline, wealth will slip away. Without alignment, wealth will become a burden instead of a blessing. God is not just interested in increasing what you have; He is interested in developing who you are. Because who you become will determine what you can sustain.

As you turn the pages of this book, slow down and process each nugget. Embrace the experience. Pay attention to what stands out to you. Reflect. Be honest with yourself. And most importantly, apply what you learn. Real transformation doesn't come from information; it comes from application.

God does not want you to stay where you are right now. If you feel behind, as if you've made too many mistakes, or you don't know where to start, please know that none of that disqualifies you. God loves you and will work with what you give Him. Know that we have been praying for you and are excited for where God will take you on this journey.

In your hands, you hold more than a book; you hold an invitation. An invitation to grow as you align your heart, mind, and money with God's truth and build something that truly lasts.

Your journey to kingdom wealth starts now.

SHELLY FOLEY

Pastor Shelly Foley is a dynamic leader with a passion to see every generation rise to positions of responsibility, stability, and strength through a strong understanding of God, His church, and their identity with Him.

For the last 20 years, Shelly has been strategically involved in various forms of ministry, including leading worship, teaching, preaching, and serving. She is committed to bringing strength to her family, church, and community with direct involvement in training, business, and ministry outreaches.

An important part of Shelly's heart is a desire to advance high moral standards and bring a powerful spiritual impact in the business arena. For 13 years, she operated a successful financial consulting business and then transitioned into the corporate finance world in 2012, where she continues to function today.

When the Math Doesn't Math

By Shelly Foley

There are seasons of life when anxiety doesn't announce itself as panic. It's not dramatic; it shows up quieter—practical, reasonable. It may even sound like responsibility and maturity—running numbers late at night, trying to stay one step ahead. For me, financial fear has often worn the mask of being "on top of things."

I'm the kind of person who can't help but do the math. It's how my brain works. I've spent my life paying attention to what's coming in, what's going out, what's due next week, and what might happen next month. And honestly, there are times that kind of attentiveness is a gift: It helps me plan, steward, and avoid being careless. But there's a point where planning crosses the line into something else, when being "wise" quietly turns into carrying weight we were never meant to carry.

The truth is that our world doesn't exactly help us stay on the healthy side of that line. We live in a fear-shaped culture. It's everywhere—on our phones, in the headlines, in conversations at work, even in the little side comments people make like it's normal: "Have you seen the price of groceries?" "I don't know how anyone buys a house anymore." "Hopefully the economy doesn't crash." "I just need to work harder so we'll be okay." Fear can become the atmosphere we breathe. Even when we don't feel like we're afraid, our thoughts and decisions can still be shaped by it.

And finances are one of the clearest places fear shows up. Almost everyone I talk to has felt it: that low-grade hum in the background. The uncertainty. The pressure. The "What if?" What if something breaks? What if I lose my job? What if the market shifts? What if I can't keep up? What if I can't provide? What if I'm not enough?

I've felt those questions, too. There were days—especially when our boys were little—when the numbers didn't look like they were going to work. My husband, Jonathan, was working at our church at the time. It was meaningful work, but it wasn't high-paying. I had stepped back professionally after our first son was born. We were committed to tithing and were trying to live faithfully. And still, there were months when I would sit at our kitchen table staring at what we had and what we needed, and I could feel that old familiar tightening in my chest: *How are we going to make it to the end of the month?* That's what fear does. It narrows your world until all you can see is what's right in front of you. It makes the future feel like a threat instead of a promise. It makes you grip tighter—tighter to money, tighter to control, tighter to your own ability to make it happen.

It's not that the needs aren't real. Food is real. Bills are real. Kids are real. Clothing and shelter are real. Jesus never pretends those things don't matter. But what He does challenge is the space those needs are allowed to occupy in our hearts.

That's why Luke 12 has become one of the most confronting, freeing passages for me—not because I didn't know it, but because I realized I wasn't actually living it.

Jesus says: *"Therefore I tell you, do not be anxious about your life, what you will eat... what you will put on"* (Luke 12:25 ESV).

And if we're honest, that can sound almost offensive at first. *Do not be anxious? In this economy? With these responsibilities? With kids and bills and a future that feels so uncertain?*

But Jesus doesn't stop there. He doesn't scold. He doesn't shame. He doesn't give a three-step plan for managing stress. He gives pictures.

"Consider the ravens... God feeds them" (v. 24 ESV).

"Consider the lilies... how much more will he clothe you" (vv. 27-28 ESV).

It's as if He's saying, "Look around. Creation lives every day depending on the Creator. And you—how much more valuable are you?"

Then God says the line that has worked its way into the deepest places of my decision-making:

"Seek his kingdom, and these things will be added to you" (v. 31 ESV).

That phrase—*seek first the kingdom*—can sound like a slogan if we treat it like one. But when your life is being pressured by worry, it becomes something else. It becomes an anchor. It becomes an antidote. It becomes an invitation to live differently, even when the world around you is spiraling.

Because what Jesus is offering in Luke 12 isn't denial. It's a different foundation. He's not saying, "Ignore your needs." He's saying, "Stop letting fear be your ruler."

He doesn't start with behavior; He starts with authority. I began to realize that worry and God's kingdom don't share authority well. Worry quietly claims control. It tells you that your security depends on your effort. It trains you to interpret every decision through scarcity and narrows your field of vision until provision feels fragile and the future feels like a threat. When worry is in charge, everything feels heavy.

Responsibility becomes pressure. Opportunity becomes risk. Generosity becomes dangerous.

Chapter 12 in Luke isn't about pretending money doesn't matter. Money matters. Stewardship matters. Wisdom matters. Responsibility matters. But what I've learned—slowly, and sometimes through tears—is that the kingdom of God has a different way of shaping a person: a different pace, posture, and kind of security.

The kingdom way doesn't eliminate responsibility, but it does allow us to walk away from the fear underneath the responsibility.

And for me, learning to "seek first the kingdom of God" has been less about becoming more spiritual in theory—and more about becoming more grounded in the Father's heart in real life. Because Jesus doesn't just tell us what to do, He reveals what God is like.

He says, *"Fear not, little flock, for it is your Father's good pleasure to give you the kingdom"* (v. 32 ESV).

For me, the questions underneath everything, especially regarding finances, are: *Do I really believe that? Do I really believe God is a Father who delights to give? Or do I live as if it all depends on me?*

THE COST OF SEEKING HIS KINGDOM

There was a season when seeking God's kingdom first didn't feel poetic; it felt like uncertainty.

My husband, Jonathan, and I were dating; he was one year away from finishing college and had a full scholarship lined up for his senior year. The path in front of him was clear: finish school, graduate, and move forward building a stable life. It was the kind of trajectory parents hope for their children, and planners appreciate. It was good, it made sense. Then God asked him to walk away. And he did—not because he was failing, the opportunity disappeared, or something collapsed, but because God asked him to. His decision wasn't thoughtless, emotional, or impulsive, but was confirmed to him again in ways he couldn't ignore.

Even writing this now, I can still feel the tension of that season. My husband-to-be was so close. One more year. One more stretch. He had a full scholarship. And he wasn't just taking a small step in another direction—he was turning away from something substantial. From the outside, it looked irrational.

We got engaged shortly after he made his decision, and it quickly became our decision. One that appeared to leave us less secure for our future. But then, in a single moment a few months later, things became clear: Jonathan's mom died in a car accident. Looking back, I realized how important it was that he was home, present, and available in a season that none of us saw coming. That one moment reframed that decision for me.

But the story didn't end there. Years later, a prophet from the other side of the country, someone we had never met, gave us a prophetic word about Jonathan returning to school. Previously, when anyone asked him if he would ever return to school, Jonathan's answer had always been simple: "Not unless God tells me to." Well, here we were, God spoke. But receiving a word doesn't automatically answer the how or the when. So we prayed, and God led us to do something bold. We put out a fleece and said, "Lord, if it's time to go back, open up the same scholarship he gave up." It had to be a full scholarship.

The next day, Jonathan called the professor to inquire about scholarships and was told that the scholarship applications had been due the week before. That felt like the door closing. But then the professor added, "If you can get it to me tomorrow, I'll put it in the stack." Months later, we received the call. Jonathan had been awarded the exact same FULL scholarship that he had walked away from.

Now we were facing a new tension: Jonathan would be going back to school, but he was our primary source of income. I was barely working at the time. On paper, it still didn't make sense, but now, something was different. For the first time, I felt the peace of God. Even though I couldn't see how it made sense financially, I knew God had opened the door, and He would provide. And somehow, He did. Door after door opened. That year, we put more money into savings than we had in the previous five years of our marriage. I call it "God math." The numbers didn't make sense. But they were real. It was one of the first times in my life when math didn't math.

That's when something in me began to shift. I realized I had quietly believed that if we let go of something secure, we would lose it—that opportunities don't come back, and stepping off the predictable path carries permanent cost. But that season gently exposed the flaw in that thinking.

Seeking God's kingdom first had looked, in the moment, like stepping off a stable path. But what was not visible is that stability doesn't always lie on the path that looks secure. Stability is always found in our alignment with God's will.

That season didn't make us reckless. It didn't make us passive or even remove responsibility. But it began loosening something in me: the quiet belief that everything depended on our ability to hold the right pieces together.

That season taught me something I couldn't have learned from a sermon. Seeking first God's kingdom doesn't mean you lose ground; it means you stop believing that you are the one holding everything together. What felt like risk was actually obedience. And obedience hadn't cost us the future—it catapulted us into it.

We didn't lose what God intended for us; we learned that His intentions were never ours to secure in the first place.

WHEN OBEDIENCE FEELS FINANCIALLY UNSAFE

It's one thing to trust God with the direction of your life; it's another thing to trust Him with your money.

The scholarship story reshaped something in me, but it didn't eliminate the everyday financial tension. We were still living month to month. We were still raising boys and navigating seasons of tight margins.

And I am not naturally casual about money. I'm an accountant—I calculate, reconcile, and project. That's how I'm built. I don't "hope it works out." I calculate whether it will. So when God nudged us financially, my first response wasn't faith. It was math.

At one church service we attended, a guest speaker was sharing about ministry work happening somewhere across the world. At the end, they invited people to give. Jonathan leaned over and said quietly, "I think we're supposed to give." I remember my immediate internal reaction: From what? We didn't have extra. We weren't sitting on margin. And we were already tithing faithfully. I knew what was in the account and what was coming out. And I didn't feel excited; I felt stretched. There's a quiet fear that surfaces in moments like that. It sounds like wisdom.

Be careful. You don't know what's coming next month. What if something unexpected happens?

Fear is rarely dramatic. It's practical. But we had learned something by then. When God nudges, it's rarely about comfort. It's about trust. So we gave around $350, which felt like a lot of money.

I won't pretend it was comfortable. I gave with tension, believing it was God—and that was enough. Even if my math didn't agree.

The next week, a check showed up in the mail. Five hundred dollars. It was from an obscure IBM dividend connected to something Jonathan's grandfather had done years before. The strange part was that we had already received that check earlier that year. This one said, "replacement check." I called to clarify. According to their records, the original check had never cleared their bank—even though I could see it had cleared ours. There was nothing they could do. So they issued another. The date on the replacement check? The day before we gave.

I just stared at it. The accountant in me wanted clear explanations, logical sequences, and clean reconciliation. But sometimes God's kingdom doesn't reconcile the way spreadsheets do. We had obeyed. And provision had already been in motion.

That moment didn't make me reckless with money. It didn't make me irresponsible, and it didn't turn generosity into a formula for me. It didn't tell me that every act of obedience would result in a financial return. But it exposed something again. I had believed generosity was safest when we had surplus, when everything felt predictable, and when we were ahead.

God was teaching me that generosity is not about surplus. It's about trust.

I need to say this clearly: Not every act of obedience results in a check in the mail. That isn't the point. The point is what happens inside you when fear no longer dictates your grip.

Every time we have opened our hands—not recklessly or irresponsibly, but obediently—God has proven Himself faithful. This has not always happened instantly or dramatically. But it has happened consistently. Sometimes, provision followed in visible ways. Other times, it came quietly. Sometimes, provision showed up in the form of peace. But over and over again, God was faithful—not because we triggered something, but because He is who He says He is.

Fear closes your hands. Trust opens them. Our world tells you to hold tightly, God's kingdom invites you to release. The more I have learned to seek first His kingdom, the more I have realized that generosity is not loss. It's alignment. Generosity is a declaration that my security isn't sitting in an account; it resides in a Father who delights to provide.

A DIFFERENT KIND OF SECURITY

I still have moments when I slip back into math-first thinking. There are times I have that instinct to tighten my grip when things look uncertain, and I still catch myself rehearsing "what if" scenarios in my head. Seeking first God's kingdom hasn't removed responsibility from my life, but it has changed where I look for security. There's a difference.

For years, I thought peace would come when the numbers worked, when there was margin, and I could see clearly how everything would play out. I've learned, however, that peace comes when I remember whose hands my life is actually in. There will still be seasons when math doesn't math, when the numbers don't settle your nerves, and obedience stretches you past what feels reasonable.

God offers us a very different kind of security—not the kind that comes from control, but the kind that comes from trust. Jesus didn't tell us to ignore our needs; He said that our Father knows our needs (Matthew 6:8). That truth has undone me more than once. Your Father knows, and He will provide. Your Father—not your boss, not the economy, not your own effort. And He will not be reluctant about it. *"It is your Father's good pleasure to give you the kingdom"* (Luke 12:32 ESV). Good pleasure—not obligation, not annoyance, not tolerance. Delight.

I think that's where this whole conversation about money lands for me. Do I really believe that God delights to care for me? Because if I do, then I can loosen my grip. If I do, then generosity isn't frightening. Obedience isn't terrifying. Stretching isn't punishment. It's an invitation to participate in His kingdom.

Maybe that's what He wants you to know today. You don't have to try harder or give more. You don't have to feel guilty about anxiety. Consider where fear has been quietly shaping your decisions, and bring that place back under the Father's care.

You don't have to pretend money isn't real. God doesn't want you to stop planning or ignore wisdom. But He does want you to release the weight of being your own provider. You were never meant to carry that alone.

Seeking first God's kingdom isn't about losing control. It's fully giving control to and trusting the One who already holds it. Even when the math doesn't math.

Kyle Negrete

Kyle Negrete wakes up every day excited to serve the world through business and generosity. An entrepreneur by day and aspiring poet by night, he played football at USC and then got a job working on Wall Street in investment banking with Blackstone. Kyle's adventurous spirit led him to move to Haiti in 2016 to run a children's home, and then in 2018, he moved his life to Austin, Texas. He's lived a life of intentional engagement and worked across several sectors (entertainment, venture capital, consulting, and commodities), but has always found the outdoors, community, and social impact at the center of it all.

Generosity and adventure have always been the cornerstones of Kyle's life. In another lifetime, he would have been a full-time cowboy pushing cattle in the West.

Open Hands

By Kyle Negrete

True kingdom generosity is the courageous decision to release what we have been given so that God's love, justice, and provision can flow freely through us to the world. We are called to live with open hands.

I left my comfortable Wall Street job in 2016 to move to Haiti. On paper, it looked like I was walking away from opportunity, security, and the upward trajectory that so many spend their lives chasing. But deep down, I felt God inviting me into something different. Something closer to His heart. I left my job and moved to Port-au-Prince to oversee a children's home with twelve incredible kids. Twelve beautiful, resilient, joy-filled children who had already lived through more hardship than most adults ever will. My job was simple in theory: Love them well. Create a safe home. Build a family. What I did not realize at the time was that those years would reshape my understanding of generosity more than any book, sermon, or financial success ever could.

About half a mile from our house was one of the largest tent cities in Port-au-Prince. The earthquake had displaced thousands of families, and entire communities were living in makeshift shelters. When people imagine tent cities, they often picture rows of tents neatly arranged. The reality was far more raw. Tin roofs patched together with scrap metal. Walls made from Samaritan's Purse tarps stretched across wooden poles. Dirt pathways weaved between homes that could barely withstand a strong rain. The heat was relentless. The smell of charcoal fires hung constantly in the air.

Children ran barefoot through the dust. Life was fragile there, but it was also deeply communal.

I began spending a lot of time walking through that community—not to bring programs or solutions, but simply to build relationships. I wanted to know names, hear stories, and sit with people. Proximity has a way of changing how you see the world. It is easy to talk about generosity from a distance. It is much harder when you are face-to-face with real lives and real needs.

That is where I met Jacob.

Jacob was one of the street kids in the community. He lived with his three brothers, one sister, and his mom. Their home was a tiny structure made from tarps and rusted sheets of tin. He had the kind of smile that made you feel like you had known him forever. From the moment we met, he had this quiet confidence and curiosity about him. Jacob quickly became my guy.

As we built trust, I began inviting him over to my house. My place was simple by American standards, but compared to the tent city, it felt like another world. Jacob loved going up to the roof. From there, you could see across the city, the mountains rising in the distance, and the ocean stretching out on the horizon. He would lean over the edge, eyes wide, taking it all in.

When Jacob came over, we would play games, listen to music, and just hang out. I tried to be intentional about how I helped. I did not want our relationship to become transactional. I did not want him to see me as a walking handout. But I always made sure he ate when he came over.

After a few visits, he discovered one of my favorite childhood staples: peanut butter and jelly sandwiches. But not just any PB and J. The proper way. Slather peanut butter on both slices of bread, then lay down a thick layer of concord grape jelly right in the middle. It is the perfect combination of sweet and salty. Jacob loved them.

Every time he came over, I would make him one, and he would devour it with the enthusiasm of someone discovering a five-star meal. One day, I noticed something strange. I had barely turned around after handing him the sandwich, and it was gone. Completely gone. It felt like I blinked and the sandwich had disappeared.

At first, I thought he was just incredibly hungry. But after a few visits, I started noticing the same pattern. He would take one bite, chew quickly, and then the sandwich would vanish. One afternoon, curiosity got the best of me. When Jacob finished his sandwich and walked downstairs, I quietly followed him outside. I slipped around the side of the house so he could not see me.

That is when I saw the full picture. Standing just outside the gate were two of his older brothers, hiding behind the wall. Jacob reached into the pocket of his cargo pants and pulled out the sandwich, which was not a sandwich anymore. It was a once bitten peanut butter and jelly wrapped in his pocket.

He handed it to his brother, who immediately turned and started running back toward the tent city. The rest of the sandwich was going home to the family. In that moment, my heart broke. At first, I felt a deep sadness. A heaviness. The reality of hunger suddenly felt much closer than statistics or headlines. This was not poverty in theory; this was a little boy saving half a sandwich so his siblings could eat.

But as I stood there watching, something else began to rise inside me—a realization. What I had just witnessed was generosity. Jacob was hungry. Yet the first thing he thought about was his family. Love compelled him to reach through the gate and take care of the people he loved. That image has stayed with me ever since.

A once-bitten peanut butter and jelly sandwich passed through a gate. That was the definition of generosity. Generosity is rooted in love. And love is always asking one question: What am I willing to give for the sake of the beloved?

Love gives.

In that moment, Jacob was not the one receiving generosity. He was teaching it. Through the heart of a son, I caught a glimpse of the heart of the Father.

Fear has a way of tightening our hands, doesn't it? It whispers that there will not be enough—not enough time; not enough money; not enough security. Fear convinces us that survival depends on control. So we are tempted to clench our fists and white-knuckle our way through life, to hold tighter to our resources, attention, influence, and opportunities. We may even quietly build walls around what we believe is ours. The world trains us to protect our territory and secure our future through accumulation. But God's kingdom operates on an entirely different economy, inviting us to open our hands.

Jesus spoke directly to this tension between fear and freedom when He said, *"Do not be afraid, little flock, for your Father has been pleased to give you the kingdom. Sell your possessions and give to the poor. Provide purses for yourselves that will not wear out, a treasure in heaven that will never fail"* (Luke 12:32-33 NIV).

God's kingdom begins with this radical truth that our loving Father has already given us everything. When that truth sinks deep into the soul, generosity stops feeling like loss and begins to feel like liberation. I have discovered something surprising on my own journey: Growing in generosity is growing in freedom against fear. Fear tells us to hold on; faith invites us to release. Fear says to protect yourself; faith requires us to trust God. Generosity becomes the battlefield where these two voices collide inside the human heart.

Simone Weil, a French philosopher, once wrote, "Attention is the rarest and purest form of generosity." Before money ever enters the conversation, generosity begins with attention. Attention to God. Attention to people. Attention to suffering. The moment we truly see the needs of the world, something begins to stir inside us. The Spirit of God awakens compassion.

And compassion demands a response. The real question is not whether we have resources. The real question is whether we have the courage to acknowledge what is happening around us.

One of the greatest temptations of modern life is distraction. Our lives are filled with noise, speed, and constant stimulation. Our calendars are packed, and our minds are occupied. Distraction quietly protects us from proximity to pain. If we never slow down long enough to see the needs around us, we will never feel the weight of responsibility to respond.

Jesus was never distracted from suffering. Scripture tells us that when Jesus *saw the crowds, He had compassion on them because they were harassed and helpless, like sheep without a shepherd* (Matthew 9:36 NIV). Jesus saw. He noticed the overlooked and the invisible, the blind man sitting on the roadside, the widow who placed two small coins in the offering, and the hungry crowd that had no food. Compassion begins with sight. True generosity requires what I would call a courageous capacity to look at the needs of the world. It is courageous because looking creates responsibility. Once we truly see, we cannot pretend that we did not.

There is a natural tendency in every human heart to shrink back from this responsibility. The suffering of the world feels overwhelming. The problems feel too large, and the darkness feels too thick. So we quietly assume someone else will deal with it—someone more qualified or with more money or influence. But the kingdom of God rarely works that way. More often than not, God places a need directly in front of us and waits to see what we will do with it. The Apostle John wrote with striking clarity, *If anyone has material possessions and sees a brother or sister in need but has no pity on them, how can the love of God be in that person?* (1 John 3:17 NIV). Generosity is not primarily about resources. It is about the condition of the heart. A heart aligned with God cannot ignore suffering. The Spirit of God pulls us toward it. Not recklessly, but courageously.

The early church provides one of the most radical pictures of generosity in human history. It was not a financial strategy or a social program, but a spiritual culture shaped by the resurrection of Jesus. The book of Acts describes a community transformed by the power of the gospel.

> *All the believers were one in heart and mind. No one claimed that any of their possessions was their own, but they shared everything they had. With great power the apostles continued to testify to the resurrection of the Lord Jesus. And God's grace was so powerfully at work in them all that there were no needy persons among them* (Acts 4:32-34 NIV).

This passage has always captivated me. Luke does not say the apostles required everyone to sell their possessions. There was no forced redistribution and no legal requirement. This descriptive language was not prescriptive law. God did not require the people to sell everything they owned and bring the proceeds to the church. Yet something remarkable happened. The people desired to share their belongings with other believers. The resurrection had so transformed their understanding of life, eternity, and ownership that generosity became instinctive. Luke continues, *For from time to time those who owned land or houses sold them, brought the money from the sales and put it at the apostles' feet, and it was distributed to anyone who had need* (Acts 4:34-35 NIV). The result was extraordinary. There were no needy persons among them.

Pause and let that statement settle. Poverty had effectively been abolished within that community. Not because of political policy. Not because of economic theory. Because of love. Because believers began to view their possessions through a kingdom lens: Everything belonged to God. Everything was available for His purposes. This is what happened when the church truly functioned like a family. Everyone abdicated their personal claim to ownership for the sake of the community's flourishing. If one person suffered, everyone responded. It became illegal to have poverty in their community—not illegal by law, but illegal by love. That is the culture generosity creates when the Spirit of God transforms a community.

Another lesson from the early church is that generosity is not meant to be abstract, but relational. The early believers did not simply donate to distant causes; they shared life with one another. They knew each other's stories and struggles. Proximity should encourage our generosity. When you sit across the table from someone who cannot pay their rent, generosity becomes personal. Looking into the eyes of a single mother struggling to feed her children makes generosity urgent. When you understand the story behind someone's pain, generosity becomes inevitable.

Jesus modeled generosity via proximity throughout His ministry. He touched the leper that others refused to approach, stopped for the blind man that the crowd tried to silence, and spoke with the Samaritan woman whom society rejected. Jesus did not operate from a distance; He moved toward people.

The incarnation itself is God's ultimate act of proximity. *The Word became flesh and made his dwelling among us* (John 1:14 NIV). God came close to us. Kingdom generosity follows that same pattern—it moves toward people, not away from them. When generosity becomes relational rather than transactional, it begins to transform both the giver and the receiver.

Our culture quietly trains us to expect reciprocity. If I show up for you, you show up for me. If I give to you, you give to me. If I support you, you support me. On the surface, that seems fair. But it is not the way of God's kingdom. Jesus confronted this expectation directly when He said, *"If you love those who love you, what credit is that to you? Even sinners love those who love them"* (Luke 6:32 NIV). The kingdom introduces a radically different motivation for generosity. Love that gives without requiring return. Love that serves without demanding recognition. Love that sacrifices without keeping score.

This kind of generosity can feel risky, unfair, and even lonely. Generosity that depends on reciprocation eventually collapses under disappointment.

Generosity that flows from love remains steady because love is always looking at what it can give, not what it can get. The Apostle Paul writes, *Each of you should give what you have decided in your heart to give, not reluctantly or under compulsion, for God loves a cheerful giver* (2 Corinthians 9:7 NIV). Cheerful giving is not transactional. It is joyful participation in the heart of God.

Something surprising happens when people begin to live generously. It becomes addictive in the best possible way. The joy of giving begins to outweigh the comfort of keeping. Jesus hinted at this dynamic when He said, *"It is more blessed to give than to receive"* (Acts 20:35 NIV). The word "blessed" here refers to a deep and abiding fulfillment.

Generosity unlocks a dimension of joy that accumulation never can. Money promises security, but generosity produces freedom. Possessions promise identity, but generosity produces purpose. The more we give, the more we discover something remarkable: Our God will continue to supply. The Apostle Paul describes this spiritual dynamic clearly when he writes, *Now He who supplies seed to the sower and bread for food will also supply and increase your store of seed and will enlarge the harvest of your righteousness* (2 Corinthians 9:10 NIV). God funds generosity. When someone becomes addicted to giving, God often supports the habit, not as a formula for prosperity, but as a partnership in the work of His kingdom. God entrusts resources to people who are willing to release them.

There are moments in history when glimpses of the kingdom break into the world—moments when communities reflect the heart of God so clearly that something sacred emerges. The emergence of the early church happened during one of those moments. For that window in time, believers looked closely at what God had called them to be. Unity replaced division. Generosity replaced scarcity. Love replaced self-interest. The believers were one in heart and mind. Imagine a world where people truly lived that way: a world where no one clung tightly to possessions, resources flowed freely toward need, and love shaped economic behavior. This is not theoretical; it happened.

The resurrection of Jesus reshaped priorities.

Sustaining that kind of culture requires constant spiritual alignment because selfishness always tries to creep back in. Fear always tries to regain control. The human heart must continually return to the source of generosity, which is God Himself.

At the root of generosity is a transformation of identity. Self-centered living begins to dissolve as our attention shifts outward toward God and others. This transformation mirrors the life of Christ Himself. The Apostle Paul describes Jesus with breathtaking clarity when he writes, *Who, being in very nature God, did not consider equality with God something to be used to His own advantage; rather, he made himself nothing by taking the very nature of a servant* (Philippians 2:6-7 NIV).

Jesus gave Himself away. His life was not organized around self-preservation but around sacrificial love. When the Spirit of God reshapes our hearts, we begin to reflect that same posture. We become less preoccupied with ourselves, and our attention turns outward toward the needs of the world. That is where true generosity is born, not from obligation but from transformation.

The world does not need more cautious generosity. It needs courageous generosity. The kind that refuses to shrink back. The kind that charges into darkness carrying the light of Christ. The kind that sees suffering and responds with love. There will always be reasons to hold back. Fear will always whisper. Scarcity will always threaten. But God's kingdom invites us into a different story. A story where open hands replace clenched fists, resources flow through us rather than stopping with us, and love becomes the organizing principle of our lives.

Jesus said, *"Freely you have received; freely give"* (Matthew 10:8 NIV). Everything we have ultimately comes from God: our time, talents, finances, and opportunities. All of it is a gift. And gifts are meant to be shared. So let love begin with you today. Do not wait for perfect conditions. Do not wait for perfect reciprocation. Do not wait for someone else to go first.

Look at the needs of the world with courage. Pay attention. And when God places something in your hands—even a simple peanut butter sandwich—hear His invitation. With love, take this resource and get this justice done.

Open your hands and step into the freedom of generosity. Because in the kingdom of God, the people who give the most away often discover they never lose anything at all. They simply become free.

> *Where the Spirit of the Lord is, there is freedom*
> (2 Corinthians 3:17 NIV).

VISION

MADE FOR FINANCIAL FREEDOM

God made you to be financially free, and having vision is where you begin.

You cannot build a new financial reality while maintaining your old habits. There is a 2.0 version of you that God designed; stepping into that version begins with seeing it clearly. Scripture tells us that without vision, people perish, which means if you cannot clearly see who you are becoming, you will remain where you are. There is a next level of your life that you are called to live out, especially in your finances. As you commit to consistent growth, you will begin to step into the version of yourself that God has already created you to be.

Understand that financial freedom begins with identity. Three areas shape your financial identity: your way of being, your way of thinking, and your relationship with money.

Your way of being determines how you act. How you think determines the decisions you make. And how you feel about money shapes your behavior around it.

I have seen time and time again that the 2.0 version of a person does not just earn more—they think differently, make better decisions, follow through, and live with intention.

Scripture reminds us, *The Spirit of the Sovereign Lord is on me... to proclaim that freedom for the captives and release from darkness for the prisoners* (Isaiah 61:1 NIV).

Some of you are called to change the entire financial trajectory of your family. Some of you will build a legacy that impacts generations beyond you. And some of you may recognize that you are the one who needs to be set free first. Wherever you are, freedom is available, and it begins with trust.

As you move forward, you are going to become more aware of your finances than ever before. That level of awareness requires objectivity. It's difficult to be objective about money; many people end up not trusting themselves because of past decisions, and some do not trust others, including systems or institutions. Know that there is One you can trust fully, and that is God. He knows your story, your struggles, and your desires, and He will guide you through this process.

Start with who you are. If you were already living in financial freedom, what qualities would you likely exhibit? You would be disciplined, consistent, organized, responsible, prepared, strategic, generous, present, and in control. These are not just actions; they are character traits. Scripture says, *"Be strong and courageous... for the Lord your God will be with you wherever you go"* (Joshua 1:9 NIV). This is wise direction.

When you define who you are, you begin to align your actions with who God called you to be. Discipline and consistency begin to flow. You cannot create a new life while remaining the same person. You must become the person who can sustain what you are building.

Your mindset shapes everything that follows. The thoughts you think daily influence your decisions, habits, and outcomes. When your thinking shifts, the trajectory of your life follows. Scripture says, *Do not be conformed to this world, but be transformed by the renewing of your mind* (Romans 12:2 ESV). Your inner dialogue becomes your outer results.

Many people carry limiting beliefs about money. They believe it is hard to make, that they will always struggle, or that they are not capable of managing it well. Take a moment and see that these thoughts are not true. They are patterns. And patterns can be changed. *God has not given us a spirit of fear, but of power... and a sound mind* (2 Timothy 1:7 NKJV). You have the ability to think intentionally, purposefully choosing your thoughts and actions.

Think of your mind as a container. New vision requires new capacity. Scripture says, *No one pours new wine into old wineskins... new wine must be put into new wineskins* (Mark 2:22 NKJV). Your old mindset may have been reactive, impulsive, or fear-based. Your new mindset must become intentional, proactive, and aligned with truth. You are in control of your thoughts, and you can direct them toward limitation or toward possibility.

God even gives clear instructions on what to focus on: *Whatever things are true... noble... just... pure... lovely... meditate on these things* (Philippians 4:8 NKJV). Begin aligning your thoughts with truth, because this is where transformation begins.

Your relationship with money is the final piece and is often where the most emotion exists. When people think about money, they feel stress, pressure, fear, or uncertainty. Most were never taught how to manage money, so it feels overwhelming. Believe that your relationship with money can change.

Even King David had to redirect his thoughts and emotions. *Why are you cast down, O my soul?... Hope in God* (Psalm 42:11 NKJV). You can move from stress to peace, from fear to confidence, and from uncertainty to clarity. This shift begins when you decide how you want to relate to money moving forward.

Define who you are becoming, what you are choosing to think, and how you want to feel about your finances. The life you build will reflect those decisions. This process requires commitment. It requires showing up consistently and doing the work. Over time, you will begin to see transformation take place, not just in your finances, but in who you are becoming.

Financial freedom begins the moment you decide who you are becoming.

JOURNAL REFLECTION

1. Who is the 2.0 version of you that God is calling you to become?
2. What are the three ways of being that define that version of you?
3. What thoughts have you been carrying that are keeping you in your current reality?
4. What thoughts do you need to begin aligning with truth?
5. What is one decision you can make today that aligns with who you are becoming?

Jeribai Tascoe

Jeribai Tascoe is an HGTV host/designer, licensed real estate agent, real estate investor, and creative entrepreneur. With a background in branding, design and development, home renovations, and real estate strategy, Jeribai helps clients navigate big decisions with clarity, creativity, and results. Outside of work, he hones his discipline on the jiu-jitsu mats, fuels his musical creativity behind the drum kit, and brings the same passion for excellence to every area of life.

Jeribai passionately desires to see men and women move beyond fear and confusion into true identity, manifesting their unique God-given greatness within. With the heart of a coach that encourages, challenges, and motivates, he operates with a grace that combines spiritual inspiration with practical wisdom and strategy to live a powerful life.

Along with serving God and others, some of Jeribai's greatest joys are in being a husband and father, and in enjoying the moments of adventure and discovery with his wife and each of his children. His heart's desire is to see men truly understand the joy and fulfillment that comes from leading with love and living a life of service to others.

TRUE WORTH

By Jeribai Tascoe

I was 14 when I earned my very first dollar by raking up what seemed to be endless layers of pine needles and fallen autumn leaves from the neighbor's yard. The piles got higher and higher as my hands turned red and grew sore inside the yard gloves that were two sizes too big. A blister was developing on my palm, and I got a splinter from the aging rake handle as I pulled the last pile together.

"I think I'm all done," I said to the homeowner.

He smiled widely and congratulated me on doing such a great job, then paid me with cold, hard cash—twenty-five big ones for five hours of raking. I still remember the walk home, pulling out the money again to look at it, holding it with my sore hands, and congratulating myself on a job well done. I had received money before, for a missing tooth or for a birthday gift from grandma, but this money was different... I earned it.

That first moment of earning did a lot for me as a young boy. I really loved how it made me feel: accomplished, valuable, and powerful. I grew up in a good home with good parents, including a father who taught me the value of working hard and a mother who taught me how to shop smart. I'll never forget my dad's familiar motto while we worked around the house: "You gotta learn how to work, son!" I wasn't handed anything. I had to earn almost everything. It was good training, and I'm so thankful for it, but my learning about earning was just getting started.

My mother, the thrift shopper and patient deal-hunter, often outfitted me with non-name-brand clothes. She bought me shoes that looked like the latest Nikes, but were cheap imitations; "Fakies," the kids would call them, regularly making fun of me for my inauthentic apparel. I would later come to understand my mother's brilliance better. Still, those early moments in life really carved something into my soul—a deep-seated desire for material possessions so that people wouldn't make fun of me or perceive me as some poor, ethnic kid. I never resented my parents for where we were financially, I always knew they worked their hardest to provide us kids a good life. Even so, I became driven, determined to prove myself.

For the next ten years, I proceeded to work and work and work. More yard work jobs. Detailing cars. Washing dishes, prep cooking, and bussing tables at a local restaurant. I worked in construction as a laborer, putting in some serious shovel time digging footings on the side of a hill with my best friend. At the end of that week, not only did I get paid, but my dad rewarded me by buying me my own steak, cooking it for me, and letting me eat it on a TV tray in the living room while we watched the baseball game together. He said I had just completed a week of "man work." Earning was working; I felt proud and accomplished, but several problems remained.

Every time I earned money, it left my hands as fast as I made it. I had so many ambitions and a never-ending shopping list of things I wanted to buy; often, I spent my money in my mind before I even finished earning it. My developing work ethic and understanding of earning were good, but it still took me years to understand the motives propelling my drive to earn. I was in what I call the EARN and BURN stage. I worked super hard for the money, but it hardly worked for me. I bought so much silly status stuff, learning later that one of my money motivators was status.

Helping to prop up that status was my first credit card. I applied for one when I was 17; it was a slick black and orange Discover card with a matte silver magnetic strip just waiting to be swiped. At first, I was careful and only bought what I could afford, paying off the balances in full, but not long after, my undeveloped discipline caved into my growing desires: the shoes, hats, paintball gear, music gear, software—almost anything I wanted was a simple, single swipe away.

Greed is hungry for speed, and I quickly started down a dangerous path of just covering minimum payments and getting smacked with monthly interest charges. To add to the already insane bonfire of bad purchasing decisions, I financed a car and new computer equipment for my newly formed graphic design business, then decided to quit my perfectly decent day job to live the "dream" of working for myself.

I was now 21 years old with four maxed-out credit cards, a car payment, office equipment payments, rent, and expenses. I was working endless hours at multiple jobs and doing freelance design work late into most nights just to keep up with minimum payments and not get buried in late charges. The only good thing I had going for me was that I didn't miss making payments, which I later discovered was a strange excuse and reason why I continued to overspend. My pride was driving me to do whatever it took to look good, not only publicly, but even on paper.

I kept thinking it was a dignified thing not to miss a payment, which, don't get me wrong, IS A MUST for anyone paying their credit cards. But I was mentally wrapping a sliver of dignity in layers of ambition, greed, and status, then deep frying all that in a vat of pride and serving it up with a side of shame. I was buying and building this life to look like I had it all together, so I couldn't afford to fail; therefore, missing a payment wasn't an option. It wasn't discipline, but a carefully crafted deception that I was eating up.

The way of a fool is right in his own eyes, but a wise man listens to advice (Proverbs 12:15 RSV).

I was the problem. I didn't listen. I wanted to do it by myself, for myself, and it was a miserable, lonely road. I had to get out of the debt hole I dug for myself. My pride would barely even allow me to pray to God to help me out of the hole I was in. "I broke it, so I'll fix it," is what I kept telling myself, all the while sliding further into the dungeon of debt.

Finally, one day it came to a head, and thank God it did. Our God is so merciful and kind; it's His goodness that leads us to repentance. I was reminded of Proverbs 28:13—*He who covers his sins will not prosper, But whoever confesses and forsakes them will have mercy* (NKJV). I was doing everything I could think of to prosper, pay off my debts, catch up, and keep my head above water, but I was leaning on my own strength, ability, and efforts. I was following my own ways and was blind to the root issues of striving, greed, and, ultimately, shame.

I had to deal with the pride first. "Lord, I need Your help. I'm a mess, I've made a mess. And most of all, I'm not trusting You." I remember praying and asking the Lord what I needed to do; He showed me three things I needed to do to get back on track.

The first thing was tithing. I was taught to tithe as a boy, and for the most part, I would give 10% of my wages each month. But as I got older, and especially when the money was tight and the bills came knocking, I would surrender God's portion of His provision to my purchases and prideful ambition.

God's portion must always come first. I had to repent. As Jesus teaches us in Matthew 6:19, I was laying up trivial, earthly treasures for myself and struggling at best to do that. I was full of the lust of the eyes and the pride of life; my heart was way off, completely focused on self and the appearance of success. So I began tithing again, the full 10%. And even when it seemed like I was going to be short on a bill, I somehow always had just enough. God was helping!

The second thing was to freeze all frivolous spending—immediately. I stopped shopping, eating out, and going to the movies every week. I had to face the facts and acknowledge where my money was going as it flooded out of my bank account. I locked it down and got disciplined about my spending habits, which led me to a life-changing personal revelation. Yes, I was buying stuff, but ultimately, I was really trying to buy happiness. I had no joy, peace, or relationship with God. I started to realize how poor I was in things that He is so wealthy in. Right then, the Lord started to shift my heart to truly want treasure in heaven. I know, I know, it sounds so virtuous and enlightened, but really, this was a huge moment of deliverance. Earthly things are temporary, but heavenly things are eternal. I had a radical shift from obsessing about earthly things to developing a hunger and desire for only godly things.

I can barely express what a mind-blowing transformation this was. My debt didn't magically disappear, the bills kept coming, and the work still needed to be done, but for the first time in years, I had peace in my heart. I knew that God was going to help me in the place where it mattered the most: the position of my heart towards Him. And as I focused on Him, He was with me, helping me ditch the debt as I slowly began to shovel my way out. He empowered me whenever the urge to shop or the temptation to strive tried to lure me back into the old pride cycles. He guided me and gave me His peace when He led me to leave a good-paying job, take a huge pay cut, and go to work for my dad in an unrelated field. He was cheering me on when I wrote that last check to pay off the last credit card, and He has strengthened me, allowing me to remain free of credit card debt ever since.

The third thing God asked me to do was surrender my identity to Him. This lesson has been a recurring one as the Lord has walked me through stages of learning to trust Him, totally rely on Him, and completely depend on Him. I was shifting from living for the approval and applause of people to living for His purposes and promises.

The first stage of this was after I paid off $36,000 in past debt in a little under two years. I know the Lord helped me stay consistent and find some creative ways to generate extra money to tackle the debt. One of these ways was to sell clothes and musical gear on eBay. I got good at rehabbing snare drums and reselling them online as a little side hustle that ended up generating enough money to really attack the credit cards and chop those down.

Then, I began to ask the Lord about making purchases. I could sense in my heart what was foolish and what was wise. This seems like a little thing, but these were moments of surrender, letting the Lord lead me and teach me.

My work life stabilized, and the Lord opened the door for me to step into working for a marketing agency doing all their graphic design and web development. This was the beginning of about a 15-year run of great abundance with good employers and smart money moves. At 28 years old, I got married, and Michelle and I began building our life together. We both worked, saved, and learned how to trust the Lord along the way.

We bought our first home in 2010 at the bottom of the recession and fixed it up. We later went on to sell the property and make a good sum of money. As we were renovating the property, I remembered how I had been renovating drums in the past while climbing out of the debt hole. Now we were doing the same, but with houses, and not to put towards debt, but to put towards investments. God had been teaching me stewardship and money management even in the middle of my darkest debt days. He is always faithful to lead us and grow us as we grow in our willingness to surrender.

The most recent stage of learning the lesson of surrender came when the Lord led me to leave the comfort of a 20-year career in the creative world without a next career in sight. I had gotten my real estate license so we could keep more of the proceeds after selling one of our renovated homes, and I had taken a part-time job with our local church to partner with others in developing various things, but my heart was unsettled again. Our finances were stable, we had savings, and Michelle's business was exploding—this was all great, but my heart was still unsettled. I wasn't making nearly as much money as I used to, but I had grown in trusting the Lord for His provision, so I wasn't doubting that He would provide. I just hadn't been this seemingly inactive since I was 14.

One night, I found myself unable to sleep, and I started pacing in the entryway of our home. I couldn't figure out what was going on inside my chest, so I started praying and asking the Lord what was happening.

"Do you trust Me?" I sensed Him asking me in my heart.

Out loud, I said, "Yes, Lord, I trust You. I'm just frustrated, I guess, because I'm not sure about my next move with my career, and I haven't made this little of money since I was 14, so what kind of man am I if I can't provide for my family?"

The Lord responded, asking a question I did not at all see coming, "Who is the provider?"

I replied, "You are, Lord. I know you're providing for us, but..."

"Who is the provider?" He asked again.

Then it hit me. The next stage of surrender had just shown up. It was time for an identity check. Up until that moment, I had endeavored to operate as any godly man would: work hard to provide for the family. But buried in there for me was this hidden root of pride that I was the one making it all happen. That, because of my "hard work," I had earned my identity as a provider, a designer, an investor, a professional this-or-that. Now that those titles were in flux, the Lord showed me how my heart found significance in the job title and pay, rather than how He sees me and treasures me as a son.

That was a monumental moment of deliverance. All those years, ever since I was a young teenage boy raking leaves, I had been drawing my sense of worth and significance from what I earned, what I was able to produce, and what I was able to create. I'll never forget dropping to my knees in the entryway of that home, asking God to deliver me from mammon. My identity was wrapped up in earthly riches, and I trusted in my own skill and ability to generate riches, which is serving mammon. I was more devoted to mammon and worshipping the false god of money, which was evidenced by where my heart was at: unsettled, worried, fearful, and prideful. When the pay was taken away, my heart fell away. But God's mercy and faithfulness are so much greater than even our own hearts.

I spent some time before the Lord that night, repenting and declaring that He was all I would ever need. He alone is worthy of my time, strength, emotions, work—everything. I had already spent 40 years reading the Bible and growing up in the church, but this was a new moment, a great awakening to the truth: God is all; God has it all; and God is worthy of it all. As the night wore on, my heart began to settle down, and I became secure in the Lord in a way that I could have never earned. He did it. He secured me. He set my feet on the right path.

God changed my heart and my life, and I know He can change yours.

No matter where you may be on your journey with your finances, your work, your debts, your business, or your bills, know that God is able. And He will be faithful to show you the way as you surrender your ways to Him. He teaches us how to be faithful stewards—servants who can be trusted with many responsibilities and who know that the Lord will help shoulder those responsibilities, businesses, and opportunities.

My prayer is that this book, with all its stories of the goodness and faithfulness of God, will drive you into His arms as His son or daughter and that you will find your true worth in Him and Him alone. He has so much for you and will always provide for your every need. Work heartily unto the Lord, trust Him in all your ways, and lean on Him even when it seems impossible. He is able, and He is worthy. He will do exceedingly above all you can ask or even think.

I pray that you encounter Him as your true worth today.

CASSANDRA ROY

Cassandra Roy is a native of Los Angeles, California. She is a product of the Los Angeles Unified School District, where she attended 36th Street School (now known as Bright Elementary School), Foshay Junior High School, and Susan Miller Dorsey High School. After graduating from high school, she attended the Fashion Institute of Design and Merchandising—earning an AA degree in Merchandising, Immaculate Heart College—earning a Bachelor of Arts degree in English, and Mount Saint Mary's University—earning a Master of Science Degree in Counseling and Guidance.

Raised by a single mother, Cassandra was instilled with the life skills that would help shape her into the person she is today—including having a strong belief in God and His Son, Jesus Christ, the courage to speak her truth and speak up for others, empathy for all, and focus on her goals.

In addition to contributing to this anthology, Cassandra is writing two children's books titled *Leilani Meets Lyle the Lizard* and *Mrs. Tuggle Finds A Rocket.*

You Are Not Alone

By Cassandra Roy

"For I know the plans I have for you," declares the Lord, "plans to prosper you and not to harm you, plans to give you hope and a future" (Jeremiah 29:11 NIV).

He will cover you with his feathers, and under his wings you will find refuge; his faithfulness will be your shield and rampart (Psalm 91:4 NIV).

There is something sacred about dreams. Over the years, I have come to believe they are one of God's tender ways of preparing us for the plans He has already written for our lives. Many times, I have dreamed something that later came to fruition, and each time it reminded me that He goes before me.

One particular dream still lingers in my heart as if it happened yesterday. In it, I was sitting around a fire pit with many women. They came from every race, background, and walk of life. Though masks hid their faces, somehow I knew they had been sent to help me. I was crying, and as each tear slid down my face, a woman silently poured water over the rocks and the fire.

At the time, I didn't think much of it, but tucked the odd but comforting dream away in the back of my mind. Little did I know that the dream was a promise. God was whispering to me that a time was coming when I would be broken and need help, and that I would not be alone. That dream gave me a quiet assurance: No matter how hard things got, I would not fail.

> *The righteous person may have many troubles, but the Lord delivers him from them all* (Psalm 34:19 NIV).

One of my longest and most painful battles has been with my finances. My relationship with money was never easy; in fact, for many years, it brought me nothing but shame and embarrassment. I carried the weight of that shame like a shadow I hid behind. But there came a point when I realized something had to change.

I grew up attending public schools in Los Angeles, on what was then known as the West Side, during the 1960s. My mother became a widow when I was just 10 years old. Losing my father left a hole in my life that I would only begin to understand many years later.

Academically, most subjects came easily to me—except math. Numbers confused and frustrated me, ultimately becoming the source of deep shame. Teachers judged me. My classmates teased me. I remember sitting in class, horrified because I couldn't solve a simple equation on the board. With each humiliation, I withdrew further and, eventually, I stopped trying altogether. I decided numbers were my enemies, and that was the end of it.

But of course, life doesn't let us escape numbers. As I grew older, I found ways to compensate. I leaned on others to solve problems, relied heavily on calculators, and when that failed, I cried in frustration. And through all of it, I prayed that God would remove the shame I carried, would lift the heavy veil, and that somehow, He would forgive me for what felt like an unforgivable weakness.

But the truth is, I wasn't just asking Him to help me with math. I was asking Him to help me with the shame itself.

After I got married, my husband and I split our expenses evenly, but the weight of managing the money fell squarely on me. Fear and anxiety would grip my heart every time I sat down to balance the budget. The numbers would float on the page, and I felt so overwhelmed that when it looked like there wasn't enough money to cover everything, I turned away from managing it, promising myself I would catch up next month.

When the next month came, and there still wasn't enough money, I did the same thing. The pattern continued. Before I knew it, bill collectors began calling. I would offer an excuse and promise to bring the account current. Then I would pay that bill, leaving another unpaid. I was too embarrassed to tell my husband what was really happening.

Finally, one day, my husband answered the phone when a bill collector called. When he confronted me, I broke down in tears and admitted I was not doing a decent job of paying the bills. So he and my mother took over managing our finances. I felt both relieved and devastated. I was a well-educated, successful woman in my 40s who was unable to manage paying bills. That realization was as painful as it was humbling.

The breaking point came years later, when, after my husband and my mother had died, I found myself drowning in debt. Not a little debt, but thousands upon thousands of dollars. The calls were so frequent I became familiar with the debt collectors; we were practically on a first-name basis. I would even ask about their families.

I knew every payday loan office within a ten-mile radius of my house, and yet somehow, every single month, I was overdrawn again. I was spinning in circles, patching holes with more holes, and the shame grew heavier by the day.

I'll never forget the time my sister, who worked for Mastercard, called me about my overdue balance. To hear the seriousness in her voice, mixed with the knowledge that she was both my sister and a representative of the very company I owed, was more than I could bear. I wanted to disappear.

I told myself three things needed to happen. First, I had to strengthen my relationship with God. I knew that without Him, no amount of planning or budgeting could heal what was broken inside of me.

> *The Lord is my strength and my shield; my heart trusts in him, and he helps me. My heart leaps for joy, and with my song I praise him* (Psalm 28:7 NIV).

Second, I had to forgive myself for my failures. If God could forgive me, I could forgive myself.

> *"I, even I, am he who blots out your transgressions, for my own sake, and remembers your sins no more"* (Isaiah 43:25 NIV).

And third, I had to find someone who could help me.

> *The way of fools seems right to them, but the wise listen to advice* (Proverbs 12:15 NIV).

I prayed for all three. And slowly, God began answering. It was then, in the middle of my desperation, that I knew I couldn't do this alone. I began searching for a financial life coach. As I did, something about one particular description made me pause. I prayed as I read, asking God if this was who He was sending to help me.

Gathering my courage, I called and left a message. I poured my heart into that voicemail, hoping that somehow, through the sound of my voice, she would hear not just my words but my pain, my desperation, my silent cry for help.

A day later, the phone rang.

"Hi, I'm Michelle Tascoe, returning your call. How can I help you?"

I will never forget that moment. The sound of her voice broke me open. I started to cry—not just quiet tears, but the kind of sobs that come from exhaustion, from years of carrying burdens too heavy for one person. I was ashamed, hopeless, and at the end of myself. But her voice gave me something I hadn't felt in a long time: comfort and hope.

I poured everything out to her: my struggles with math in school, the emptiness created by the losses of my husband and my mother, and even how I had tried to fill that emptiness with shopping. I confessed that retail therapy had become my bandage, my way of soothing wounds I didn't know how to heal. I told her I was tired of the spiral, of destroying myself, and of being an emotional wreck who could not be trusted.

Michelle listened. She didn't interrupt, scold, or judge. She simply listened. And in that listening, I began to feel a small seed of dignity returning to me.

When I reflected on how I ended up with insurmountable debt, I realized that whenever I became stressed, I shopped. Shopping was my drug of choice. I had a hole inside—one I believed shopping for new clothes would fill. When I shopped, the focus was on me. When I wore a new outfit, people complimented me, and I basked in those compliments.

As I surrendered to God and the Holy Spirit, I came to understand that it was not about the garments I wore, but about what was emanating from within. What people were truly seeing was what lived inside of me.

Then I remembered the dream about the women around the fire pit. And I realized that meeting Michelle was its fulfillment. God had promised I would not be alone, and now I had met a woman who was pouring water on the fire of my shame.

My healing journey was not quick, and it was not easy. There were many tears, many moments when I wanted to give up. But with each conversation, each small step, Michelle helped me build not just a financial plan, but a new way of seeing myself. She reminded me that I was not a failure. She reminded me that forgiveness—even self-forgiveness—is a gift God gives freely.

I began to learn that my worth is not tied to numbers in a bank account, my dignity can never be erased by debt, and my past mistakes have not destroyed my future.

God works through the most unexpected means. Sometimes, He sends us dreams to prepare us, and sometimes He sends us people—strangers who become lifelines. Other times, He waits until we have reached the end of ourselves so that we will finally turn to Him with empty hands and an open heart.

Today, I am still on the journey. I am not perfect, and I still face challenges. But I walk with far less shame and far more faith. I have learned to ask for help and accept grace. And I have learned that no matter how deep the pit feels, there is always a way out when we turn to God.

I am now entering an exciting phase of my life as I realize in a deeper and more meaningful way that I can truly do all things through Christ, who strengthens me (Philippians 4:13). My past is in the past, and through my experiences, I have learned lessons that have shaped me and brought me to where I am today.

I contribute where I am now to God's grace and mercy. When I look back over my life, I see His hand guiding me even in moments when I did not fully understand what He was doing. His love and patience have carried me through seasons of joy and seasons of deep challenge. God's plan is always greater than anything I could design for myself. Overcoming my struggles with money has given me a new lease on life.

Recently, I celebrated my 75th birthday. When I was growing up, my mother was a single parent who often worked two jobs just to make ends meet. Yet, no matter how difficult things were financially, she always made my birthday feel special. Every year there was a celebration, and every year I had a new outfit. My mother made those outfits herself, carefully sewing each one with love. She continued doing that until she developed cataracts and could no longer sew.

The thing is, those birthdays were never about extravagance or expensive gifts, but about love, intention, and the joy of celebrating life. To this day, I am overjoyed to celebrate my birthday each year because it reminds me not only of my life but also of the love and sacrifice of my mother.

This year's birthday celebration was no exception. In fact, I like to say that every day in February is National Cassandra Month. Most of those celebrations do not cost anything at all. For example, I may spend a day watching a new television show I have been curious about or take a trip to visit a free museum. Sometimes the celebration is simply taking time to reflect on how blessed I am to still be here.

During my birthday celebrations this year, something very meaningful happened. My friends, former students, and sorority sisters took the opportunity to tell me how they felt about me and what our relationship has meant to them. Their words were both humbling and encouraging, and they reminded me that the seeds we plant in others' lives do bear fruit. Sometimes we do not see the results right away, but the impact is there. Each word spoken to me during those celebrations gave me strength and renewed motivation to pursue the goals I have set for myself this year.

As I was planning my birthday celebrations, I initially envisioned two days of what I thought would be epic events. However, when I added up the numbers and considered the costs, what I was planning to ask my friends to spend on my behalf did not sit right with my spirit. I knew that asking others to spend what I could not personally afford would be insensitive. That realization caused me to pause. The best thing I knew to do was to pray about it.

As I prayed about what to do, I experienced a struggle between what I wanted to do and what I felt was the right thing to do. It was the struggle between trusting the Spirit's guidance and trusting my ego, or what I like to call E.G.O.— "Edging God Out." I thank God that in that moment, the spiritual and right choice won easily. After prayer and reflection, I reorganized my plans and sent out new invitations with different venues that were more thoughtful and reasonable.

I've learned that the true joy of celebration does not come from the extravagance of the event, but from the fellowship, laughter, and love shared among the people who come together. When we resist the temptation to let ego guide our decisions and instead allow the Holy Spirit to speak to us, life becomes much richer and more meaningful. And in those moments, we receive clarity and understanding about what God truly has in mind for us.

As I look ahead to this year, I realize that this stage of life represents an entirely new chapter for me. During a recent conversation with my pastor, she asked me what my plans were for the future as I move forward in life. I must admit that her question caught me by surprise. While I had been thinking about the future, my ideas were not yet fully formed.

However, one Scripture has become central to how I approach both my daily life and my long-term goals. Jeremiah 29:11 (NIV) reminds us: *"For I know the plans I have for you," declares the Lord, "plans to prosper you and not to harm you, plans to give you hope and a future."* Whenever I begin to feel overwhelmed or discouraged, I return to this verse and remind myself that God is always on my side.

Part of my future includes completing and publishing my first children's book, *Leilani Meets Lyle the Lizard.* Writing this book has been a dream that has lived in my heart for some time. Another goal is earning my pastor's license in the Four-Square Church. I have always wanted to serve as a pastor in some capacity, but for many years, the timing simply did not seem right. Now I understand that the time has come. Every experience I have had has prepared me for this calling and has positioned me to be a blessing to others.

Today I serve as a member of the leadership team at my church, NewLife LA. My pastors, Todd and Michelle Clease, have encouraged and supported my growth as a spiritual leader. I currently serve as the Baptism Coordinator, an usher, and a prayer warrior.

If someone were to ask me what my greatest joys in life have been so far, two things would come immediately to mind. The first is seeing my son, David, grow into the remarkable person he is today. He is kind, principled, and a gifted artist. Watching him become the man he is today has been one of the greatest blessings of my life.

The second joy has been working with Michelle Tascoe. Her patience and unending kindness have helped me learn how to manage my finances and budget more effectively. She has taught me the importance of setting achievable goals and extending grace to myself when I fall short. I may not yet be exactly where I want to be financially, but I am no longer where I used to be. And for that, I am grateful.

When I first entered my seventies, I began to believe that perhaps I did not have much left to offer. Negative thoughts tried to convince me that I was simply getting old and was no longer useful. Thankfully, before those thoughts could take permanent residence in my mind and spirit, I turned to prayer.

I asked God what He had in mind for me in this season of life, and He healed me in greater ways than I could have imagined.

I placed my trust in God, and He heard my prayers.

If sharing my story helps even one person take that first brave step toward healing, then all my years of struggle will not have been in vain. If you turn to God, He will cover you with His feathers. Under His wings you will find refuge. You are not alone.

HEALING

BREAKING FINANCIAL SHAME

As you move forward to getting your finances on track, healing must be addressed. Freedom begins when you release what you've been carrying for far too long, allowing God to heal what has been shaping your decisions.

God purposely placed desires inside you, and it is time for you to step into them. You already sense that you were created for more—you know you are meant to grow, increase, and be a resource for God's kingdom. That inner knowing is evidence of something God has already planted within you.

Often, the area in which we struggle the most becomes the very place we experience the greatest breakthrough. I know this personally. There was a season of financial destitution in my life when it was difficult to manage what little I had just to make it to the next paycheck. I had learned how to survive in lack, but I had not yet learned how to live in freedom. That began to change when I encountered a new way of thinking that gave me permission to believe that my past did not define my future.

One of the greatest barriers to financial freedom is financial shame. Many people try to move forward while still carrying the weight of the past. They take action, but something continues to pull them back into the same patterns. When the root of the issue is not addressed, new results do not last. True transformation requires healing at the source. It requires us to forgive ourselves or others.

Joseph's story in Genesis reflects this clearly. Joseph had a vision for his life, but his journey included being betrayed, rejected, and enduring hardship. Although his own brothers had sold him into slavery, God continued working through every part of his life. Joseph was eventually placed in a position to lead and steward resources during a time of famine. When the moment came to face those who had hurt him, Joseph had a choice. He could hold onto resentment, or he could trust the bigger picture of what God had done and choose to release the shame he had endured.

Joseph proclaimed to his brothers, *"You intended to harm me, but God intended it for good to accomplish what is now being done"* (Genesis 50:20). Forgiveness allowed Joseph to step fully into his purpose. If he had held onto the offense thrust upon him, it would have limited his ability to lead, provide, and walk in the fullness of what God had for him.

Unforgiveness does not stay contained. It affects how we think, make decisions, and move forward. Bitterness can quietly take root and block growth, shaping your perspective and limiting your capacity to receive what God is trying to do in your life.

Sometimes, we must forgive other people, and other times we must forgive ourselves. We often carry more frustration toward ourselves than toward anyone else. We replay past mistakes, hold onto regret, and allow guilt to define how we see ourselves. That weight can keep us stuck.

Ask God, *Create in me a pure heart, O God, and renew a steadfast spirit within me* (Psalm 51:10 NIV). When you bring your shame and blame before God, He restores what has been broken and clears the way for you to move forward.

As we forgive, our perspective begins to shift. We begin to see possibilities again. Healing and freedom meet. When we release what has been holding us back, we create space for what God wants to build in our lives.

Freedom is not just about what you are moving toward. It is also about what you are willing to release. When you let go of the past, you step into a new level of clarity, confidence, and purpose.

As you choose to forgive, fully and completely, you will begin to experience a level of freedom that changes how you see yourself and how you approach your finances. You will no longer be building from pain. You will be building from the truth.

When you release the past, you finally have the capacity to build your future.

JOURNAL REFLECTION

1. Who comes to mind when you think about your hurt? Write down their name(s).
2. If someone came to mind that you thought you had already forgiven, don't resist it. Allow yourself to recognize if any unforgiveness is still there. What are you still feeling when you think about them?
3. Now take a step deeper as you seek God's power to forgive. What are you ready to release?
4. Search your own heart. What do you want God to forgive you for? What has been heavy on your heart that you have not brought fully to Him?
5. Ask God for His forgiveness and allow Him to begin to restore your heart and clear the way for you to move forward.

April Snook

April Snook is a certified Christian life coach, speaker, and podcast host who has spent 25 years helping people learn how to do real life with the REAL God. Through speaking, podcasting, and coaching, she shares inspirational and instructional personal stories that stir a deeper thirst for God and make faith practical, personal, and accessible.

April's passion is helping women hear God when life gets loud—when distractions, pressure, and inner noise make it difficult to discern His voice. She teaches women how to recognize the Holy Spirit's guidance, renew their thinking, and partner with God in everyday moments, not just in spiritual settings.

Through her coaching and content, April equips women to break free from mental cycles, regain joy and peace, and live fulfilled, Spirit-led lives. Her approach is warm, practical, and faith-rooted, empowering women to discover that God is already speaking and they are already equipped to hear Him.

Learn more at TheWellHouseLife.com.

LEAVING LIMITATIONS

By April Snook

It's amazing how we can pinpoint the very moment a major shift happens.

I'm not talking about those win-the-lottery moments that instantly alter your circumstances or the subtle changes of building income where—due to diligence and sweat equity—you find yourself so far from where you started: thankful, but measurable.

I'm talking about the kind of increase that has little to do with your circumstances and everything to do with who you are—those moments right in the middle of the messy and the mundane that transform how you experience life. When your situation is still the same and your need is still present, but everything is redefined—because something in you has taken root.

This is my wealth story—the moment my entire life and legacy shifted, although I only had $30 in hand. The story where God took my moment of need, surpassed it by providing my want, and taught me how to do life with Him. It's the foundational revelation that delivered me from scarcity, reframed need into opportunity, and launched every adventure, every victory, and hope for every dream. It's the testimony that keeps me dreaming bigger when most people are slowing down, settling, and believing the lie that they have to live smaller as they grow older.

Regardless of whether you are believing God for your next million dollars or enough to pay the mortgage this month, there is a richer way to live—a life filled and fulfilled regardless of need. My story is not about getting rich quickly; it's about getting quickened to the richness of who God is and that He is within you.

I had only $30 in hand.

It's been almost 20 years since that day, but I remember every detail—far more than the room and the chair where I sat at the table. I remember the sunlight streaming through the curtain, the sound of Public Television in the background, and most of all, the feeling of disbelief that this was my life.

I was raised going to church and living in a comfortable home—two things I am thankful for. Yet at that moment, I was a long way from home. When my husband and I were ready to build a family, we decided to live off one income so I could stay home and raise our kids. We believed, just like with the tithe, that God could do more with our one income in faith than with two incomes in line with societal norms. Let me just say—we were right.

A few years in, we had two little kids and a whole lot of hopes and dreams. My husband would make the money, and I would make it stretch.

On this particular day, I had an empty fridge, an empty pantry, and only thirty dollars for groceries. I had run our kitchen down as far as I could before I needed to go to the store. I never thought of us as poor, but that day, I felt a poverty identity knocking at my door with piles of evidence in hand, demanding access. Still, I had faith for our future. I believed God had good things for us and that we would actually get there. But this day, the future was too far away. I needed to see the goodness of God right where I was.

As I sat at my dining table—which touched both couch and kitchen—I grabbed my notepad to make my grocery list. This was going to be basic, not abundant; doable, not delicious. Thirty dollars back then might have been more than it is now, but it still wasn't enough.

On my table was also my Bible. In a very "spiritual" act of procrastination, I thought I would read a little. Honestly, it was just to delay facing the awful feeling of being "poor" and to check the box that I had read my Bible that day.

Now, before I get too hard on myself, I will say—even though there were times I was just going through the motions—I praise God that I had developed the diligence of reading Scripture. Routine or not, I was there! God had the opportunity to speak, and I had the opportunity to hear.

As I flipped open my Bible, it opened to Psalm 103. I'm sure my first thought was, Oh no! It's so long. But I didn't get more than five verses in before I was stopped by the Holy Spirit.

> *Bless the Lord, O my soul,*
> *and all that is within me,*
> *bless His holy name!*
> *Bless the Lord, O my soul,*
> *and do not forget all His benefits—*
> *who forgives all your iniquity,*
> *who heals all your diseases,*
> *who redeems your life from the pit,*
> *who crowns you with steadfast love and mercy,*
> *who satisfies you with good*
> *so that your youth is renewed like the eagle's*
> (Psalm 103:1-5 ESV).

STOP! When I read verse five, I felt a desire reach out from the page, grab my heart, and come out of my mouth as a sigh and the words hidden under that breath of, "I want that."

When I said those words, I heard a thought: *Write down what you want.*

I looked at my blank list and quickly dismissed it: I can't afford what I want.

Then I heard it again: *Write down what you want.*

Three times I argued with the thought, citing my reality—I had only thirty dollars. And then I knew: it wasn't a thought at all. It was the voice of God. The voice of God sounds like a thought that comes up from your heart, not down from your head. It's a still, small voice (1 Kings 19:12). It's not coming from outside you but from His place right inside you.

I had known His voice from early childhood, but I was no longer a child believing for turtles and toads on our family farm. This was real life, and I had to feed my family.

In obedience, I picked up my pen and paper to write down what I wanted—what would be "good" to me, as the Scripture said. But nothing came to mind. I could have filled the notebook with all the cheap foods I didn't want that day: beans, rice, peanut butter, chicken—oh, I hated chicken at that point! I had joined a food co-op with a friend to get chicken on the cheap, straight from a processing plant. One box of random chicken parts, yellow with feathers still attached, was enough to realize I was no pioneer woman.

Staring at the empty page, I did something beyond my own wisdom. My imagination was out of practice, and I needed help to think beyond my own limitations. I turned to God and asked, "God, what do I want? What would be good to me?"

Who knows us better than the One who created us? He knew what I would like, and He also knew what He had already prepared for me.

> *Delight yourself in the Lord, and he will give you the desires of your heart* (Psalm 37:4 ESV).

We receive the desires of our hearts as we delight in the Lord, setting our eyes and minds on Him. That delight is attention with intention—of joy, thanksgiving, and faith—giving our God access to our imagination station that produces wants, dreams, and desires.

So I sat and listened. Two items rose up in my heart: lamb and shrimp. My mouth watered at the thought. Nothing else came, so that's what I wrote down. Then I added the other things we needed: milk, eggs, butter, bread, cereal... Do you know what wasn't on my list? Chicken!

I finished writing, ripped the page from my notebook, held it up to heaven, and said, "Father, Your Word says that You satisfy my mouth with good things. I receive this now in Jesus' name." I folded the list, put it in my pocket, got my kids, and headed to the grocery store.

My heart teetered between excitement and anxiety as I approached the store. I could feel the spark of faith, birthed from God's promise, reaching for fulfillment—but my mind analyzed, doubted, and tried to keep me "safe" and small: *What if God didn't have time to prepare the store? What if I don't receive what I'm believing for? If I'm wrong, this could seriously damage my faith moving forward.*

The struggle between the mind and the heart, the soul and the spirit, is the battleground where victory is gained by faith or lost by reason.

I placed my little ones in the cart, list in hand, thirty dollars in my purse, with my faith and cart aimed toward the seafood counter—my Canaan land, my land of promise. I encouraged my heart, whispering quietly, "My mouth is filled with good things."

I didn't bother even looking at the food, only the price tags. And there it was: $1.34 per pound. This was a price I could afford. My heart leapt! Behind that sign were giant Gulf prawns!

I called the clerk over to ask if that price was correct. He checked and said, "I'm so sorry. We switched stuff around last night and forgot to change the sign. Those are usually $9 per pound."

He left my side, and for a moment, it felt as though time slowed. My desire, my will, and my hope were at a crossroads. What felt like an entire board meeting between my members—my mind, my spirit, and my will being the deciding vote. Do I let go or hold tight? I felt a dogmatic majority overruling reason, and that voice was the voice of faith. Under my breath, I whispered, "No! I won't let go, in the name of Jesus! I receive my mouth filled with good things."

Suddenly, the man stopped mid-step. He turned to me with a smile: "Ma'am! Hold on! We received so much of these shrimp yesterday. I'll give you as much as you want at that price!"

I bought five pounds of shrimp—a substantial part of my budget, but far less than one pound normally would have cost. Glory to God!

I continued to the meat section, with my faith soaring and a bounce in my step. With my eyes toward the prize, I zoomed past the chicken without even a courtesy glance. As I searched the meats, another employee came over and said that a leg of lamb had just been marked down in the discount area. There it was—my "good thing."

I left the store with everything on my list—for the thirty dollars I had.

Twenty years later, this story still brings my eyes to tears and my heart to worship. That day, our account didn't instantly change—but I did. I had heard God's voice, believed His promises, put feet to my faith, and, as a result, ate the good of the land.

Arriving home, I piled the groceries on the table, now crowding my Bible, still open to Psalm 103, and heard God clearly say, "You are no longer limited by your husband's income. You will only be limited by your faith—your ability to believe Me."

Faith comes from hearing, and hearing through the word of Christ (Romans 10:17 ESV).

As we fellowship with the Holy Spirit through Scripture, allowing Him to teach us, not only does our revelation of Him grow, but our sensitivity to His voice, capacity to believe, and ability to receive Him grow.

The GOOD NEWS of the gospel is all good news! We weren't created to do life alone; we were created to do life with God, and Jesus made that possible. His name tells us everything: Emmanuel—God with us (Matthew 1:23).

If you haven't made the shift to becoming God-is-inside-of-me-minded, or as I like to say, "God inside minded," I encourage you to make that adjustment this very moment. His Holy Spirit—the same Spirit that raised Christ from the dead—is literally within us. It's not just for crises or for eternity—it's for today. There's a lot that goes into "life," from the mundane to the major, and God wants to be invited into all of it: lunch, laundry, raising kids, building a business. God cares about what you care about, because God cares about you!

The revelation of kingdom wealth is a love revelation of relationship with God.

> *Grace and peace be multiplied to you in the knowledge of God and of Jesus our Lord, as His divine power has given to us all things that pertain to life and godliness, through the knowledge of Him who called us by glory and virtue, by which have been given to us exceedingly great and precious promises, that through these you may be partakers of the divine nature, having escaped the corruption that is in the world through lust* (2 Peter 1:2-4 NKJV).

I learned that day how to do life with God, in all things at every moment! I can confidently say after living this way for over twenty years that I can have whatever I want WHEN I get my want from Him.

The last part of 2 Peter 1:4 says, having escaped the corruption that is in this world through lust. Do you know how to eradicate lust in your life? Stop restricting God to only your needs and start inviting Him to be involved in all your ways—that includes your wants.

> *In all your ways acknowledge Him, and He shall direct your paths* (Proverbs 3:6 NKJV).

As the years went by, our family grew to six, and my husband went from being a faithful employee to owning his own production company in Dallas. As an almost empty-nester, having had the privilege of raising my children to adulthood, I have now stepped into my dream of ministry and running a thriving Christian coaching practice, teaching women these very principles of freedom, hope, and fulfillment. We went from God doing more with our little to God blessing us with more. We also taught our kids to live this way: Ask God what you want, receive it by faith, and listen for the steps to take. Nothing is too big for God, and nothing is too small for Him either.

Hundreds of stories later, it's not about the "thing," it's about doing every day in every way with God. When God is in your everything, nothing owns you but Him, including comparison, jealousy, and envy. With God, you're no longer limited by income, education, or the number of mouths you have to feed, but only by your capacity to believe God and be led by His Spirit.

Kingdom wealth is directly connected to your internal relationship with God and His way of doing things. The rules of His kingdom overrule and override earthly reason. Jesus says in Luke 17:21 (NKJV), *"The kingdom of God is within you."* Pray and trust in John's prayer in 3 John 1:2 (NKJV): *Beloved, I pray that you may prosper in all things and be in health, just as your soul prospers.*

God's promises for my future renewed my soul (mind, will, and emotions) in those early years so I could see us prospering years down the road. I knew we would get there! But that day, when I sat in the very reality of our scarcity, God wanted to give me a kingdom revelation: Jesus is not only the God of Sundays or some days, He is the God of right now—this moment—today!

A scarcity mindset looks to validate its lack of opportunities, but a kingdom mindset sees scarcity as an opportunity for faith.

> *And God is able to make all grace [every favor and earthly blessing] come in abundance to you, so that you may always [under all circumstances, regardless of the need] have complete sufficiency in everything [being completely self-sufficient in Him], and have an abundance for every good work and act of charity* (2 Corinthians 9:8 AMP).

The word "able" has two meanings. One is ability, which I hope we can agree God has all of; the second meaning is opportunity. While God has the ability to make all grace abound toward us, that we would have all sufficiency in all things, we are the ones who give God the opportunity to show up in our lives in this way. In the previous verses, Paul outlines the heart posture and life habits of generosity and joyful giving that please God and align us with kingdom provision.

And this we also know:

> *But without faith it is impossible to please Him, for he who comes to God must believe that He is, and that He is a rewarder of those who diligently seek Him* (Hebrews 11:6 NKJV).

You can leave limitations behind by seeking God and giving Him the opportunity to show up in your life. Pray with me: *Holy Spirit, I invite You into every place of my life, show me where I've been on autopilot or listening to the voice of scarcity. Open my eyes to see Your promises, fill my heart with Your desires, and expand my imagination to dream with You. Thank You for living inside me and doing every piece of life with me. In Jesus' name, I pray. Amen.*

Now, I encourage you to take some time and process all you've just read and all the Holy Spirit is speaking to you. You may even want to journal your thoughts. Remember, God is not just the God of "someday"—He wants to meet you in your everyday, from mundane to main things, He wants to do life with you! Take time to pause, listen, and invite Him into your own story. Use these questions as a guide to reflect on and respond to:

1. Where in your life might you be on autopilot instead of engaging your Co-Pilot, the Holy Spirit?
2. Identify an area of your life where scarcity feels the loudest. How could this very place be reframed as an opportunity to trust God in faith?
3. Which promises in Scripture speak directly to the areas that God is calling you to trust Him in?

Blessing, friends, as you practice dreaming, hearing, believing, and obeying the voice of the Holy Spirit, leaving limitations behind and doing life with God.

Kim Garro

Kim Garro, born and raised in California, is 59 years old. A successful retired entrepreneur, she co-founded an RF & Microwave manufacturing business and an almond farming venture alongside her husband for eighteen years.

Kim is a proud mother of three children and grandmother to seven wonderful grandchildren. For the past six years, Kim has served in public service as a California Notary Public, Loan Signing Agent.

Deeply committed to her faith, Kim has been a lifelong follower of Jesus Christ since she was 11. Driven by a passion to make a positive impact both in her community and beyond, she actively serves in recovery ministries such as Celebrate Recovery, Alcoholics Anonymous, Alateen, and Al-Anon.

Kim also finds joy and fulfillment through her personal interests and creative pursuits, including gardening, canning, and quilting.

Claiming Eternal Wealth

By Kim Garro

Have you ever wondered why you were born to the parents you have? Were you truly desired or the result of an accident? I wrestled with those questions. I also asked God why my parents were abusive, didn't love or nurture me, and caused me so much pain.

Over time, I've discovered that the keeping power of Jesus and the truth of God's Word are the greatest treasures I possess. And His Word assures me that I was not born by chance, and neither were you. God formed each of us intricately, knitting us together in our mother's womb. He created each of us as unique, wonderful individuals, fully known and predestined by Him.

> *For You formed my innermost parts; You wove me in my mother's womb. I will give thanks to You, because I am awesomely and wonderfully made; Wonderful are Your works, and my soul knows it very well* (Psalm 139:13–14 NASB).

This chapter is a reflection on how my early moments of faith laid the foundation for a lifelong journey of trust, hope, and eternal wealth in God's kingdom. Eternal wealth isn't measured by money, possessions, or worldly success, but by the priceless inheritance of faith in Jesus Christ and the promises of God's Word. It's a testimony that God's Word, even when seen through a child's eyes and understood out of biblical context, can sustain and strengthen us forever.

I was born into poverty to parents who were 15 and 16 years of age. My mother was orphaned by her father's death due to cirrhosis of the liver, and her mother's death as a result of a drunk driver. My biological father disavowed me from birth, never acknowledging my existence.

My mother and I lived in a foster home. When she was pregnant with me, she attended a Bible study (at the church I now attend and serve!) where a man named Allen prayed over me, the unborn baby in my mother's womb; I believe those prayers changed my destiny. I was raised in that foster home for the first four years of my life; during that time, I know that was God revealing His plan for me.

Eventually, my mother and I moved to a small house in Section 8 housing by the tracks, where "peeping Toms" looked in the windows at night. Mom worked long hours as a waitress while I was cared for by the neighbor girls, wherein I suffered sexual abuse and was forced to smoke cigarettes. Later, Mom married a man who, despite suffering from bipolar disorder and manic depression, was unmedicated. He and my mom were also addicted to drugs and alcohol.

As a blended family, I had two stepsisters, one stepbrother, and, later, a half-sister. All of whom could never do wrong in my stepfather's eyes and were, therefore, never punished for their behaviors. My coping mechanism was to live in a "fantasyland" as Cinderella. It was fitting; I was named as the stepchild, enduring the endless chores and all the rejections that came with it. I believed that one day, my "prince" would come and take me away from the painful upbringing filled with abuse and trauma.

I was molested repeatedly by my stepbrother starting at age 7, which became the "secret" I had to keep. I stuffed that secret and pain so far down in my soul that I was drowning in silence. I kept silent for decades, not knowing how to process what was happening or even recognizing that what I endured was unforgettable abuse. Instead, I carried the shame and confusion alone, afraid to speak out or seek help.

During the highs and lows of my stepdad's bipolar, manic rages, I lived on eggshells, never knowing what would set off the bomb. He took the slightest look or sound I made as sarcasm and chased me around the house, which ended in him beating me with his hand or whipping me with his belt, inflicting me with bloody wounds. Even when he wasn't home, I was often sent to my room to wait for him to return to perform the whipping.

I tried to pad my bottom with extra clothes or blank out my mind to separate myself from what was happening, but if he didn't see me cry, the beating escalated. There were times I would wake up in the morning with my panties off and no memory of the night before; this still disturbs me to this day.

My stepdad decided he didn't want a "fat" stepdaughter; therefore, I had to do weigh-ins on Sundays. If I didn't weigh an amount he decided on, then I had to wear a dress to school. As a result, I viewed myself as fat and a failure for not making weight. I never considered myself to be good enough, and I became bulimic. Before a weigh-in, I would exercise excessively, starve myself, and take diuretics to lose weight. After a weigh-in, I would binge eat for three days. Then the cycle would repeat itself. This went on for years.

Mother stood by, allowing the abuse to take place and never protecting me, as she herself endured abuse. She also physically and verbally abused me, saying things like, "I wish I had had an abortion," "With a kid like you, who needs enemies," and "You will never amount to anything." One time, she slapped me so hard across the face that I passed out and fell, cutting my head open. She wanted to stitch the wound closed herself!! Of course, because how would she explain the cut to the emergency room doctor? Fortunately, she did not stitch it closed as I put up a huge stink. I still have that physical scar today.

Enduring those experiences and unresolved emotions left deep, deep heart wounds and scars, which actually became a catalyst for my journey of faith and healing. For three years, my parents tried sobriety and started attending church—the same church started by the pastor who initially taught Bible study at the foster home where I first lived. Now only God could orchestrate those details. Those three years were the very best of my childhood memories. When I was 11 years old, we attended a church family camp, where I accepted Jesus Christ as my Savior and was baptized and filled with the Holy Spirit. I was forever changed by my encounter with Jesus that day.

Still, I cried myself to sleep many nights as I asked Jesus why I had the parents I did, why they were abusive, why they didn't love me, and how I was to honor them as He commanded. Despite the pain and the rivers of tears I cried daily, wondering when my prince was coming to take me away, I always found peace as I talked and cried to Jesus.

I clung to three Scriptures in God's Word I heard at church that became my spiritual anchors. Although I didn't fully understand their depths at the time, their truths were profound, shaping my understanding of God's provision, love, refuge, strength, and assurances. Their power and promise carried me through every challenge life threw my way.

> *For the word of God is alive and active. Sharper than any double-edged sword, it penetrates even to dividing soul and spirit, joints and marrow; it judges the thoughts and attitudes of the heart* (Hebrews 4:12 NIV).

The first Scripture I held fast to was Jeremiah 29:11-14 (NIV): "*For I know the plans I have for you," declares the Lord, "plans to prosper you and not to harm you, plans to give you hope and a future. Then you will call on me and come and pray to me, and I will listen to you. You will seek me and find me when you seek me with all your heart. I will be found by you," declares the Lord, "and will bring you back from captivity. I will gather you from all the nations and places where I have banished you," declares the Lord, "and will bring you back to the place from which I carried you into exile."*

These verses reassured me that God's plans for my life were good and that one day I would prosper, even though my present circumstances felt dark, traumatic, hurtful, and hopeless. It taught me that, despite my endless tears, I could find hope by seeking God wholeheartedly and that the abuse inflicted on me was never God's plan; it was a result of my parents' brokenness and actions. God saw me and was listening to me; He was always with me. Jesus, my Prince, would get me out of the captivity of hell I was living in.

The second Scripture that carried me was John 8:32 (NIV): *Then you will know the truth, and the truth will set you free.*

As a child who was forced to keep the family secret of molestation, this verse spoke to me personally in a way that was out of context biblically. Yet, in an astounding way, the Holy Spirit brought me solace through these words, assuring me that God knew the truth of what was happening to me, I wasn't crazy, and He was going to set me free from it.

Later in life, I discovered that John 8:31-32 actually conveys that true discipleship involves consistently living according to Jesus' teachings, which leads to knowing Jesus, the Truth, and experiencing freedom from the bondage of sin and falsehood. It emphasizes that those who believe in Jesus and remain steadfast in His Word will not only be identified as His disciples but will also experience the liberating power only He can provide.

I do not want to gloss over the miracle that Jesus, through His Words and the Holy Spirit, gave me exactly what I needed when I needed it, comforting me with His care and love, even as I applied the Scripture out of context. Understanding these verses on a different level later only enhanced their biblically intended meaning: The Truth that truly sets us free for eternity is Jesus. Yet His love for me in my time of pain—and for eternity—is liberating on a level that is impossible to describe. His ever-present words remind me that knowing Him and His Truth sets me free from a future of bondage to sin and from the lies and pain of my past.

> *Jesus said to him, "I am the way, and the truth, and the life; no one comes to the Father but through Me"* (John 14:6 NASB).

The third Scripture I clung to is 1 Corinthians 10:13 (NIV): *No temptation has overtaken you except what is common to mankind. And God is faithful; he will not let you be tempted beyond what you can bear. But when you are tempted, he will also provide a way out so that you can endure it.*

This verse talks about temptation. Being mistreated and abused can certainly tempt us, but per His promise, God will provide a way for us to endure whatever we go through, giving us the strength and means to remain loyal to Him.

God saw the abuse and pain I was suffering; He knew it was more than I could handle on my own, but He gave me the strength to endure and know that a way out was coming. You see, God brought me a job around the corner from our house when I was just 13. For four overnights a week, I cared for a child who was 9. This job gave me funds to make my mandatory contribution to our household finances—paying the water bill and purchasing my own clothes and personal toiletries. More importantly, it gave me four nights of reprieve from the abuse—"a way to endure."

At age 16, I purchased my own car and insurance; I saw working and being an overachiever as a way out. I became one of four managers at a local fast-food restaurant and worked 12-hour shifts. After saving money and accumulating house items, finally, the time came; I emancipated myself from my parents and moved out, renting a room from a family. Life was still hard as I continued with school and work, but the abuse finally stopped. I will never forget the words my stepdad said as I walked out the door: "I guess you finally drew a line in the sand."

Although I moved out, I desired to be obedient to God and His Word, especially His command to honor my parents; if I did, God had another promise. I still choose to honor them today with my forgiveness. Due to circumstances, I was not there when my mother passed, but I did serve my stepdad for four months, taking care of him with my stepsister until he passed, ushering him into Jesus' arms as I worshipped and read God's Word to him.

> *"Honor your father and mother"—which is the first commandment with a promise—"so that it may go well with you and that you may enjoy long life on the earth"* (Ephesians 6:2-3 NIV).

Childlike faith is pure and unshakable, built on trust rather than understanding, obedience rather than doubt. For me, honoring my mother and father was not turning them into Child Protective Services, but rather, walking away and offering forgiveness. I learned that my parents did the best they could with what they had. They didn't have much; they came from an orphanage, rejection, mental illness, poverty, addictions, and broken relationships. They were emotionally unavailable to be parents or role models who could teach me and love me; instead, they chose to numb themselves. After I moved out, my stepdad eventually tried to kill my mother with a shotgun, and their relationship resulted in divorce.

After the divorce, my mother spiraled in her alcoholism and died by suicide on November 20, 2003.

Decades later, I fell into the typical Adult Children of Alcoholics (ACoA) and Dysfunctional Families combined with Adverse Childhood Experiences (ACE) statistics, with an ACE score of nine. I married an alcoholic, became an alcoholic, and dealt with character defects such as perfectionism, people-pleasing, trust issues, and relationship intimacy. I will save that for my three-book writings, or another chapter of God's miracles in my life. I am still a work in progress, but God said to me in several prophetic words, "I am healing your heart." And I am trusting that process.

And we know that in all things God works for the good of those who love Him, who have been called according to his purpose (Romans 8:28 NIV). In this Scripture, God answered all the questions I said I wrestled with at the beginning of this chapter—and then some. Although I don't understand why I was born to parents who abused me, I can trust that even in that, God was working. And I know that God desired me and always had a plan for my life.

My cherished childhood Scriptures are more than just words. God is using them to heal my heart, lay the foundation of my spiritual life, and give me the strength to endure and hope in the Truth that will set me free.

Years of hard work, integrity, and a strong work ethic grounded in faith and morals blessed my husband and me with entrepreneurial success. Building and selling our businesses allowed us to retire early at 45, living debt-free and frugal. We continue to give generously, serving Jesus Christ and claiming eternal wealth through His truth.

True wealth is not having worldly possessions, but having the eternal promises of God's Word—that's what I refer to as eternal wealth. I look forward to living a long time on earth, but I also look forward to living eternally with Jesus Christ after my earthly body passes away.

Eternal wealth is rooted in God's divine promises. It's the inheritance that no thief can steal, and no storm can destroy. My early lessons of faith revealed that the greatest riches are found in knowing Jesus Christ as my personal Lord and Savior and trusting in His Word, regardless of my circumstances. As I've matured and seen God show up for me again and again, His truth has become my bedrock.

Sharing these Scriptures and my personal story is part of my healing journey. It's a testament that no matter what any of us go through, God's promises and love can restore, heal, and renew us. Your past does not define your future. God's plans for your life are extraordinary and filled with hope and purpose. Simple trust in God's Word continues to grow within me as I use my pain for His glory and pray to bear fruit through challenges, blessings, and seasons of growth.

Faith is a treasure that comes from hearing and believing God's Word; it leads to miracles and victory. Our salvation is not something earned by our own efforts, but a gift received through faith in Jesus Christ, who came into the world to save sinners; to save me. Through His death and resurrection, He offers eternal life as a gift to all who believe in Him. As we trust in Him and His finished work on the cross, we are forgiven, redeemed, and empowered to live victoriously. This gift of salvation leads to new life and miracles, illustrating God's love and faithfulness to those who believe.

> *This means that anyone who belongs to Christ has become a new person. The old life is gone; a new life has begun!* (2 Corinthians 5:17 NLT).

If you haven't accepted Jesus as your personal Lord and Savior, pray this prayer sincerely from your heart:

Lord Jesus, I believe you are the Son of God and that You died on the cross for my sins. I ask You to forgive me and come into my heart. I accept You as my Lord and as Savior. Thank You for loving me and giving me eternal life. Help me to follow you and live for you every day. In Jesus' name, I pray. Amen.

Goals

Designing Your Wealth Future

Goals help you look ahead. With your vision clear, your decisions will start to align with what you are building. What you define, you begin to build.

There are goals inside of you that are waiting to be brought to life. These are not random ideas. They are seeds that God has planted within you, and it is time to nurture them and allow them to grow into the life you are meant to live.

I remember when I first began to write down my goals. At the time, they felt far beyond what I could see as possible. I wrote down goals to build a six-figure business, own a home, buy a car with cash, invest in real estate, and create a life that felt stable and free. What I did not realize then was that writing those goals down was the beginning of a completely different future.

Scripture says, *Take delight in the Lord, and he will give you the desires of your heart. Commit your way to the Lord; trust in him and he will do this* (Psalm 37:4-5 NIV). When your heart is aligned with God, your vision expands. You begin to see what is possible beyond your current circumstances.

Over time, my initial goals began to take shape. With consistency, faith, and aligned action, I began to accomplish what once felt impossible. Each milestone created the confidence to expand further. What started as a single step turned into a completely different life. That progression did not happen overnight. It was built through clarity, commitment, and a willingness to keep moving forward.

Many people struggle to set goals because they are focused on where they are instead of where they are going. When your attention is fixed on your current limitations, it becomes difficult to see beyond them. Your starting point does not define your ending point. What matters is your direction.

Jesus gives us a clear principle when He says, *"Suppose one of you wants to build a tower. Will he not first sit down and estimate the cost?"* (Luke 14:28 NIV). He was speaking about planning. When you take the time to think through what you are building, you position yourself to follow through.

Your goals should reflect the life you are building across every area. Financial goals are important, but they are not the only goals that matter. Your professional goals, home goals, and life goals all work together to shape your overall vision.

When we take the time to define our goals clearly, our decisions begin to align with those goals. We begin to prioritize differently, spend differently, and use our time more intentionally. Clarity creates direction, and direction creates momentum.

There is also a direct connection between time and money. When we are disorganized with our time, we are often disorganized with our finances. When we are intentional with our time, our finances begin to reflect that same level of intention. The way you spend your time shapes the results you experience.

Scripture reminds us to stay focused on what matters. *Turn my eyes from looking at worthless things* (Psalm 119:37 ESV). That which you give your attention to will either move you forward or hold you back. When you begin to focus on what aligns with your goals, your life will begin to reflect that focus.

Think beyond short-term results. Some people define long-term as one to two years, while others think in five, ten, or even longer timeframes. Both perspectives are valuable. What matters is that you are clear on your next step. Every structure is built in stages, and your life will be built the same way.

As you set your goals, remember that growth is a process. You may not see everything come together immediately, but that does not mean it is not working. Consistency over time creates results that feel exponential.

Scripture says, *Your word is a lamp for my feet and a light on my path* (Psalm 119:105 NIV). As you seek God and stay aligned with His direction, He will continue to guide your steps.

Your future is not something that happens to you; it is something you build. Your goals give you direction. Your decisions move you forward. Your consistency creates results.

As you define your vision and commit to it, you will begin to see your life shift in ways that once felt out of reach. What begins as a written goal becomes a lived reality.

When your vision is clear, your life begins to align.

JOURNAL REFLECTION

1. Take inventory of where you are financially. What debt do you currently have? What assets do you have?
2. Define your professional goals: What are you building/want to build in your work?
3. Define your home goals: What do you want to create when it comes to where you live or invest?
4. Define your life goals: What brings you fulfillment? What do you want to experience, create, or give?
5. Take inventory of your time. In light of the above answers, what do you need to stop doing that is not moving you forward? What can you start doing to create what you seek to build?

BRITTANY STEHLE

Brittany Stehle is a Jesus-loving, faith-driven entrepreneur and devoted mom of five based in Temecula, California. Saved by grace, she is passionate about building kingdom wealth with purpose, obedience, and integrity. Her faith is deeply woven into her approach to motherhood, marriage, health, and business ownership, guiding both daily decisions and long-term vision.

Brittany is the owner of a thriving private preschool in Temecula and is actively preparing to open a second location in Orange County, with additional growth already in the works. As an entrepreneur, she views wealth as stewardship, believing financial freedom and abundance are tools God uses to serve families, strengthen communities, and expand kingdom impact.

With a strong interest in health and wellness, fitness, and nutrition, Brittany is committed to caring for her body as a temple while pursuing excellence in leadership and life. She loves learning new ways to integrate her faith into everything she does and who she is. She is continually striving toward generational impact, financial freedom, and Christ-centered abundance.

The Ultimate Business Partner

By Brittany Stehle

From a young age, I wanted to build something of my own, something truly meaningful—a business or a private school. I was ambitious, motivated, spiritual, and wanted to make an impact in the world.

I grew up with wealth. My dad was a record producer and radio station owner. We had maids, nannies, and a limo driver; we traveled, shopped, and lived life without limits. By the world's standards, life was perfect. But money doesn't heal wounds or guarantee peace. A resistance to generosity, strained relationships, and pride stole the joy in my family. Although we were a Catholic Christian family, and my mother's charitable side impacted me deeply, we did not live with a biblical view of money, including respecting it as a blessing from God. Over time, my mother became depressed, my parents divorced, and my family went from having $15 million to almost nothing, proving that wealth is fleeting.

> *Honor the Lord with your possessions, and with the first fruits of all your increase; so your barns will be filled with plenty* (Proverbs 3:9-10 NKJV).

When my parents' marriage ended, money couldn't fix the brokenness. However, God, in His mercy, began refining me, showing that true wealth isn't in a bank account—it's in stewarding what He gives and aligning with His kingdom.

At 43, I live the dream I had when I was a child. I own a large, unique, and thriving preschool and kindergarten, called Wild Roots Holistic Learning Center, which is expanding into multiple locations thanks to the Lord's guidance. The journey hasn't been easy, but everything changed when I surrendered fully to Jesus. What once felt like stress and turmoil shifted and was replaced by peace, blessings, and growth. As 2 Corinthians 9:8 reminds us, *God is able to make all grace abound to you, so that... you may abound in every good work* (ESV).

Though I always called myself a Christian, I never truly applied His Word or sought a personal relationship with Him until recent years. I once believed I didn't need help from anyone, not even God, but now I know I wouldn't be here without Him. In truth, I might have lost it all if I hadn't surrendered my life and future to His will.

HOW WILD ROOTS BEGAN

After earning a master's degree in education with a Montessori diploma, I opened an in-home daycare while caring for my three young children. I set up a beautiful classroom with an assistant teacher and a group of children, thinking this would be my long-term path, until demand grew so high that I added sessions and created a waitlist. It became clear that God had bigger plans.

My mother's proceeds from selling our childhood home provided the investment to open a larger childcare center in a commercial building. Everything fell into place, including funds, a welcoming landlord, and the initial 17 students who had been part of my home program. Within a few years, the school grew to five classrooms, and eventually seven classrooms serving infants through kindergarten. Wild Roots became more than a school; it was a thriving community of staff, families, and children—a place I felt called to preserve.

For we are God's handiwork, created in Christ Jesus to do good works, which God prepared in advance for us to do (Ephesians 2:10 NIV).

Shortly after opening the school, I went through a divorce, and my school became my oasis, giving me purpose and focus. I later endured a tumultuous relationship that almost cost me everything. During this time, I felt distant from the Lord, only to realize it was I who had strayed; God never left my side. Eventually, I found the courage to leave the abusive situation and embrace the blessings that awaited me.

I wouldn't trade the heartache of those years, because every challenge paved the way for kingdom wealth and abundance beyond my dreams. The greatest lesson is that no matter my independence or resilience, I would have nothing without my heavenly Father and His grace. If I could speak to my younger self, I would say, "Surrender to Jesus, and He will guide your path better than you could ever imagine."

"Whoever wants to be my disciple must deny themselves and take up their cross daily and follow me. For whoever wants to save their life will lose it, but whoever loses their life for me will save it" (Luke 9:23-24 NIV).

BUSINESS OWNERSHIP NEEDS GOD

Owning a business is no small task. Some days feel like a marathon, others like a circus, and often both at once. Running a school means every decision impacts staff, families, and hundreds of children. As someone who struggles with perfectionism, anxiety, and self-worth, I constantly need the reminder that Jesus is not only my Lord, but He is also my Savior.

The Lord saves me daily—from myself and from what the enemy tries to steal. Protecting my life, business, and children is a constant mission. My advice to other business owners is simple: Make Jesus your Lord and trust Him fully. Pray about every decision, big or small, until it becomes a sustaining rhythm. Having the Lord of Hosts with you changes everything. He fights for you, even in moments that otherwise would be overwhelming.

For years, I was a single mother, a domestic abuse survivor, and a sole business owner. Outwardly, friends and family called me Superwoman. Inside, I was terrified and exhausted, carrying responsibilities that felt impossible to manage alone. I longed to feel the strength and blessing everyone saw in me, but I lacked peace. I learned that without Jesus, abundance is impossible, and progress can stagnate.

Once I placed Jesus as King of my heart and owner of my life and outcomes, He removed obstacles, provided guidance, and turned situations that could have broken me into sources of growth and peace. He is my Good Shepherd, guiding me back whenever I stray.

> *"The thief does not come except to steal, and to kill, and to destroy. I have come that they may have life, and that they may have it more abundantly. I am the good shepherd. The good shepherd gives His life for the sheep"* (John 10:10-11 NKJV).

God has placed unique talents in each of us; when we use those gifts for His glory, they become powerful tools for building His kingdom. Every ability I possess—overseeing, managing, problem-solving, inspiring, creating, envisioning, and acting with perseverance and ambition—is a gift from my heavenly Father.

The Bible reminds us, *Each of you should use whatever gift you have received to serve others, as faithful stewards of God's grace* (1 Peter 4:10 NIV), and to *work at it with all your heart, as working for the Lord, not for human masters*

(Colossians 3:23 NIV). When we faithfully cultivate the gifts God gives us, He honors our efforts.

Although I have many strengths, I struggle with debilitating anxiety and have battled a victim mentality. God lifted me from that low vibration and taught me that when I choose to operate in excellence and give all glory to Him, opportunities and resources flow—not because I chase them, but because I am walking in the purpose He designed for me.

That is the essence of building kingdom wealth; it is not merely accumulating money, but cultivating God-given gifts to create abundance that honors Him, blesses others, and expands His kingdom.

AT THE EDGE OF "NOT ENOUGH"

Running a business as a single mom tested every ounce of me, especially when work deadlines conflicted with my family schedule, causing inner turmoil in decision-making. *Should I let my kids down or sacrifice business success?* Those times were frequent, but so were God's interventions. Once, rain resulted in a rescheduled baseball game I didn't want to miss. Another time, a big meeting was delayed by the other party at the last minute, allowing me time with my children.

And when payroll was due and the numbers simply didn't add up, I'd pray, pace the floor, cry, and wonder, *Lord, how will this work?* And then, almost out of nowhere, provision would show up: an unexpected tuition payment, a grant, or a workers' comp refund check. Each moment was God's gentle reminder: "I've got this. Lean on Me."

> *"Fear not, for I am with you… I will strengthen you, Yes, I will help you, I will uphold you with My righteous right hand"*
> (Isaiah 41:10 NKJV).

Over time, I realized the pattern: The grace of God provided. When I tried to carry everything in my own strength, I spiraled into stress. But when I handed it over to God, peace always followed. Some of the greatest tests of my faith came during seasons of financial strain, when I desperately needed a miracle just to make it to the next month. Every single time, God reminded me that I am not running this show alone. Jesus is—and always has been—my business partner, comforter, and shepherd. *The Lord is my shepherd; I shall not want. He makes me to lie down in green pastures; He leads me beside the still waters. He restores my soul* (Psalm 23:1-3 NKJV).

Through the Holy Spirit, I find calm, guidance, and perspective. Challenges that once felt crushing are now opportunities for growth. He continually reminds me that we are not to carry the weight of ownership alone. Although business feels heavy, with Jesus, it is also holy. In every instance of feeling scarcity, God provides lessons and grows faith.

One Sunday morning at church, after a discouraging week, the weight of business finances pressed on me so heavily it felt physical. My prayers were raw: "Lord, maybe I'm failing. I don't know how much longer I can keep going. Please, show me the way."

In that moment, the pastor's message felt spoken directly to me, a reminder that God always provides and worry has no place when we trust Him. The Holy Spirit rushed over me, lifting the heaviness off my shoulders. Peace flooded my heart, and I felt God whisper, "You are not doing this alone. Your school is protected. I will provide and give you the strength and grace to grow abundantly."

> *"Look at the birds of the air; they do not sow or reap or store away in barns, and yet your heavenly Father feeds them. Are you not much more valuable than they?"* (Matthew 6:26 NIV).

THE POWER OF FAITH

At the core of building kingdom wealth is faith—faith in Jesus as King, Savior, and guide. When I place Him first through prayer and Scripture, my perspective shifts. Aligning with His will allows me to lead my business and serve my community from peace and clarity rather than stress. Prayer clears my head, the Word strengthens my spirit, and faith opens doors that personal striving never could. *Commit to the Lord whatever you do, and He will establish your plans* (Proverbs 16:3 NIV).

I am headstrong, and surrendering my ambitions to God is challenging, but doing so has brought blessings far beyond financial provision. Faith transforms leadership into service guided by Jesus' heart and positions us to receive His abundance. Even in low points, I've learned to trust with gratitude, knowing that life's crumbs can lead to unexpected blessings.

As my school flourished beyond my expectations, God called me to dream bigger. What began as a vision for one community has now grown into a blessing for many more children and families. Success is meant to multiply. Just as seeds in good soil bear fruit, creating generational impact flourishes through His goodness.

> *"If you diligently obey the voice of the Lord...The Lord will command the blessing on you in your storehouses and in all to which you set your hand"* (Deuteronomy 28:1,8).

Some of the greatest blessings of this journey have been the people God has placed alongside me—dedicated staff, encouraging friends, and mentors who point me back to truth. One of these impactful individuals was a financial advisor who helped me navigate my business finances and change some deep-rooted money habits. Over time, God changed our working relationship into a business partnership. She not only guided me to correct my course but also recognized the work God had led me to create and joined me in opening new locations and eventually franchising my school. This partnership was the answer to years of prayer, showing that God brings the right people at the right time, often through unexpected circumstances.

Solitude has also been a blessing. Quiet moments with God have allowed me to reflect on His plans and see how everything He has walked with me through has led to true financial freedom, faith partnerships, and kingdom wealth. He whispers wisdom, steadies my heart, and reminds me that He is steering the ship. I feel His presence daily, in both hardship and victory, and I thank Him for guiding all my business decisions.

> *Be still, and know that I am God* (Psalm 46:10 NKJV).

JOY, GRATITUDE, AND KINGDOM IMPACT

Walking with the Lord, I've learned to celebrate small and big wins alike, not with self-congratulations, but with gratitude. I celebrate everything, from full classrooms to divine business partnerships, as God's provision. Even the heavy challenges offer reasons to rejoice, because those moments reveal God's faithfulness all over again—each time with increasing clarity.

It amazes me how everything changed once I began entrusting every business and personal matter fully to God. He has opened doors to greater success and provision to the point where worry no longer weighs me down. He has abundantly sustained my school for years. When I surrendered—giving Him ownership of my finances, business, and life—I watched Him move mountains on my behalf and point me in the direction of godly and uplifting relationships.

From the moment I wholeheartedly placed my life and business in my Father's hands, He guided me into fresh innovations, meaningful relationships, and divinely orchestrated opportunities. Looking back, I realize that if I had remained fearful and closed off, I would have continued spiraling in loss and hopelessness. Instead, I have discovered peace, joy, and clarity in my work that far surpass anything I ever knew when I was striving on my own, apart from Him.

Kingdom wealth isn't just financial—it's joy, peace, relationships, and eternal impact. It's realizing that money is simply a tool in God's hands, not a trophy of my success.

> *"Give, and it will be given to you: good measure, pressed down, shaken together, and running over"* (Luke 6:38 NKJV).

Looking back, I see that this business has never truly been mine. It has always been God's—His vision, His provision, His glory. My job is simply to steward it by serving people faithfully and trusting Him with each outcome.

Kingdom wealth isn't about chasing dollars at any cost. It is about aligning every decision, every dollar, and every day with God's purposes. When He's your business partner, success is measured not just in profits, but in eternal impact. This is the kind of wealth that never runs dry.

No matter how much progress I make, all kingdom wealth begins and continues with gratitude and the recognition that God is the ultimate source of every blessing. I have learned to pause, acknowledge God's hand in every detail, and give Him the glory. But giving thanks and giving glory is only part of the equation.

Building kingdom wealth also requires sacrifice—offering our time, talents, and resources to serve God and advance His purposes. Whether it is dedicating hours to mentor others, investing in programs that benefit families and communities, or using financial resources to support His work, true stewardship involves putting God first in all areas of our lives. Romans 12:1 reminds us: *Therefore, I urge you, brothers and sisters, in view of God's mercy, to offer your bodies as a living sacrifice, holy and pleasing to God—this is your true and proper worship* (NIV).

Giving glory to God changes how I view my work. When I offer up every decision, every new program, and every relationship as an act of worship, my focus shifts from my ambition to His purpose. Money and success then become tools for kingdom impact. James 1:17 says, *Every good and perfect gift is from above, coming down from the Father of the heavenly lights, who does not change like shifting shadows* (NIV). Recognizing that all gifts—talents, opportunities, resources—come from God keeps me humble, grateful, and focused on multiplying what I've been given for His glory.

Each time I pause to acknowledge God's provision and offer myself fully—my time, my abilities, and my resources—I am reminded that kingdom wealth is never just about accumulation. It is about stewardship, obedience, sacrifice, and the joy of seeing His purposes unfold through the work of our hands.

God has led me to the most important relationships I could ask for after years of hardships and feeling alone. He led me to a Christian business partner who is bringing Wild Roots to a whole new level. He also led me to my new husband, a true partner who supports not only our home and family life, but also my business, allowing me to focus with a clear mind and a peaceful heart. His encouragement and shared faith in Jesus make every challenge easier to face, and together we walk in alignment with God's purpose for our lives.

God orchestrates relationships for our good when we follow His lead—and especially when we treat our relationship with Him as the most important one of all. He is our ultimate friend, confidante, provider, mentor, guide, and yes, business partner.

> *And we know that in all things God works for the good of those who love him, who have been called according to his purpose* (Romans 8:28 NIV).

Dee Miller

Dee Miller is a speaker, bestselling author, podcast host, and the founder of MJM Ministry (mjmministry.com). Dee has a passion to work with others who believe changing the outside of themselves will bring happiness and peace to their internal selves. She also supports parents and churches as they navigate the transgender landscape, knowing that we all bear God's image and are created in His likeness.

MJM ministry was born out of the desire to see everyone embrace themselves as God created them to be and to bring the truth of God's Word to the belief that following our feelings will bring happiness.

MJM ministry was named after Dee's parents, Mary and John Miller. Dee had stopped all communication with her family while living as a transman, but her parents rushed back into her life at the precise moment the door was reopened.

Dee authored chapters in Women World Leaders' books *Unshakable: God Will Sustain You* and *Restoration: God Brings Beauty from Ashes.* She also writes for Voice of Truth magazine.

Stay connected with Dee at Dee@mjmministry.com.

It All Belongs to Him

By Dee Miller

I was ready to leave my parents' home. To be out in the world on my own—free to make my own choices. My mom sat me down to teach me how to make a budget, making me think extensively about the details and budget for non-everyday expenses like haircuts and postage stamps. But the one thing she did not teach me was how to put God first in everything I did. It would not have mattered, as I did not believe in God's existence. Although I was always a generous giver to a person in need, you could not ask me to give it to a church or anything a church wanted money for. My heart was hard to anything that acknowledged that God was real.

I had a great-paying job and believed I was set up to be successful. I was comfortable with the amount of money I was making and the balance in my bank accounts. Then I started the pursuit of changing my gender, and, financially, my life also began to change. I moved to a new city, away from my good job, and my expenses doubled overnight as I was spending money trying to buy myself happiness. Living as a transgender man required me to pay for everything out of pocket.

My accounts slowly drained dry—I was not making enough money to fund my dream of becoming a man. So I began to fund my life by using credit cards, digging a hole of debt I would never be able to pay off. My mind was consumed with how to pay for essentials, mainly rent.

"So don't worry about these things, saying, 'What will we eat? What will we drink? What will we wear?' These things dominate the thoughts of unbelievers, but your heavenly Father already knows all your needs" (Matthew 6:31-32 NLT).

Regarding my gender change, I began to understand that I was chasing a fairytale. No matter what I did to my body, I would never be male. I could even spend time on a surgeon's table, but that would not make me male. It was not a path that was going to be blessed by God. Although Jesus taught us, *"Seek the Kingdom of God above all else, and live righteously, and he will give you everything you need"* (Matthew 6:33 NLT), this was a foreign concept that was about to become the focus of my life.

As my life hit rock bottom, I was facing homelessness. I needed help. Where my help came from was a surprise.

I accepted Jesus as my personal Savior, stopped my pursuit to change my gender, and started going to church on Sundays. When the offering basket was passed during service, I would place a check for five dollars in it—I felt that was my duty to help keep the lights on. I knew the church was asking for a tithe, which is ten percent of my income, but my heart was still hard towards what the church wanted.

That church congregation never accepted me, and soon, I could no longer ignore the stares I received each time I walked through the doors. After a time of no one reaching out to befriend me, I found I did not have the strength to endure. My whole life had been turned upside down; I was overwhelmed by everything and had no support. Soon, I found myself hospitalized with a breakdown. Great; more bills. But this was the moment God began to move noticeably in my life. Although I had not been in contact with my family for almost six years due to my own choice, my hospitalization opened the door for our relationship to be reestablished.

When my parents realized my financial circumstances, they stepped in and paid off my creditors. Just as Jesus has paid my debt for all my sins, my parents stepped in to rescue me from disaster. The difference is that Jesus knows I can never pay Him back. My parents only took the pressure off, but required me to sign legal papers promising I would make good on my debt. Still, I was grateful to know I would have a safe place to lay my head every night.

Before long, the door opened for me to get a lucrative second job. This was not a minimum wage job with a few hours here and there; I was working four hours, four nights a week, and making the same hourly wage as my full-time job. I still had not returned to church—I had been hurt by the people of a church, and I had put their actions over who God is—but my path in life had changed.

I soon made the decision to change employers, opening the door for me to meet people who went to church near where I lived. I slowly worked up the courage to attend and was quickly befriended. I began attending service 'weekly and then getting involved in other ways.

With my financial debts paid off, I was still keenly aware of how easily I could get back in debt, so when a man I attended church with offered a class on finances, I was intrigued by what I might learn from him. His success was apparent—he owned his own company, drove nice vehicles, and had plenty of expensive toys. I will never forget Lesson One: It all belongs to God. That mindset put me on a path to learning that if I keep my hands open, not clenched to secure what I think I own, it is easier to focus on God and not what I have—or more importantly, what I have convinced myself I do not have.

I slowly increased my church giving to ten percent. As I did, my faith grew as God provided for my every need. One Saturday, I took a single mom to purchase a Christmas gift for her oldest child. As we spent time together, I was gaining an understanding of how much need she had for herself and her three children. By the end of the day, I had paid for three gifts, groceries, and her dry-cleaning bill, so she could pick up the clothes she had been unable to retrieve. The amount I spent was easily four times more than I intended to.

That Monday morning, as I looked at the balance in my checkbook, I took a deep breath and said to God, "I just used my car payment to help this family." I had a sense of calm that it would be ok. My faith in God's provision for all my needs had grown tremendously.

The following Sunday morning, a lady walked up to me with an envelope of cash. Her only words were, "God told me to give this to you." Inside the envelope was the exact amount I needed for my car payment. The wisdom I gained surrounding the moment was that I had the time to drive around and do all the necessary errands, and the other person had the finances but not the time. What do you have an abundance of that you are willing to give?

My trust in God's provision continued to grow. I felt challenged to understand what God truly desired from me. Proverbs 11:24-25 (NLT) states, *Give freely and become more wealthy; be stingy and lose everything. The generous will prosper; those who refresh others will themselves be refreshed.* I refreshed a person in need. In turn, I was given exactly what I needed in that moment. I would be remiss not to point out how I felt at the end of that day: I knew I had done well. It felt good to give—give my time and money. I was grateful I had money in my account to do everything we did. I knew that if I had kept my fist clenched around my little, I would have never seen God provide the way He did.

This experience caused me to dig in even deeper to seek God's heart. In Genesis 4, we learn that Cain presented some of his crops as a gift to the Lord, but when Abel brought his firstborn lambs to the Lord, the Lord accepted Abel's gift. Cain was upset, and God told Cain to do what was right. The difference was that Cain brought God *some* of his crops, while Abel gave God his *firstborn.* God did not have Cain's heart; perhaps he was giving out of obligation or even keeping his fist tightly clenched around his best crops, merely offering God his leftovers.

I began to give God my first fruits, the best of everything I had. I saw each pay raise as a financial blessing. I gave the increase of my first check on top of my ten percent. If I ever received a financial gift, I would find a way to give someone in need a blessing out of my abundance. I wanted to keep my hands open, reminding myself that it all belongs to God and I am only a servant for what He wants to accomplish.

The way I now live my life is based on Proverbs 30:8b-9 (NLT): *Give me neither poverty nor riches! Give me just enough to satisfy my needs. For if I grow rich, I may deny you and say, "Who is the LORD?" And if I am too poor, I may steal and thus insult God's holy name.* To do this required learning the difference between what I think I want and what I need.

When my father died, I had the privilege of speaking at his funeral. My father and I did not get along in my youth. He worked all the time, so I rarely saw him. There were several times I scanned the horizon to see if my dad was attending an important event. His hard work paid off with several promotions, which led to my parents having a comfortable life. I was bitter, however. I wanted my dad, not his money. But his routine was to arrive home on a Friday night as I was leaving to be with friends, hand me a twenty-dollar bill, and tell me to have a good time. I took the money, but not with a grateful heart.

In his later years, my dad would often say to me, "I guess we are spending your inheritance." Though my parents were still frugal in many ways, they were able to afford luxuries to make their lives comfortable. My siblings and I were happy they were doing those things; Dad earned the money; he should be able to enjoy his retirement years.

As I matured, I learned to ask my dad questions, which led to my understanding some of the difficult choices he believed he had to make, such as choosing work over attending my activities. His job was to travel; that was not his choice, his career had led him in that direction. He worked for 40 years for the same company. After he died, I learned how lucrative his retirement package was—an amazing blessing for his years of dedication.

Dad preceded Mom in death by a few years, and he left an incredible legacy for his family. His work ethic is evident in all his children and grandchildren, and his wisdom—which at times felt outdated—was not disregarded; his intentions were understood.

As I was driving to be with Mom when she was living her last days in Hospice, I had a conversation with God. I had never wanted my parents' money; I wanted them in ways that they seemed unable to give of themselves. Although I had zero indications as to what my financial inheritance would be, I told God He could have it all. I knew He was asking me to start a ministry and that whatever amount I would receive could be used for His kingdom's purposes.

My mom was adopted, but she had never wanted to discuss it, leading us to believe she knew very few details surrounding her adoption. But as we cleaned out her home, we found all the adoption papers. My grandparents had filled out paperwork almost a year before Mom's birth. They described in detail what they were hoping for beyond a girl, and they were given their heart's desire.

I researched the place Mom was adopted from and found out that it was a historical site still in existence. It had been built during the Civil War for children who were orphans of war. I decided I wanted to see it to witness my mom's humble beginnings—the start to her life that she was ashamed of. I recognized that my mom had been stuck in the feelings of not being wanted instead of recognizing how much her adoptive parents longed for her.

I learned that after my mom's birth, my grandparents promptly jumped in the car to make the six-hour drive across the state to pick her up and adopt her. They had treated my mother like a true princess—she was loved and well cared for. Notably, they were considered wealthy in the depression era.

As I sat on the grounds where my grandparents first met my mother, I could not help but meditate on Psalm 139:16 (NLT): *You saw me before I was born. Every day of my life was recorded in your book. Every moment was laid out before a single day had passed.* My mom had been adopted by people who served God, and upon their death, she inherited farmland, which had grown increasingly valuable over the years.

It took time to settle my parents' estate. Besides my mom's inherited land, she and my father had purchased two additional farms during their life together. My siblings and I had to look at all our options: The farms were rented out and could provide a steady income, but neither my siblings nor I had any knowledge of how to farm. As much as we wanted to keep the farm Mom had inherited, it became obvious that we could not. Auctioning off the land was the right decision.

I knew God wanted me to retire early from my job and start a ministry. I gave my employer plenty of notice that I was moving on. I still planned on giving God the entire inheritance, but He had other plans. To stop working, I was going to need something in the bank. He only wanted His portion.

I began the ministry, naming it MJM, which stands for Mary, John Miller. My parents and I went through a lot in our lives—while we were together and during our time apart. I had tossed them away when they did not agree with my choices, but when I needed them, they stepped back into my life as if no time had passed. They did not have to leave me anything in their will. And because of my rebellion and the heartache I caused them, I did not expect to receive a dime. However, I did get a portion equal to my siblings.

My parents were godly people. They did not hold a grudge against me. Just as Jesus has paid my eternal debt, He also does not hold a grudge against the years I did not believe in Him. Once I changed my life to follow the instructions of the Lord, everything else started to settle.

Those who listen to instruction will prosper; those who trust the Lord will be joyful (Proverbs 16:20 NLT).

I have never been happier in my life than I am now. Because of the inheritance, I was able to buy my first house. While most people are downsizing in their mature years, my home provides a base of operations for MJM Ministry. It is a true blessing to have a place to host those who desire to meet with me. I consider God the owner of the home, and He has charged me with keeping it in order.

I do what I can to make my home welcoming to those God sends to meet with me, even putting in a coffee bar so we can have coffeehouse drinks to sip on as we chat. I often hear my visitors say, "I do not know why I am telling you this." I know why. It is the presence of the Lord that gives them clarity for what they need to say, what needs to come off their chest, so that, together, we can find the path toward the solution God is leading them to.

When I look back at my financial journey with God, I see that it all started with those five-dollar checks that I gave to the church out of an obligation to "keep the lights on." God had patience with me while I learned how He wanted to take care of me. He was not upset with the length of time it took me to give Him my whole heart. If you are feeling a nudge to be even a little bit generous, trust the feeling. Trust God. You'll be amazed at where He can take you.

Today, I live completely by faith. I am in a place where I must trust his provision. He is my employer, and I work only for Him each day. My hands are open for God to fill and empty as He desires.

After all, it ALL belongs to Him.

VISIBILITY

MASTER YOUR MONEY FLOW

We cannot master what we cannot see clearly. When you are willing to see where your money is going, you begin to take ownership of it. Visibility creates responsibility.

God is on your side when it comes to your finances. The same God who was with Joseph is with you today. Scripture says, *The Lord was with him... and gave him success in whatever he did* (Genesis 39:21-23 NIV). God showed Joseph kindness and favor, and He desires to do the same for you. That favor was not random. Joseph was entrusted with responsibility, and he carried it well. In the same way, recognize that you have been entrusted with your finances. Whether you have fully stepped into that responsibility or not, it belongs to you. You have the opportunity to steward with God what has happened, what is happening, and what will happen financially in your household.

We experience financial transformation when we take ownership. Stop waiting for circumstances to change and begin to take responsibility for what is in your hands, and everything will begin to move in a new direction.

One client I worked with came to me after he was laid off. He had three children and was the primary provider for his family. They had a mortgage, very little retirement savings, about $45,000 in credit card debt, and a small amount of savings. They needed a way forward, and they needed it quickly. As I listened, I could clearly see what was missing—not effort, desire, or even income. They were missing visibility.

Visibility, the ability to see clearly, is the missing piece in many financial situations. Most people do not know where their money is going. They earn income, and before they fully realize it, that money has already been spent. They find themselves living paycheck to paycheck, covering expenses, making minimum payments, and slowly falling further behind without realizing how it is happening. Over time, this creates a cycle that feels impossible to break.

Lack of visibility keeps people stuck. When you cannot see clearly, you cannot lead effectively. But when you gain clarity, you begin to take control. Jesus said, *"You will know the truth, and the truth will set you free"* (John 8:32 NIV). Although this "truth" is referring to Jesus Himself, it can also apply directly to our finances: When we know the truth about where our money is going, we position ourselves for freedom.

Resistance often gets in the way of visibility. My coach used to say, "Change is not hard. Resistance to change is hard." Many people avoid looking at their finances because they do not want to face what they might find. I want to encourage you to lean into this moment instead of resisting it. Growth requires you to step into a level of responsibility you may not have operated in before. You are capable of doing this. You can learn new skills, make new decisions, and completely change your financial trajectory. The key is to not quit.

Scripture shows us a powerful picture of what it means to see clearly. When a blind person receives his sight in the Bible, there are natural and spiritual applications. As you begin to look at your finances honestly, you will begin to see clearly in a new way. What once felt confusing will begin to make sense.

This clarity requires seeking God. I think about David, who consistently inquired of the Lord when facing decisions. Even in difficult situations, he chose to seek God rather than rely on fear or pressure. David's focus remained on God, even when others around him were overwhelmed by circumstances. I want to encourage you to do the same. When you look at your finances, do not only look at the numbers. Ask God to show you what you need to see. Invite Him into the process.

When my client committed to this process, everything began to shift. We worked together to create full visibility, build structure, and develop a plan to eliminate debt. Over time, he sold his home, paid off his credit cards, relocated his family, and stepped into new job opportunities. When we spoke again, he told me that he had always known about God, but now he truly knew God was real because he saw how everything aligned at the right time. Every detail came together in a way he could not have orchestrated on his own.

This is what happens when you combine responsibility with faith. You do your part, and God meets you in it. Jesus says, *"One who is faithful in very little is also faithful in much"* (Luke 16:10 ESV). Faithfulness begins with what you can see and manage right now. As you grow in that, your capacity increases.

Financial confidence begins with visibility. When you can clearly see where your money is going, what you owe, and what you have, you begin to make decisions with confidence instead of fear. You move from reacting to your finances to leading them. That shift changes everything.

As you step into this level of clarity, you will begin to experience peace where there once was stress, direction where there once was confusion, and confidence where there once was uncertainty. You will begin to lead your finances instead of feeling controlled by them.

JOURNAL REFLECTION

1. Look at your finances without avoiding anything. Where is your money currently going? What are your monthly, quarterly, and yearly expenses?

2. What debt do you currently have? Which debt can you focus on paying down/off first?

3. What savings and assets do you currently have?

4. Now look at your income. What is coming in each month? Is it consistent, or does it vary?

5. As you reflect on all of this, ask yourself one more question: Where have I been avoiding looking at the truth?

Gabriela Walerczyk

Gabriela Walerczyk is a wife, mother, and woman of faith who believes ordinary people are capable of building meaningful, impactful lives when they trust God and take consistent steps forward. Based in Texas, she is passionate about developing people, strengthening families, and helping others create financial margin with integrity.

Gaby's journey has been shaped by seasons of rebuilding, growth, and surrender. Through mentoring and leadership, she encourages men and women to pursue excellence without compromising their values, embrace discipline as a gift, and build from a foundation rooted in Christ.

Gaby believes leadership begins at home and that faith and work are deeply connected. Together with her husband, Lance, she seeks to model unity, resilience, and long-term vision grounded in Ecclesiastes 4:12.

Gaby writes with honesty and conviction, inviting readers to grow, believe again, and trust that God establishes what we faithfully place in His hands.

BUILDING WEALTH WITH INTEGRITY IN CHRIST

By Gabriela Walerczyk

A good name is more desirable than great riches; to be esteemed is better than silver or gold (Proverbs 22:1 NIV).

For most of my life, I thought wealth was about money: A bigger paycheck. A bigger house. A better life. And while money is a tool God uses to provide and bless, what I have learned is that real wealth is built on something much deeper—integrity, identity, and obedience to Jesus.

My entrepreneurial journey began in sixth grade when I sold Menudo pins and posters. That early spark was more than a side hustle; it was a dream taking root. Even as a child, I wanted to create value, to exchange something meaningful with the world, and to build something that mattered.

But the reality was not as glamorous as the dream. I started and failed. I quit before I really started. I earned money and lost money, and it always seemed to slip through my fingers before I could make a real impact.

There came a moment when I woke up and realized, *This is not where I thought I would be.* My plans, my choices, and even my excuses had led me to a place where I felt stuck. Maybe you have felt that way too, when you look around at your life and wonder, *How did I end up here?*

That is when I had to ask a bigger question: What does the Bible say about building wealth while becoming a new creation in Christ? Because money without Jesus is meaningless, but money with integrity and purpose becomes a legacy.

ACTION STEPS:

1. Ask yourself: Am I measuring wealth by money alone, or by integrity and obedience to Jesus?
2. Write down one area of your life where you feel stuck; pray for God to show you His bigger purpose.
3. Meditate on Proverbs 22:1 and ask, *What kind of name am I building today?*

LIFE HAPPENS FOR YOU

For years, I carried the mindset of a victim, asking, *Why did this happen to me? Why is life so hard? Why can't I catch a break?* But the Holy Spirit began to show me that life was not happening to me; it was happening for me. Every struggle, every disappointment, every failure was not the end of my story but the soil where God was preparing new growth.

Instead of asking, *Why me?*, I started asking, *What can I learn from this? How is this shaping me? How can God use my experience to bless others?*

That shift changed everything. I realized that because of my pain, I now have compassion. Because of my mistakes, I now have wisdom. Because of my story, I now have authority.

> *Therefore, if anyone is in Christ, the new creation has come. The old has gone, the new is here* (2 Corinthians 5:17 NIV).

Saul's transformation into Paul in Acts 9 is one of the most powerful pictures of this truth. Saul was a persecutor; he was feared and despised. But when he encountered Jesus, his entire identity changed; he became a new person. That same truth is available to us today. No matter your past, no matter your story, when you are in Christ, you are not defined by what you've done or has been done to you; you are defined by who Jesus says you are.

ACTION STEPS:

1. Write down one painful event and reframe it by asking, *How did God use this for my growth?*
2. Pray 2 Corinthians 5:17 daily, claiming that you are "I am a new creation in Christ. The old has gone, the new is here."
3. Share your testimony with someone who needs hope this week.

LEARNING DISCIPLINE AND INTEGRITY

Once I stopped living as a victim, I had to learn what it looked like to live as a woman of integrity. I did not grow up knowing how to do that. I had to learn step by step.

I started with the little things: I asked my now husband how he kept his car so clean. I practiced making my bed, cleaning my house, and organizing my closet. These might sound small, but they built something bigger in me: discipline.

Jesus said, *"Whoever can be trusted with very little can also be trusted with much"* (Luke 16:10 NIV).

If I could not be faithful in the small things like showing up on time, keeping my word, or stewarding my home, how could God trust me with wealth, leadership, or influence?

Motherhood became another turning point. I did not plan my daughter, but God did. Psalm 127:3 (NIV) proclaims, *Children are a heritage from the*

Lord, offspring a reward from him. My daughter was God's reward to me, and the Holy Spirit used her to change everything in me. My desires shifted. My vision expanded. My values deepened.

I became obsessed with building a legacy, not just for me, but for my daughter and her children after her. Proverbs 13:22 (NIV) states, *A good person leaves an inheritance for their children's children.* That verse is burned into my heart.

If you want to grow, you must put yourself in rooms with people who are doing better than you. And if you are going to model success, make sure it is someone worth modeling—I chose the Proverbs 31 woman. She was wise, strong, diligent, and a blessing to her household and community.

ACTION STEPS:

1. Start with one small thing this week: make your bed, keep your car clean, or stick to your word.
2. Ask God to show you one area of your life where He wants to grow your integrity.
3. Read Proverbs 31 and write down three qualities of the woman you want to model.

RENEWING YOUR MIND FOR WEALTH

The first time I really made what I thought was a lot of money was when I was in my 20s. By 1997, I had become an apprentice in a high-end hair salon in Los Angeles. What I discovered surprised me: I was not a bad student; I just needed the right teachers. I thrive in a hands-on environment, and I learned from some of the best stylists in the industry.

I mastered the art of beautiful hair and learned how to run a business. I studied personal development and dabbled in the law of attraction, though I did not yet know how different it was from God's Word. I set a clear goal: to earn $10,000 a month. And I reverse-engineered it.

I took excellent care of my clients, and it worked. Within months, I was earning $10,000 a month in a beautiful Santa Monica salon. I bought myself an SUV and paid for my daughter to attend private school.

But here is the truth: I was not tithing. I was not saving. I was not investing. For every $10,000 that came in, $10,000 went out. A few years later, I looked back and realized I had nothing to show for it.

The Lord spoke of this: *"You earn wages, only to put them in a purse with holes in it"* (Haggai 1:6 NIV). That was my life. I knew how to earn money, but without honoring God, money never stayed.

> *Honor the Lord with your wealth, with the firstfruits of all your crops. Then your barns will be filled to overflowing* (Proverbs 3:9-10 NIV).

In 2008, after more than a decade in the hair industry, I walked away. Everyone thought I was crazy. Why leave a successful business to start over in the travel industry? But I knew God was stirring something new in me. Proverbs 16:9 (NIV) teaches, *In their hearts humans plan their course, but the Lord establishes their steps.*

That is what He was doing. God was redirecting my steps.

I moved to Texas in pursuit of the American dream. What I discovered is that you can earn money and still not keep it. You can build a business and still not have peace. You can chase success and still feel empty.

Romans 12:2 tells us, *Do not conform to the pattern of this world, but be transformed by the renewing of your mind* (NIV). For me, renewing my mind meant shifting from "I have to" to "I get to."

ACTION STEPS:

1. If you do not tithe, start today by giving God your firstfruits.

2. Write down your financial patterns. Do you have holes in your pocket?
3. Replace one "I have to" statement with an "I get to" statement, and live it out this week.

THE WEALTH OF INTEGRITY

Proverbs 22:1 says a good name is worth more than silver or gold. The world tells us to chase money, but money fades. Markets crash, businesses close, promotions get passed by. But integrity never depreciates. A good name, rooted in righteousness, humility, and love, leaves a legacy long after the dollars are spent.

For a long time, I thought wealth meant arriving. But what I discovered is that wealth is really stewardship. It is about how you live, how you lead, and how you honor God with what you have been entrusted.

One of the most practical ways I changed my view of wealth and integrity was through the discipline of 75 Hard, a program that requires following five rules for 75 days. For me, this was not about weight loss. It was about proving to myself that I could finish what I started. That I could honor my word to myself. That I could do hard things and become stronger for it.

Doing the program taught me that I could accomplish hard things—and that what I thought was hard was not really hard at all. Once I made the decision, there was no negotiation. It simply became my new normal. And each time I completed one "new normal," I stacked another on top of it. Before long, I realized I was not just changing my habits; I was changing my identity.

An object in motion stays in motion, and when I chose consistency, even when it felt like nothing was changing, something inside me was changing. I was building character.

Wealth is not just in what you hold in your hand. It is in who you are becoming.

I did not need to wait until someday to step into the person God was calling me to be. I could become her now.

Dr. Benjamin Hardy teaches that your future self is your greatest guide. Instead of looking at who you have been, you look forward and ask, *Who am I becoming?* And then start living today as if that future self is already here.

That is also the gospel. Second Corinthians 5:17 says you are already a new creation in Christ. Not someday. Now.

Stepping into your future self means chiseling away everything that is not really you. It means letting go of old self-images, breaking off limiting beliefs, and releasing the words people have spoken over you that do not align with what God says about you.

I've learned to stop saying "I know" and start saying "Anything is possible." Because with Jesus, anything truly is possible.

> *I can do all things through Christ who strengthens me"*
> (Philippians 4:13 NIV).

When I looked at my future self, the woman who earns a significant income, builds a legacy, leads with integrity, and blesses others, I realized she was not waiting for me to get ready. She was waiting for me to decide.

Set a goal so big you need Jesus. That is how faith grows. Know your why, and the how will show up.

ACTION STEPS:

1. Write a letter from your future self describing the life you are living in Christ.
2. Identify one limiting belief and replace it with a Scripture-based truth.

3. Set one goal that is so big you need Jesus and commit it to prayer.

FROM BROKENNESS TO BUILDING LEGACY

Looking back, I can see the thread of God's redemption throughout my story.

In Joel 2:25 (NIV), the Lord declares, *"I will restore to you for the years that the locusts have eaten."* That is what He has done for me.

That verse became more than words on a page for me—it became a promise I could hold onto. For years, I felt like I had wasted time, missed opportunities, and lost resources. But God reminded me that nothing surrendered to Him is ever wasted. What I thought was gone forever, He was able to redeem.

Restoration is not just about getting back what has been lost; it is about God multiplying what remains and using it for His glory. God restored my confidence, my joy, my vision, and my purpose. The lost years became the training ground for the life I am living now.

He took my brokenness and turned it into wisdom. He took my pain and turned it into compassion. He took my mess and turned it into a message.

Part of that redemption came in a way I will never forget. There is a saying, "When the student is ready, the teacher will appear." That was my story. I reached a point where I knew I was not where I wanted to be, but for the first time, I had peace about it. I trusted that God could change everything in a moment. And He did.

I still remember the day my phone rang. I knew the call, and yet I also knew it was more than just a phone call. It was an answer to my prayers. The prophet Isaiah said, *"Before they call I will answer; while they are still speaking I will hear"* (Isaiah 65:24 NIV). I experienced the evidence of that promise. Everything shifted, and I knew God had heard me.

The call I received was not just about money. It was about my name, my integrity, and my identity in Christ. It was about my family, my marriage, and my children. About leaving something behind that will outlive me.

Wealth is not evident in what you accumulate. It is about what you steward. Being wealthy is becoming the person God designed you to be, so that you can bless others.

Sometimes, it requires the courage to keep believing even when it looks too late—that's faith. Faith is believing God's promises even when your reality has not caught up yet.

ACTION STEPS:

1. Write down one prayer you have been waiting on and thank God as if He has already answered it.
2. Reflect on Joel 2:25. Where has God already restored lost years in your life?
3. Share a redemption testimony with someone who needs hope.

VICTIM TO VICTORIOUS

Moving to Texas was a big deal. I only had a handful of acquaintances and was leaving behind the village that had helped me raise my daughter and keep me together. It was my safety net, and walking away from it stretched me in every way.

On the outside, my life looked like everything I had prayed for, but on the inside, I knew there was more. It would have been easy to give up on my entrepreneurial career, get a steady job, and forget about my dreams. But I refused to believe this was how my story would end.

Being an entrepreneur had awakened big dreams and big goals, and I was not willing to let them die. I knew God had better plans for me. So when the phone call came, it was everything I had been praying for and more. It was the partnership I had asked God for. It was the system and the strategy that would provide stability and security. And it was the opportunity to do what I loved most: help people. But I also realized I first had to put my own oxygen mask on, so I could show up strong for others.

The Lord says, *"Before they call I will answer. While they are still speaking I will hear"* (Isaiah 65:24 NIV). That is exactly what He did for me.

Change is not hard. It is a decision. The word "decision" comes from the Latin word decidere, which means "to cut off." A true decision means cutting off every other option. It means there is no plan B. You move forward with faith, fully committed.

I decided that I was no longer going to live as a victim. I decided that integrity would be my wealth. I decided that I would become my future self now. And here is the good news. You can too.

You do not have to wait until you have more money, more success, or more answers. You do not have to wait until your past feels distant or for someone else to validate you. With Jesus, you already have everything you need. You are a new creation. You can do all things through Him.

So today, choose to step into the future self God is calling you to be. Decide that your good name, integrity, and faith will be your wealth. Because life is not happening to you; it is happening for you. And when you live as a victor in Christ, your wealth will not only bless you, it will leave a legacy that will bless generations to come.

ACTION STEPS:

1. Make one firm decision today and cut off every other option.
2. Declare Philippians 4:13 over your life: *I can do all things through Christ who strengthens me* (NKJV).
3. Write down one legacy action you will take this week to bless the next generation.

The blessing of the Lord brings wealth, without painful toil for it (Proverbs 10:22 NIV).

KETURAH WILK

Keturah Wilk and her husband, Shamariah, are a dynamic team who utilize their God-given talents to manage and operate multiple businesses successfully. Married for 23 years with four incredible children, they began their friendship and partnership in high school.

The Wilks answered God's call in 2010 to start a small business. Combining Shamariah's construction knowledge with Keturah's business training, they have since expanded their portfolio to include three additional construction-related companies. Their vision is rooted in faith and includes a commitment to providing employment and personal growth opportunities for their employees, delivering quality products to their customers, and stewarding God's companies as they trust in His provision beyond what they can imagine.

The Wilks have a clear mission: "His Kingdom come; His will be done."

YOUR KINGDOM COME

By Keturah Wilk

Counsel and stewardship are two biblical principles that have guided me and ushered God's kingdom into my life here on earth. Let me introduce myself. My name is Keturah Wilk; I am writing so that my husband, Shamariah, and I can share with you the great testimony of our lives as stewards of all that God has entrusted to us as we've lived our lives praying and seeking His kingdom.

Shamariah (or Sham for short) means "kept of God," which basically explains our entire life. We have been kept by God in so many ways that it is beyond humbling. As I put words to these pages, I am overwhelmed and in awe of how good God has been to us and how He continues to bless us every day and in every way.

Sham and I have known each other since we were children; we were raised in the same church by wonderful God-loving parents. Our story together began on a bus when he was 15, and I was 14. He played catcher on the baseball team, and I played second base on the softball team. Our teams rode the bus together, where we quickly became lifelong best friends. One of the greatest gifts of our lives was that God allowed us to find each other early and kept us from heartbreak and rejection. We became a great team, which has translated into every area of our lives.

Our financial journey began early in our marriage. I earned a degree in business and accounting, and Sham worked for our church, becoming skilled in every construction trade imaginable; expertise that would later be invaluable in our business structure. A few years later, I was working in public accounting, and Sham was contemplating going into general construction when we learned the value of counsel. While deciding what his next steps were, Sham reached out to a trusted counselor who told him, "Go work for different contractors, see how they do things—how they run their business, treat their employees, etc." Sham took that counsel and began working for a few reputable contractors in our area, learning and gleaning from them as he grew his own skills, gaining confidence and experience in carpentry.

During this same time, our church asked us to get trained in biblical financial principles, another amazing gift in our journey. We studied the Word to find out what God thought about money. Soon after, we began counseling others on these principles, witnessing through them and learning firsthand that how we handle money impacts our relationship with the Lord.

We also continued to seek counsel for our own lives as our finances grew and changed. Many of our friends were also newlyweds who were starting families and purchasing homes. At one point, we, too, had an opportunity to buy a home. We could have "made" it happen; however, after seeking counsel, we decided to wait.

> *Without counsel, plans go awry, But in the multitude of counselors they are established* (Proverbs 15:22 NKJV).

Receiving counseling can be tough. The advice we received regarding purchasing a home at that point was not what we wanted to hear: words like "wait," "be patient," and "don't overextend yourself." But, after seeking guidance directly from God to ensure we were acting wisely and in His will, we followed the difficult-to-hear words. As a result, God kept us from a difficult path and began to unfold one of our greatest blessings.

Soon after, the housing market crashed. We watched with great pain as many of our peers found themselves "upside down" on their mortgages, some losing everything. God shielded us from that fate.

A few years later, we received an opportunity to move into a beautiful property—the one-time caretaking quarters for an extravagant cabin across the street. We rented the property for a ridiculously low amount and saved the difference of what we previously had been spending on rent. Sham took care of the cabin, which was owned by a wonderful couple, for nearly ten years, treating it as if it were his own property. We were learning stewardship firsthand.

I regularly prayed that God would give us the house that had become our home. We had our four beautiful children there and enjoyed the most amazing yard in the middle of the forest, where we would host others and invite God's presence. I asked the homeowner every year if we could buy the home, and every year he said no.

Finally, one year, out of the blue, the homeowners called us to their cabin. All four of us were seated on the back deck when the homeowners presented Sham and me with an astonishing proposal for us to purchase the house; it was a deal we still can't believe ten years later.

The gentleman told us, "You've taken such good care of the property, you made it your own, we want you to purchase it plus all the acreage around it."

I remember thinking, "Wow, this is just like the Scripture in Matthew 25:21 where God says, 'You were faithful with a few things, I will put you in charge of many things.' I guess these godly financial principles really work!"

Little did we know that we were sitting on seven additional acres of land that were part of the purchase. Everything truly is the Lord's. *To the Lord your God belong...the earth and everything in it* (Deuteronomy 10:14 NIV). What an amazing truth to live in. Once Sham and I acknowledged God's ownership and control, we could do our part, stewarding what He allowed us to. We came to learn that God didn't design us to shoulder the responsibilities that only He can. This is why Jesus tells us, *"Come to Me, all who are weary and heavy-laden, and I will give you rest. Take my yoke upon you...For My yoke is easy, and my burden is light"* (Matthew 11:28-30 NIV).

God owns everything. And the home that He has allowed us to live in is a blessing that keeps on blessing us more and more. Sham has used his skills to expand and improve the property over the last few years. He built a home for his parents on the property so they are nearby—blessing our kids, us, and our parents. He built an amazing outdoor area where we host youth groups, worship services, and baptisms, and play and have fun as we sit around the fire and fellowship about the Lord. The land has become a place where God's presence truly resides.

The fact that our rent had been so inexpensive and we acquired the property for a surprisingly low price was the hand of God on our lives; He was setting us up for what He had in store next.

A few years before, God had led us to start a general construction company. He had also asked me to leave a job I loved in public accounting to stay home with our two young children and help Sham start the business. This was a tough ask for me. I had built a successful career, acquired my clients, and really loved what I did and the people I worked with. I had to lay down my pride and submit to what God was asking.

The rest of that story is a chapter for a different book; for now, suffice it to say that in God's wisdom and sovereignty, He met us in our obedience. We went on to have two more children— four kids in total—in five quick years. All while starting a business during a recession. We trusted God, and He provided. We combined Sham's entrepreneurial drive, charisma, and construction knowledge with my business background, and we hit the ground running. Sham is one of the most influential people I know; he displays this in coaching youth sports while teaching the Word of God and leading our now many employees. We truly are a powerful team when working alongside God!

We ran God's modest business, Cornerstone Construction, out of our house for years. Steadily plodding, year after year, while raising our four small children.

> *Steady plodding brings prosperity* (Proverbs 21:5 TLB).

God promised us through prophetic word that "business would be an avenue for salvation"—a promise that we are watching unfold right before our eyes today. Each year, as we steward what is in front of us, God continues to grow the company.

We had talked about someday acquiring other businesses, and God unfolded a vision for a business model that made perfect sense to us, but getting there seemed so far off. Then, in 2021, we were approached by a subcontractor with whom Sham had established a long-standing working relationship over the years. He asked if we wanted to purchase his flooring company.

We had been setting aside capital for "something," so when this opportunity presented itself, we began to seek our most important Counselor, the Lord. Then we sought financial counsel from our business mentor and my former boss. We sought legal counsel from an attorney, and we sought spiritual counsel from our pastor, who had also run a successful business for years. These counselors have proven to be safeguards for us, and their counsel usually lines up with what we believe God is leading us to do.

Acquiring this business proved to be a time-consuming, learning process; we both learned more than MBA students. We went through financials, had professionals go through the financials, and sought the Lord. Even in my reluctance, God made it very clear that we were supposed to purchase the business. A year of negotiations, financing applications, and due diligence culminated in a visit to the attorney's office to sign the papers.

In November 2022, we owned a flooring retail and installation store. There were so many "coincidental" things that tied us to this business already that we did not know going into it. Little things that the Lord allowed to reassure us that He was ordering our steps.

> *A man's mind plans his way [as he journeys through life], but the Lord directs his steps and establishes them* (Proverbs 16:9 AMP).

We used the capital we had set aside for the down payment on a business loan for the flooring store. As we went through negotiations, we were surprised to find out the down payment would be considerably less than what we originally planned for. We took the difference in savings and put it aside in case we needed it for operating capital as we got the flooring store off the ground. While the first few months came with many challenges, God met us every step of the way. It required a lot of hard work, long hours, learning curves, patience, and a reliance on the Holy Spirit to guide us. During these challenging times, we would remind ourselves that the businesses were God's and we were stewarding them. Jesus promises us that if we partner with Him, He takes the burden. I just love how it is written in The Message Bible: *"Walk with me and work with me—watch how I do it. Learn the unforced rhythms of grace. I won't lay anything heavy or ill-fitting on you. Keep company with me and you'll learn to live freely and lightly."* (Matthew 11:28-30 MSG). God is so good and truly wants us to live an abundant life!

At the end of 2022, we had two huge contracts in place for new home builds. We were also under contract with a local cabinet maker, who contacted Sham and said, "I'm closing shop." He was walking away. Sham, with his entrepreneurial, never-quit, always-find-a-solution mentality, offered to run the business for him until our contracts were seen through, so we could honor our contracts with the homeowners.

The cabinet owner responded with, "Why don't you just buy the business from me?"

When Sham brought this proposition to me, I, of course, said, "You are crazy. We have a thriving construction company. We JUST bought a flooring store. We have four very busy, amazing children. What are you thinking? Surely this couldn't be ordered by the Lord."

So, we brought this to the Lord in prayer, we went back to our counselors (who also thought we were crazy), and we did our due diligence. What made it abundantly clear was this: We asked the owner what he wanted to sell the business for, and he gave us a number. The amount was the exact amount of money that we had not used for the down payment on the flooring store and had set aside for "something." That was a good enough answer for me. That purchase was considerably easier after all we had learned the year before—the dos and the don'ts, pitfalls to avoid, how to draw up contracts and entity structures.

Then, in May of 2023, yet *another* subcontractor came to Sham—this time, it was our painter. It was a similar scenario; he wanted to retire—to sell his business. Once again, we followed counsel, and the Lord opened the doors. We simply walked through the doors in obedience. In a few short months, God had expanded His business from six employees to thirty-two.

In the past few years, we've come to realize that when God wants to expand something, He will do it if we are willing to submit to His expansion. In our submission, we continue to learn that our work is actually to serve God.

> *Whatever you do, do your work heartily, as for the Lord and not for people... It is the Lord Christ whom you serve* (Colossians 3:23-24 NASB).

We are often asked, "How do you do all of it?"

Each time we answer, "By the grace of God."

But because God was so gracious, so very generous, here I am. And I'm not about to let His grace go to waste. Haven't I worked hard trying to do more than any of the others? Even then, my work didn't amount to all that much. It was God giving me the work to do, God giving me the energy to do it. So whether you heard it from me or from those others, it's all the same: We spoke God's truth and you entrusted your lives
(1 Corinthians 15:10-11 MSG).

In those verses, we know Paul was talking about working to preach the gospel, but we should live our lives as if everything we do is preaching the gospel. Whether it be our work, play, or service, everything should be an avenue of salvation for those we come in contact with.

We quickly realized that while these businesses would grow and become profitable, we weren't in the construction, flooring, cabinetry, or painting business. We were in the people business. Every employee and their families, every subcontractor, and every customer had become a part of our lives. They were now in our sphere of influence.

The focus on people has been our driving factor for how we conduct business. It keeps us striving to work hard, lift, advance, and make these individuals a part of something bigger than themselves, leading them to become who they were truly made to be. Is it always easy? Not at all. But we have the greatest example: Jesus, who teaches us that serving is far greater than anything else we can ever do. What a contrast from our society and culture.

Whoever wishes to become great among you shall be a servant (Matthew 20:26 AMP).

It is challenging at times to balance efforts to be profitable with an unselfish concern for employees. Entitlement and instant gratification are so prevalent in our society. We have found that to combat this, we must absolutely follow Scripture and treat our employees (who are ultimately God's employees) with dignity and act in a just manner.

It says in Colossians 4:1, *Masters grant to your slaves justice and fairness, knowing that you too have a Master in heaven* (NASB). In other words, *[Employers] grant to your [employees] justice and fairness.* It can be heartbreaking when we offer people the opportunity for growth, experience, and development, yet they refuse to take it. These are the times when our submission to God is so important; when we do our part, we can trust that God will meet the needs of His business. God has always met our needs and been so gracious to us. He has provided wonderful employees, some of whom have been with us for years. Operating a business God's way is the right way.

As we write this chapter, we are in another time of expansion and explosive growth in our current operations. The Holy Spirit is leading us as He fine-tunes, dissects, and realigns our stewardship of His businesses. He is asking us to examine our hearts constantly.

> *Search me, O God, and know my heart; Try me, and know my anxieties; And see if there is any wicked way in me, And lead me in the way everlasting* (Psalm 139:23-24 NKJV).

We know how much God values these businesses and the individuals who work in them. We know He wants prosperity that comes as we focus continually on Him, His kingdom, and His ways. God's eternal perspective is far above anything we can imagine.

Now to Him who is able to do exceedingly abundantly above all that we ask or think, according to the power that works in us (Ephesians 3:20 NKJV).

Yes, Lord. We set aside our own agendas, however lofty they are, and we will follow Your direction. We will partner with You. As we do, I know we will witness things happen here in our lives that can only be explained by Your powerful Spirit at work in us. For Your kingdom will come, and Your will shall be done—on this earth and in our lives as it is in heaven.

CLARITY

THE WEALTH BLUEPRINT FOR EVERY SEASON

Allow your financial patterns to come into focus. When you understand what is coming, you are able to plan and move with confidence. Clarity turns intention into direction.

If you do not have a plan for your money, someone else will have a plan for it, and most of the time, that plan will not align with what God has for your life. I have seen people who work hard, earn income, and yet feel like their money is constantly slipping through their hands. The issue is not always income; it is often the absence of a clear and intentional plan.

There was a time in my life when everything felt out of control financially. I had credit cards in collections, my car had been repossessed, and I was doing everything I could just to survive day by day. There came a moment when I reached the end of my own ability to figure it out. I cried out to God and asked Him for help because I knew that what I was doing was not working. That moment became a turning point for me.

The heart of man plans his way, but the Lord establishes his steps (Proverbs 16:9 ESV). God is waiting for us to invite Him into this area of our lives. When we seek His direction, He brings clarity where there was confusion, revealing a path forward.

Clarity is built through intentional planning. When you begin to plan your finances with purpose, you move from reacting to life to leading it. Scripture gives us a powerful picture of this through the example of the ant. *Consider its ways and be wise! ... It stores its provisions in summer and gathers its food in harvest* (Proverbs 6:6-8 NIV). There is wisdom in preparation. There is stability in thinking beyond the present moment.

Over time, I developed consistent rhythms with my finances. I created weekly and monthly routines that allowed me to stay aware of what I had, what I needed, and what was coming next. Through that consistency, I began to save money for the first time in my life. As I saw progress, my confidence grew. Scripture reinforces this principle: *On the first day of every week, each of you is to put something aside and store it up, as he may prosper* (1 Corinthians 16:2 ESV). Small, consistent actions lead to lasting results.

I shifted how I saw myself—from someone struggling to someone who could lead in this area. Scripture says, *The noble make noble plans, and by noble deeds they stand* (Isaiah 32:8 NIV). How you see yourself will determine how you show up and the decisions you make.

As I continued to grow, I learned to align my plans with God. I stopped making decisions based only on what I wanted and began seeking what He wanted. *Commit to the Lord whatever you do, and he will establish your plans* (Proverbs 16:3 NIV). That alignment brought peace and direction into my finances.

Diligence became another key part of this process. Financial clarity comes from steady, intentional action over time. Scripture says, The plans of the diligent lead to profit (Proverbs 21:5 NIV). When we commit to the process, even when it feels uncomfortable, we begin to experience real change.

Financial clarity brings confidence. When you know what is coming throughout the year, you are no longer caught off guard. Many expenses feel unexpected, but in reality, they happen consistently. Holidays, car maintenance, insurance, and other recurring costs show up year after year. When you do not plan for them, they create stress. When you prepare for them, they become manageable.

The shift from reactive to proactive living changes everything. When you are reactive, you are constantly responding to problems. When you are proactive, you anticipate what is coming and prepare for it ahead of time. That preparation creates stability.

Clarity is not something that happens overnight. It is built through consistent attention, intentional planning, and a willingness to grow. As you continue to show up in this process, you will begin to experience a level of confidence and peace that you may not have thought was possible.

JOURNAL REFLECTION

1. What expenses come up throughout the year that you already know are coming? Do you plan for holidays, birthdays, car maintenance, insurance, travel, and other recurring expenses?
2. Where have you felt the most financial pressure throughout the year? What seasons tend to feel the heaviest? What patterns do you notice?
3. What would it look like to plan for these expenses ahead of time? What would need to change for you to feel prepared instead of reactive?
4. What would it look like to approach your finances with consistency throughout the year?
5. Reflect on your habits. Where have you been consistent or inconsistent? What is one area you need to become more disciplined in?

FAITH GUMEDE

Faith Gumede is a distinguished luxury real estate advisor known for her integrity, strategic insight, and deeply client-centered approach. As a licensed REALTOR® with Luxe Haven Estate, affiliated with Keller Williams Beverly Hills, she represents buyers, sellers, and investors across some of the nation's most competitive and prestigious markets.

With an academic background as a former nurse and premed student at UCLA, Faith brings a rare level of care, precision, and discipline to her work. She approaches every transaction as both a financial and emotional milestone, guided by transparency, data-driven strategy, and an unwavering commitment to protect her clients' best interests.

Faith specializes in Beverly Hills, West Hollywood, Sherman Oaks, Malibu, and Calabasas, while maintaining a presence in Miami. Known for her sharp negotiation skills and calm, confident leadership, she delivers results in high-stakes environments while ensuring a seamless, elevated client experience.

Her journey from Ridgefield, Connecticut, and Rhode Island to Beverly Hills has shaped a broad understanding of property ownership across diverse markets. Faith also shares market insights online, believing real estate builds stability, growth, and a lasting legacy.

GUIDED ALL ALONG

By Faith Gumede

There are moments in life when you realize that the path you are walking was never entirely your own to design. There is a quiet understanding that something greater has been guiding you—through the good days, the confusing seasons, and even the storms that once felt overwhelming.

For me, that realization has come through my relationship with God, whom I often call my "Daddy God."

I didn't always understand that name the way I do now. But at the age of 18, my life adjusted in a way that forced me to experience God differently. My brother and I had to move out of the home we grew up in, and suddenly, I found myself navigating independence at a very young age. What once felt like stability became uncertainty overnight.

My parents believed strongly in preparing us for adulthood at a young age. They wanted us to be independent, capable, and grounded. So my older brother and I were each given our own homes—just down the road from one another.

On the outside, it looked like such a blessing. And it was. But internally, it felt heavy. I was nervous and scared. And for the first time, I truly felt alone.

I remember the quiet more than anything. The kind of quiet that feels loud when you're not used to being alone. Even small things would make me uneasy—sometimes even the dog moving around the house would startle me. I wasn't used to that kind of stillness. I knew I wasn't truly alone—my brother was right down the road, and my parents always reassured me they were just a phone call away. My brother and I would often have weekly dinners together to stay connected.

But still... I felt alone.

There were nights I would call my mom, not because something was wrong, but because I didn't understand. I wondered, *Why do I have to do this so early? Why is independence so important? Why does this feel so uncomfortable?* It didn't make sense to me at the time.

But in that space—in that quiet and discomfort—I began to rely on God in a way I never had before. In that season, my relationship with God became deeply personal. I needed a protector and a provider. I needed guidance, comfort, and reassurance in ways I had never experienced before. And in that space, God became everything to me—my Father, my covering, my source of peace.

That is where "Daddy God" came from. It wasn't just a name—it was an experience. What once didn't make sense to me—why my parents pushed independence—began to reveal itself as preparation. God was drawing me closer to Him, teaching me that even when everything around me felt uncertain, I was never truly alone.

My relationship with God became my anchor.

A FOUNDATION OF FAITH AND SERVICE

I grew up in church. My grandfather was a pastor, and from a young age, I watched what it meant to serve others. I saw my grandfather pour into the community, host charity events, and give without hesitation. His example shaped me deeply, planting a desire in me to help people—to be present in moments where others needed support the most. That calling naturally led me into healthcare.

I pursued nursing with discipline and commitment. I wanted to make a difference, to be someone who could show up for people during their most vulnerable moments.

During my time as a critical care nurse, I experienced moments that stretched me in ways I never expected. One particular case involved a patient undergoing open-heart surgery. His body had been opened, his life literally in the hands of the medical team. During the weeks I helped care for him, everything I had studied and trained for came together. I poured everything I knew into providing him with the proper care he needed.

But beyond the training, I realized something deeper: I had to rely on Christ to be effective in the way He had called me to be.

There are situations where knowledge alone is not enough, when strength must come from somewhere beyond yourself. That experience taught me how to gather not only my skills, but my faith—to remain steady when everything around me felt intense.

Working in healthcare taught me empathy and patience. It taught me how to listen, how to care, and how to remain calm when others felt overwhelmed.

And in that space, God was allowing me to grow closer to Him and become a more mature Christian.

WHEN GOD REDIRECTS YOUR PATH

After I served for about five years in critical care nursing, I found myself in a new season of life. I had recently gotten married, and the demands of my career were beginning to take a toll on my body and my energy. At the end of each day, I felt exhausted—not just physically, but mentally and emotionally. And I began to sense that something was changing. I brought that feeling to God in prayer. I asked Him for direction, clarity, and peace in making a decision.

Slowly, I felt His response: It was time for a new chapter.

That realization wasn't easy. I had invested years into becoming a nurse. It was part of my identity. Letting go of that path required surrender. I sought counsel from leadership in my church, and through prayer and confirmation, I came to understand that I had fulfilled my nursing assignment and God was calling me into something new.

STEPPING INTO THE UNKNOWN

Real estate wasn't entirely unfamiliar to me. Growing up, my dad had investments and had exposed me to the idea of ownership, business, and leadership. He always encouraged us to pursue self-employment and to think beyond traditional paths.

Still, stepping into that world myself felt completely different. Healthcare had structure. There was always support—supervisors, colleagues, systems in place. You always knew who to go to for answers.

Real estate was different. In real estate, no one checked my work. There was no constant oversight. My success—or failure—was directly tied to my own actions.

I remember the moment it truly hit me that I was on my own. That realization was both empowering and overwhelming.

My first clients challenged me in ways I wasn't prepared for. Communication was difficult. Expectations were high. There were moments when I felt completely out of my depth. There were even times—right in the middle of transactions—when I wanted to quit.

Even when I reached escrow, when things should have felt secure, I felt pressure rising. Problems seemed bigger than me. I questioned whether

I was capable and whether I belonged in that space.

And yet, in those moments, I felt a quiet nudge from the Holy Spirit: *Trust Me.*

BUILDING KINGDOM WEALTH

As I navigated this new business terrain, one Scripture became a constant for me: *Trust in the Lord with all your heart and lean not on your own understanding* (Proverbs 3:5-6 NIV). I realized that I didn't need to have everything figured out, but I needed to trust the One who did. Day by day, I kept going. Deal by deal and challenge by challenge. And slowly, things began to fall into place.

As I built my business and adjusted to married life, I studied for my real estate exam. I walked into that exam room with faith, praying and asking God to guide me and give me clarity. I was the first one to finish the test. And I passed on my first attempt. When I spoke to other agents who had taken the test multiple times, I realized something: This wasn't just God showing me my ability; it was confirmation from Him that I was exactly where I needed to be.

As I began working with clients, I noticed something unexpected: I wasn't just closing deals; I was helping people.

Still, there were rough patches. One client early in my career challenged me in a way I had never experienced before. From the very beginning of our business relationship, communicating with him felt almost impossible. Every interaction felt distant. He wouldn't answer calls, and texts were short—sometimes not even full sentences. I would text paragraphs upon paragraphs of information to him, and sometimes all I would get in response was a thumbs-up emoji.

This kind of communication was foreign to me. Uncanny, even. I had never experienced anything like it—especially with someone I was supposed to be building a working relationship with. I found myself constantly trying to understand: *Is he uninterested? Is he just busy? Am I doing something wrong?*

There was no clear feedback, no conversation to read, and no connection to build on. And in real estate—where everything is built on relationships—that felt like a major obstacle. I didn't know how to navigate it.

So I did the only thing I knew how to do. I leaned into my faith. I began sharing Scripture with my client. Occasionally, I would send a worship song—just trying to create some connection or opening. This was not something I normally do, but I felt led to do it in that moment, even though I did not know if he was receiving it... or ignoring it. I wasn't trying to force anything—I was just following what felt right in my spirit.

Over time, something started to change. The client began to respond, to open up. And he told me that somewhere along the way, he had forgotten about God. That, in the process of building his life, gaining success and wealth, he had lost sight of the One who made it all possible. He had simply... forgotten.

In that moment, everything became clear to me: I wasn't just there to help him buy or sell property. I was there to remind him of God. To remind him where his blessings came from and that success without connection to God is incomplete.

In that moment, God was nurturing a flame in me. I began to understand why I am here: Not just to build a business. but to carry God into spaces where He is often forgotten. To be a light in spaces where faith is often absent. To carry His presence into the marketplace.

That is kingdom wealth.

Kingdom wealth is not just about money; it is about stewardship, influence, and aligning with God. And it is about impact.

Kingdom wealth is recognizing that everything you have—your gifts, opportunities, and resources—has been entrusted to you by God for a greater purpose.

For me, building kingdom wealth means inviting God into every part of my business, knowing I don't have to make decisions based on pressure but grounded in His peace. It means I can walk away from opportunities that aren't aligned with His will, even when they look good on the surface.

Experiencing kingdom wealth means I treat people as more than transactions. And it means I listen—not just to clients—but to the Holy Spirit. There have been moments where I've had to pause and ask: *God, is this You? Or is this just an opportunity?* I've learned that not every opportunity is an assignment.

Kingdom wealth requires discernment; it also requires integrity. Because wealth built without God may *look* successful, but it won't carry the same weight, the same peace, or the same longevity.

When wealth is built with God at the center, it becomes something different. It becomes a tool. A tool to impact lives, create opportunities for others, and reflect God's character everywhere, even in spaces where He may not be acknowledged.

Kingdom wealth occurs when business becomes ministry, success becomes purpose, and we use our circumstances to reflect God's glory.

Success is not just about transactions; it is about transformation.

GROWTH, IDENTITY, & LETTING GO OF APPROVAL

As my career grew, I began to encounter another reality: Not everyone will understand my journey.

It has always been important to me to fully understand what I'm doing. I ask a lot of questions, stay curious, and refuse to give up. That doesn't always make sense to others.

In an industry driven by reputation, I wanted to build something different. I didn't want to just make money—I wanted to build relationships. That desire set me apart, maybe even confused people. But I stayed committed because my goal was never to please people, but to please God.

From a young age, I was aware when something didn't align with my values. Even when I faced peer pressure, I never felt drawn to compromise who I was. That same conviction followed me into business. Over time, I learned that you do not need to convince everyone of your calling. Purpose is not something you negotiate with people; purpose is something you walk in with humility and conviction.

Progress felt slow in some seasons. There were, and still are, times when things—even in my personal life—required deeper attention, more prayer, and more surrender than I expected. It wasn't just about building a business, but about being refined.

During one of those seasons, I felt a deep need for guidance—not just professionally, but spiritually. I began searching for a Christian mentor, someone who could speak into both my faith and my future. That's when I found Michelle Tascoe. I remember the day we had our first call scheduled. It was a particularly difficult day for me. Emotionally, I felt drained. Mentally, I felt overwhelmed. Spiritually, I felt like I was at the end of myself.

When her call came through, I ignored it. I thought, *I am not in a place to talk to anyone right now.*

A few moments later, she sent a simple text: <Hi, I just tried to call you.>

Something in my spirit shifted. It wasn't loud, but it was clear—a gentle push to respond. So I answered.

Within the first few seconds of the call, I noticed something different. Michelle's voice carried joy. She was warm, light, and full of life in a way that immediately contrasted how I was feeling in that moment. And suddenly, I realized something: *Even here, I can experience joy. Even in this season, I am not stuck in how I feel.*

That conversation marked a turning point for me. From the very beginning, it felt divine—like I had known Michelle already and God placed her in my life at exactly the right time. In that moment, God reminded me again: *You are not alone.*

Those seasons of waiting, stretching, and uncertainty weren't wasted time. They were preparing me, shaping me into the person I needed to become—not just for where I was, but for where God was taking me.

Prayer became more than a routine; it became a lifestyle. I spoke to God throughout the day—while driving, working, and thinking. I filled my environment with worship and stayed rooted in His presence, which kept me grounded and aligned with His will. When you stay in God's presence, distractions lose their power, comparison loses its grip, and fear loses its voice.

Looking back, I can see clearly that every closed door had a purpose. What felt like rejection was often protection, and what felt like delay was preparation. God was strengthening, refining, and positioning me.

> *And we know that in all things God works for the good of those who love him, who have been called according to his purpose* (Romans 8:28 NIV).

That truth became my foundation.

LEAVING A LEGACY OF KINGDOM WEALTH

God helped me grow more into His image as I began to understand that faith and ambition are not separate—they are meant to work together.

My faith shapes how I do business. It guides my decisions, influences how I treat people, and anchors my integrity. Success built without integrity will not last, but success built on character creates something that can sustain and multiply.

Today, I no longer measure success the same way I used to. Success is not just about income or achievements; it is about alignment with God, impact for His kingdom, and obedience to His will. Our assignments are bigger than business; as God's children, we have been given the opportunity to build something that reflects His kingdom here on this earth.

I want to build and leave behind true kingdom wealth: a legacy of visible faith, where integrity is non-negotiable, people are seen and valued, and God is present in every space I enter.

As I reflect on my journey, one truth remains: God has been guiding me all along—even when I didn't understand it and the outcome felt uncertain, and especially when He required my surrender.

My story is still unfolding, but now I walk with a different understanding. Building kingdom wealth is not just about what we gain; it is about how we live, who we become along the way, and how we impact others.

The development of true kingdom wealth occurs when we allow our lives, our work, and our ambitions to reflect God's presence in the world.

So when you feel uncertain and like your path doesn't make sense or you are walking into the unknown, seek God's will, trust Him, and respond in obedience where and how He is calling you. You do not need to understand every step to move forward with confidence.

Trust that your life has purpose; your loving Father created you.

Trust that your challenges are shaping you; Jesus is walking across the rocks and through the fire with you.

Trust that the doors meant for you will open at the right time; the Lord is your master, and He is in control.

And above all, trust that when you walk with God, you are never walking alone. The Holy Spirit is within and around you. Seek Him.

Sometimes, the greatest breakthrough is not a moment of success, but the quiet realization that God has been guiding you all along.

LAUREN MUELLER

Lauren Mueller is an entrepreneur, single mother of four, business owner, and devoted leader who blends faith, purpose, and identity in all she does. Originally from California and now living in St. George, Utah, Lauren has over 25 years of experience in health care, supported by a nursing degree and a background in real estate. She owns a shop in Utah that has become a place of ministry, where she shares the gospel and has witnessed God perform countless miracles.

Lauren's life work centers on empowering women spiritually, personally, and professionally. She has traveled internationally to Africa, preaching and ministering to women in Kenya, and continues to serve faithfully within her local church. Lauren has led Rooted Bible studies, launched women's business groups, and coached women to step boldly into their God-given calling.

Through surrender, Lauren has experienced profound breakthrough and freedom, overcoming insecurity and fear while witnessing God's faithfulness throughout her journey. She loves hiking, sports, evangelism, and travel, and believes that movement with faith, saying yes to God, and living fearlessly are tools for transformation and healing lives.

Do It Afraid

By Lauren Mueller

Have you ever wondered if God is truly real? I'm here to tell you—not only is He real, but He is also faithful, true to His Word, undeniably good, and ready to walk with you through any fear or trepidation.

If you had told me that, by 2025, I would be secure in my identity in Christ, a homeowner, running a successful business, healthy, happy, and surrounded by my four amazing children, I would have laughed and looked at you with disbelief.

But here I am. Living proof that God's promises are real.

> *For my thoughts are not your thoughts, neither are your ways my ways, declares the LORD. For as the heavens are higher than the earth, so are my ways higher than your ways and my thoughts than your thoughts* (Isaiah 55:8-9 ESV).

I love that Scripture—not just because it's true, but because I'm living proof that God is exactly who He says He is. I say that with confidence because if God had allowed me to walk out my own small, limited, and self-focused plan, my life would have been sad and boring compared to all He had in store. And knowing that, why wouldn't I give my life to the King of kings, whose ways are far better than mine?

The truth is, I wasn't even sure I wanted to be a mom. I figured I'd probably have kids one day, but I didn't feel a natural, deep, burning desire for motherhood. I was a businesswoman. God had placed a calling on my life for the marketplace.

That passion—the dream to build and lead, to create and grow—has been with me for as long as I can remember. Even in the seemingly insignificant jobs I once saw as irrelevant—selling meat, flipping pizzas, washing hundreds of sticky buckets, and pruning grapes—God was stirring something inside of me. I didn't realize it at the time, but He was building a desire for more... for purpose... for impact.

And He was shaping a story far better than the one I could have written for myself.

> *Who [with reason] despises the day of small things (beginnings)? For these seven [eyes] shall rejoice when they see the plumb line in the hand of Zerubbabel. They are the eyes of the LORD which roam throughout the earth* (Zechariah 4:10 AMP).

Today, I am truly passionate about living fully alive and free from fear.

Recently, God placed a burden on my heart to help other women—or anyone, really—who finds themselves paralyzed by fear. Fear is a thief. It comes straight from the enemy of your soul, and its goal is to keep you stuck, trapped in small thinking, small living, and far from the life God designed for you.

Fear wants to rob you of purpose, boldness, and joy. It wants to keep you from stepping forward into the destiny that was freely given to you by God.

Throughout my story, I faced fear countless times; if I had decided to give in, I wouldn't be where I am today. But each time I chose to *do it afraid,* I grew, healed, and moved closer to the life God had called me to live.

There is no fear in love, but perfect love casts out fear. For fear has to do with punishment, and whoever fears has not been perfected in love.

We love, because He first loved us (1 John 4:18-19 AMP).

Discovering our identity in Christ and embracing His perfect love for us is the only way you and I will ever become the women of God we were created to be.

I want to share with you glimpses of the different seasons of my life—moments that, without the loving and intervening hand of God, I wouldn't be here to write about today. My story is filled with both high peaks and deep valleys, enough to fill several books. But here, I'll highlight the significant moments from each chapter.

For most of my adult life, I battled with deep insecurity, self-hatred, rejection, and fear. It wasn't until much later that I began to truly discover my identity in Christ and walk in the freedom that comes from knowing Him. God had marked me from the beginning, and throughout the darkest moments of my life, He was keeping track while turning ALL things for my good.

And we know that in all things God works for the good of those who love him, who have been called according to his purpose (Romans 8:28 NIV).

At the tender and vulnerable age of 22, I found myself pregnant. Having been raised to save sex for marriage and given an abstinence promise ring by my father at age 14, you can imagine the crushing guilt and shame I felt for making a choice so opposite to what I knew was right. As a young, single mom, it seemed inevitable that I would become another welfare statistic. I couldn't see any way out of the mess I had created. But God...

Six months after my son was born, I met an incredible man who would later become my husband. Yet, even in marriage, the insecurities buried deep in my heart still quietly steered my decisions. The first few years of motherhood didn't come naturally to me. I often resisted being at home, confined to a role I hadn't chosen for myself. I felt trapped, unfulfilled, and as though I was losing more pieces of who I once was with each passing day. I had dreamed of running a business, making money, and building something remarkable with my life. I couldn't see the significance of the role God had entrusted to me—the immeasurable value of being a mother. I longed for worldly importance and success.

After my second son was born, I threw myself into building a business while my children were still young, even going so far as to stamp a Christian logo on the name of my newly launched clothing company. But the truth is, I can't recall ever putting God first or truly inviting Him into my work. I was running a business without love, and before long, I had become little more than a clanging cymbal—noise to everyone around me.

> *If I speak in the tongues of men or of angels, but do not have love, I am only a resounding gong or a clanging cymbal* (1 Corinthians 13:1 NIV).

As the years passed, I had four children. I began accepting my role as a mother a little more with each season, but the burning desire for business never left me. Spiritually, my walk with the Lord was an up-and-down journey. I often felt like I was on an emotional roller coaster, driven by insecurity and sustained by worldly idols that I used to cope with my fears, unhappiness, and self-doubt.

During this tender and complicated season of juggling motherhood and business, I picked up a book called *Redeeming Love*. At the time, I wasn't a reader, but I would hide behind the sofa in our living room just to steal a few uninterrupted moments with its pages. The story gripped me deeply, and only days after finishing it, I felt the courage to confess to my husband a hidden sin I had been carrying for over a year.

I never imagined that living in disobedience would eventually contribute to the heartbreaking end of my 12-year marriage. However, the moment my marriage ended was also the moment my full surrender to God finally came. In my eyes, I had single-handedly destroyed my life—for the second time—but now, it was time to give Him everything: my hopes, my fears, and my dreams; my very life.

If I could encourage any action through my story, it would be this: Surrender your life to Jesus—confess your sins and walk in the way of the Lord; let Him heal you. His way is always better.

> *Therefore confess your sins to each other and pray for each other so that you may be healed. The prayer of a righteous person is powerful and effective* (James 5:16 NIV).

I quickly moved out of our family home—the one I had shared with my husband, our four children, two dogs, ten chickens, a cat, and a goat—and into a friend's trailer just a few miles away. At the time, that small, unkempt trailer felt like a peaceful palace to me. (That, in itself, is another miracle story.) I had hit rock bottom—emotionally, spiritually, physically, and financially.

I took a job caring for an older woman in our small town of Sonora, California. The work was grueling on my body, but God used it to redeem my life and set me on a path toward financial freedom. One day, while lifting the frail 80-pound woman, two discs in my back slipped, leaving my right leg paralyzed. The sciatic pain was unbearable, and I was rushed to the hospital.

The surgeon told me they had to operate immediately or I'd risk losing all use of and feeling in my leg. Then he said something that still gives me chills: He was a renowned back surgeon from Pleasanton who "just happened" to be there that day, and it was a miracle he was even on duty. God had gone before me.

Looking down at my foot, limp and dangling, I knew surgery was my only choice. At the same time, my divorce was in full swing, and my husband was in Hawaii with all our children. I was utterly alone. But in that lonely place, God surrounded me with women from my church—the body of Christ—who became my lifeline.

Because the injury happened at work, my medical costs were covered, giving me a small measure of financial stability. But the months following surgery were some of the hardest of my life. I spent weeks without my children, unable to run, and at times unable even to dress myself. I was financially and emotionally bankrupt, living in my palace trailer. There were dark moments when I thought I might drink myself to death there. But deep down, I knew that if I didn't cling to God—as my Husband, my Savior, and my Great Physician—I wouldn't make it out alive.

In desperation, I took paint and colorful markers and began writing truths and Scripture across the white canvas walls of my rat-infested trailer. I knew that if I didn't wake up each morning and see God's truth, I might not get out of bed at all. And yet, His loving grace met me every single day. By His Spirit, I found the strength to care for my children and pursue a new dream—becoming a realtor. I chose to seek and trust God in the middle of my storm, believing He had good things planned for me even though I couldn't yet see them. In that season, my faith grew.

Living rent-free in that trailer for six months allowed me to save enough for a down payment on my first home—though I didn't know it then, it would be the first of many. With constant surrender and a heart that wouldn't quit, I would purchase four homes in four years—WOW, God! During that first house-hunting process, however, I grew frustrated with God as I missed out on getting house after house. The enemy whispered in my ear, *Is God really good?* But in the spring of 2019, I purchased a fixer-upper that, at the time, was my dream home. Only later did I realize that God had said "no" to all the other homes because He knew my heart's desire and was holding out for His best.

That home became the foundation of my real estate journey, allowing me to build several thriving businesses and save for the future God had in store. Since fully surrendering my life to Him, I have seen miracles and wonders beyond anything I could have imagined.

As I continued growing my business, I learned to invite the Holy Spirit into everything I did. He gave me supernatural wisdom and began to open doors for me that no one could close. In the years that followed, I was able to purchase two more homes and launch two additional businesses on the land God had given me. It was ONLY by His grace through my surrender.

Whenever you are seeking God's direction, ask Him to reveal your gifts, passions, and godly desires. Take inventory of what He's placed in your hands and look for ways to grow income and opportunity right where you are. Say "yes" to the dreams and visions He has already placed inside of you. Ask Him for revelation while staying connected to your identity in Christ. And most of all, if where He is taking you makes you nervous... *DO IT AFRAID!*

> *There is no fear in love. But perfect love drives out fear, because fear has to do with punishment. The one who fears is not made perfect in love* (1 John 4:18 NIV).

When I began this journey, I didn't have the "right" education to grow a business. Yet through the wisdom of the Holy Spirit, I learned how to handle people, run my operations, and create lasting financial freedom for my children. His guidance was, and still is, the key to everything.

He has entrusted me with the privilege of ministering to 14 women while remaining present in the marketplace, and this has now become my full-time ministry. God is able to do the most unimaginable things. The decisions we make—good or bad—not only affect ourselves but also bless future generations. My children, members of my community, and countless others have been blessed through this journey. With God, all things are possible.

> *Enter through the narrow gate; for the gate is wide and the way is broad that leads to destruction, and there are many who enter through it. For the gate is narrow and the way is constricted that leads to life, and there are few who find it*
> (Matthew 7:13-14 NASB).

As I read the Bible, I see a long list of imperfect people—not flawless, but faithful. Though imperfect, these people were willing to say "yes" to God. They walked with Him, even when they were afraid, and allowed God to redeem their mistakes as they moved forward, allowing grace lead their lives.

Courage isn't the absence of fear—it's the resilience to make strides in life despite our fear. I live by a phrase that has shaped my life and fuels my passion for coaching others: *Do it afraid.* This is the heartbeat of my message—the place I love leading from the most—helping others step into their calling, even when fear is threatening to hold them back.

Whether it's starting a business, going on a date, trying something new, traveling, or stepping into ministry, I am deeply passionate about helping people break free from fear. If you're waiting for fear to leave before you take that first step, you might be waiting a long time.

Most of what I've accomplished in life, I've done afraid. And truthfully, I still feel fear—but I know God is for me, not against me. Knowing that His perfect love casts out fear makes partnering with God while overcoming obstacles possible. So I move forward, partnering with Him in everything I do.

> *What, then, shall we say in response to these things? If God is for us, who can be against us?* (Romans 8:31 NIV).

My encouragement to you is this: Confront the lies holding you back. Face your fears; ask God to pull them out by the root. Thank God for giving His life in ransom for yours, and simply receive His love. And above all else, *do it afraid.* Fear has a way of creeping into almost everything we try to do. And honestly, that's no surprise—of course the enemy doesn't want you to succeed. Scripture teaches us to resist the devil, and he will flee.

> *Submit yourselves, then, to God. Resist the devil, and he will flee from you* (James 4:7 NIV).

I've learned that the presence of fear often means I'm headed in the right direction. It's a sign that God is about to stretch me, grow me, and draw me closer to Himself. Fear reminds me of how much I need Him. Think about this: If you could do everything without fear, why would you need a relationship with your heavenly Father?

Do it afraid.

When I meet someone new, two of the first questions I love to ask them are, "What are you most afraid of right now?" and "Are there any fears that are holding you back?" These questions open the door to deep, honest conversations and often reveal where someone is in their journey with God.

Take a few minutes and ask yourself those questions, and then ask God if He wants you to do whatever He is calling you to, even though you are afraid.

Remember, He wants your progress, not your perfection. If you allow Him, He will strengthen you. If you commit to taking a step, He will help you lift your foot. Trust Him. You will be glad you did.

STRUCTURE

BUILD YOUR BUDGET WITH PURPOSE

Structure creates stability. As you begin to align your money, structure will protect what you are building.

Failing to plan for your finances will always leave you reacting to them. When there is no structure, money flows in different directions without intention, and over time, that creates instability. Most people are not taught how to plan financially, yet money impacts nearly every area of life. It affects where you live, how you provide, what opportunities you have, and how you experience life. When people approach their finances with structure and purpose, everything begins to shift.

Planning requires preparation, and preparation builds stability. When you are prepared, you are not easily shaken by unexpected expenses or changing circumstances and can move from reacting to leading.

We are all called to work and provide. *"The one who is unwilling to work shall not eat"* (2 Thessalonians 3:10 NIV). There is dignity in work and responsibility in earning. There is no sustainable shortcut to financial freedom. True stability is built through consistent effort, wise decisions, and faithful stewardship.

Where you are right now is not permanent. It can be tempting to feel discouraged with our current situation, thinking we have missed our opportunity or made too many mistakes. But our future is not determined by our past; it is shaped by the decisions we make from this point forward.

God created you with the ability to choose how you live. *"Rich and poor have this in common: The Lord is the Maker of them all"* (Proverbs 22:2 NIV). While circumstances may differ, each person has the opportunity to grow, build, and create a different outcome through intentional decisions. Where you are today reflects the accumulation of past choices. Where you go from here will reflect the choices you begin to make now.

Structure begins with intentionality. When we are not intentional with our time, we are often not intentional with our money—the two are closely connected. We are given 24 hours each day; how we use that time determines the direction of our lives. When we live with purpose, our finances often begin to align.

Aspire to live quietly, to mind your own affairs, and to work with your hands... so that you may ... be dependent on nobody (1 Thessalonians 4:11-12 RSV). This verse speaks to discipline, focus, and responsibility. When you are intentional with your time and your work, you create the foundation for financial stability.

Structure in your finances comes through a clear and organized plan. A budget is not just a list of bills; it is a comprehensive plan for using every dollar. Often, people stop at tracking their fixed expenses, not taking the time to plan for the rest of their spending. Without that full picture, we continue to spend money without direction.

A structured spending plan assigns every dollar, giving your income a plan, intentionality to your expenses, clarity in your financial decisions, and allowing financial freedom to take shape. With structure, we no longer guess or hope things work out. We lead our finances with direction.

Your intention matters in this process. When people are clear on what they are building toward, they make stronger decisions. Whether your goal is to pay off debt, build savings, invest, or create new opportunities, clarity will guide how you structure your finances. Without intention, it is easy to fall into patterns that lead to frustration and a lack of progress.

Discontentment can lead to a lack of structure as it drives impulsive spending and keeps people in cycles of financial pressure. When there is a sense of dissatisfaction, people often look for temporary relief through spending, which creates short-term comfort but long-term strain. Breaking that cycle requires a shift in both mindset and behavior.

Scripture speaks directly to this topic: *I have learned to be content whatever the circumstances* (Philippians 4:11 NIV). Contentment does not mean settling; it means having peace while you are building. When you operate from contentment, your decisions become more intentional, and your finances begin to reflect stability instead of reaction.

As you build structure in your finances, you will move from making impulsive decisions to making intentional ones. You will move from scarcity thinking to an understanding of provision. You will move from reacting to leading. These shifts create long-term change.

God's promise remains steady through this process. *My God will meet all your needs according to the riches of his glory in Christ Jesus* (Philippians 4:19). As you plan, prepare, and steward what you have been given, you will experience both provision and peace.

JOURNAL REFLECTION

1. What does your current spending actually look like? Do you know where your money is going each month? Where have you been spending without a clear plan?

2. What are your fixed expenses—the non-negotiables you are responsible for each month? What variable spending is happening that you have not planned for? Where do you see money leaving without intention?

3. What patterns do you notice in your spending? Are you intentional or reactive with your money?

4. How do you spend your time each day? Is it aligned with what you are building? What do you need to stop doing that is not serving you? What do you need to start doing that aligns with the life you are creating?

5. What are you building toward?

SHANNON GLEASON

Shannon Gleason is a wellness coach with over 12 years of experience helping individuals align their spiritual, physical, and financial lives with God's design. She built a thriving business that, at its peak, generated $3 million in monthly sales.

Even in her strongest months, Shannon gives God the glory—crediting Him for aligning her with wise mentors and bringing clients eager to partner in health, an area she continues to pursue with humility. The Lord has been her faithful business partner and parenting partner every step of the way.

While growing her business, Shannon navigated single motherhood to four—including one child with significant disabilities—protecting her family through domestic abuse and the uncertainty of the COVID pandemic. In those refining years, she deepened her relationship with the Lord, embraced her God-given identity, and grew in healing, freedom, and spiritual authority.

Shannon lives in Oregon and treasures time with her children above all else. The greatest demonstration of God's wealth in her life has been the opportunity to be a stay-at-home mom, building a legacy as her children witnessed her growth while she ran her coaching business from home.

An Unlikely Calling

By Shannon Gleason

God is my protector and provider.

I know this because He has taken some of the deepest struggles in my life and used them for good. What once felt like a constant thorn in my side became the actual catalyst for the unlikely calling He had for me.

My thorn—the constant, annoying tension in my life—was my relationship with both food and finances. And, naively, my identity was deeply wrapped up in both.

From a young age, food became comfort. It calmed my nervous system, and over time, that comfort turned into a pattern that followed me into adolescence and adulthood. I battled my weight from puberty onward, often looking back at childhood photos and wondering, *What happened to me?*

At the same time, my relationship with money was just as complicated.

Although I grew up around wealth, I did not have a healthy understanding of it. Money was present, but it often came with what I recognize now as a scarcity mindset. I didn't know how to use money, manage it, or make it grow aside from just good luck, good timing, and hard work. Despite the abundance around me, it created a confusing dynamic. Money intimidated me. I didn't understand stewardship and often leaned toward spending without thinking long-term. Money felt emotional, not purposeful.

Going into my young adult years, having left support from home as most graduates commonly do, I was so uncomfortable with knowing what to do with my money. This discomfort caused me to spend money to make me feel better, in a weird way. It was like selective adulting, which left me in debt and needing to be bailed out by my parents. I blamed myself and fell into depression. Growing up, we lived a lifestyle that, from the outside, looked fortunate—what some might describe as a trust fund life. My grandmother was incredibly generous and loved to give, often donating to buildings and charities where her name would be displayed. I remember feeling proud of that.

But behind the scenes, the emotional reality was more complicated, creating an unhealthy, rebellious thrill. When I had money, I spent it as if it were burning a hole in my pocket. There was always provision, but not always peace. I was given opportunities that many would dream of: a brand-new car at 16, being a debutante, and experiences that felt "princess-like" on the surface. Yet internally, there was still a sense of lack. It never quite made sense.

Looking back, I can see that I was living with a scarcity mindset in the middle of visible wealth. I had an orphan-like relationship with money—where identity, security, and provision didn't feel fully anchored. I just didn't know how to "feel" about money or God, so for many years, I was wandering, not just financially, but spiritually as well. I had grown up in a great church, but I didn't yet have a personal relationship with God or understand a more personal application of God's plan, design, and purpose.

That changed in 2001.

In the days surrounding the tragedy of 9/11, I heard the testimony of a woman whose husband died in the crash on the news, who spoke with such peace about eternity; she knew he was with God, and she wasn't afraid to die. Something about her certainty and peace deeply impacted me. I wanted that kind of relationship with God. I fell to my knees and recommitted my life to God right then and there.

That moment marked a turning point. It shifted the trajectory of my life from wandering and making many mistakes to seeking, from confusion to surrender. It was the beginning of God reshaping not just my faith, but also my identity, mindset, understanding of money and provision, and the practice of stewardship in all areas of my life.

I was a born-again Christian, and I was a sponge. I got involved in the community at my new church and participated in multiple studies. I became renewed in my life from the inside out.

In 2003, I participated in a financial Bible study through Crown Financial Ministries. That course, based on biblical teaching, changed my understanding of money. For the first time, I learned that everything belongs to God—my money, time, energy, and family...even my thoughts. I wasn't an owner; I was a steward. Change was not easy. Facing my financial reality brought up shame and regret from years of misunderstanding money (looking back, I recognize I lacked grace for myself). But the Holy Spirit met me in that place—not with condemnation, but with guidance, encouragement, and freedom.

Immediately, I began to put new practices into place—budgeting, tracking expenses and income, and making intentional decisions. I actually got a thrill from paying off debts and being faithful with my finances rather than carelessly spending. I leaned on God's truth for guardrails and direction. The change in my life required sacrifice, but I could feel God redeeming something in me.

My obedience wasn't just about finances; it was about trusting God. That season required me to confront not just my finances, but my beliefs and unhealthy patterns. I began to see that stewardship is not about perfection, but about alignment, which itself gave me peace!

My sacrifices were real. I changed how I made decisions and reestablished habits. But for the first time, I felt like I had a clear direction to walk instead of wandering in confusion. Even saying "no" to myself started to feel great, because my joy didn't come from buying things anymore; instead, He was my joy.

Most importantly, God wasn't asking me to have it all figured out. He was asking me to trust Him step by step.

THE DESIRE THAT SHAPED EVERYTHING

In 2004, I became pregnant with my first child. I instantly loved being a mother.

I was also working full-time as a teacher. Regarding stewarding my time, I had an uneasy realization that I was spending 40+ hours a week caring for other people's children while someone else cared for mine. I missed my son constantly. Time was an asset I'd lost to debt and obligation; being a working mom and utilizing childcare seemed normal, but a deep desire began to grow in me: I longed to be home with my children, and steward my time and motherhood better. But financially, that seemed impossible.

My husband and I were living paycheck to paycheck, and even though I'd started making strides financially, I had brought $20,000 in student loan debt into our marriage. My husband managed the finances, and he reminded me often that we couldn't afford for me to stay home unless something changed.

So, I prayed—and cried. Often. For six years, I prayed for a way to be home with my children.

In 2010, God answered my prayer in an unexpected way.

My husband received a job opportunity that asked us to relocate, and at the same time, I was laid off from my teaching position. Because of the move, I was finally able to stay home. It felt like a miracle.

Yet even in that answered prayer, our funds were tight. My husband controlled the finances and gave me a strict household budget to manage. There were clear limitations, and at times, the financial boundaries felt restrictive, controlling, and even overbearing. But I was so grateful to be home that I learned to work within the necessary parameters. I became resourceful—stretching, prioritizing, and making intentional decisions with what I had. I cooked meals, planned carefully, and created a home filled with love and intention. Even though I didn't fully recognize it then, God was using that season to teach me stewardship under pressure and within limitations.

Despite my submission, the fact that I wasn't leading financially, but responding without full visibility or authority, affected my confidence more than I realized.

A few years later, everything shifted again. On Christmas Eve, my husband lost his job unexpectedly; our stability disappeared overnight, and we entered a season filled with uncertainty. I had no choice except to trust God. I leaned into worship, prayer, and community. My focus became my children and trusting that God would provide.

Three months later, my husband was offered another job opportunity that paid less than he had been receiving previously, and was in yet a different location. He took the job while I temporarily stayed behind with the children.

What felt like disruption was actually God preparing me. I was learning to step back and take an honest look at my world, and my place in it.

A TURNING POINT

During this season, between moving and my husband starting his new job in a different state, I noticed that a neighbor had transformed her health. She had lost a lot of weight and seemed full of joy. Curious, I asked her what she had done. She told me she had worked with a health coach.

Wanting this for myself, I called the coach immediately and began a wellness program. After decades of trying every diet imaginable, I had given up hope. Yet this inspiring example had sparked hope inside of me.

Within days, I began dropping weight, and I felt so good, too! The first relief I noticed was in my feet. For the first time in years, I could step out of bed without pain in my arches from carrying excess weight. But the real transformation wasn't just physical. It was mental.

The program emphasized building new habits of health—similar to what I'd done with my former financial habits—learning to pause and make intentional choices rather than eating mindlessly for comfort. "Stop. Challenge. Choose." Those three words became powerful for me. In less than six months, I lost 75 pounds.

Friends and acquaintances began to notice my transformation and started asking what I was doing. At first, I referred them to my coach. But then she suggested that I could coach them. She said that people would rather walk alongside someone still on the journey than be instructed by someone who had already arrived.

At first, I didn't see myself as a coach. But as I prayed about it, I began to realize that this could be more than just helping others—it could also be a way to contribute to my family financially while still being present for my children.

When I received my first significant paycheck within just three months, I was in disbelief. I thought there had been a banking mistake. But there wasn't. For the first time, I experienced what it felt like to create income—something I had never fully stepped into before. I wasn't familiar with surplus, with having more than just enough to get by. It felt unfamiliar, even uncomfortable at first. But it also felt empowering.

I wasn't just depending on provision—I was participating in it. My role expanded from caring for and stewarding my home, marriage, life, and children to also stewarding finances and stepping into the possibility of building something.

I saw myself differently. God was inviting me into a new level of stewardship and leadership.

> *"One who is faithful in a very little is also faithful in much"*
> (Luke 16:10 ESV).

I began sharing my journey openly, taking my then and now pictures and examples to Facebook; soon, simple conversations grew into a thriving business. Helping others find freedom from weight, shame, and unhealthy patterns brought me incredible joy. I loved being a cheerleader for my clients, and their gratitude gave me such a high. I would cry out, "Is this too good to be true?"

The shame I had carried for years began to break. My pain had purpose. My struggle became a bridge to help others. I began to see my value differently.

I wasn't just someone who struggled—I was someone who could lead, support, and create impact.

And as my impact grew, so did my income. This wasn't just a business—it was a lifeline.

Clients would reach out from all different places in their journey. Some were struggling physically, others emotionally, and many both. I would receive messages filled with gratitude, breakthrough, and joy.

There were moments when people would tell me they felt confident and free again for the first time in years. And I realized something powerful: This calling is so unusual, but I love how God has redeemed the thorn of both unhealthy weight and finances. The same areas in which I had struggled became the very areas where I could now lead.

However, even as my business grew, bringing joy, accomplishment, and fulfillment, my personal life became increasingly unhealthy. Besides working, I was also a full-time at-home parent to my four babies, including a son with attention deficit disorder and another with significant developmental delays. What wasn't shared in these Facebook posts was the painful reality that my marriage was filled with domestic abuse—patriarchal spiritual abuse, physical abuse, and financial abuse.

But God met me there.

> *He became my comfort, my counselor, and my provider.*
> *The Lord is my shepherd; I shall not want.*
> *He makes me lie down in green pastures.*
> *He leads me beside still waters.*
> *He restores my soul.*
> *He leads me in paths of righteousness*
> *for his name's sake.*
> *Even though I walk through the valley of the shadow of death,*
> *I will fear no evil,*
> *for you are with me;*
> *your rod and your staff,*
> *they comfort me.*
> *You prepare a table before me*
> *in the presence of my enemies;*
> *you anoint my head with oil;*
> *my cup overflows.*
> *Surely goodness and mercy shall follow me*
> *all the days of my life,*
> *and I shall dwell in the house of the Lord*
> *forever.*
> (Psalm 23 ESV)

My kitchen became my place of prayer. Worship filled our home. And I leaned on the Holy Spirit daily for strength, guidance, and peace. Fixing my eyes on Him helped me stop seeking love, approval, and value from a husband who didn't treasure me.

STEPPING INTO PROVISION

In 2019, my marriage came to an abrupt end after years of abuse. I became a single mother and was awarded full custody of my four children. I was relieved and felt set free, but also sad at the death of a dream and the impact on my children. Also, I became fully responsible for providing. It was overwhelming. I had to set up my own accounts, manage finances independently, and step into a level of responsibility I wasn't really allowed to carry before. I was earning, but not in charge.

I lacked confidence. But I also recognized something powerful: God had been preparing me. Through my business, through stewardship, through every season—I was equipped for such a time as this. And now, I had to walk in it.

Stepping into full financial responsibility was both empowering and intimidating. For the first time, I was making my own decisions and carrying the full weight of providing for my children. I literally would talk to Jesus and seek Scripture regarding every decision.

There were moments of fear. Moments when I questioned if I could really do this. But there was also something else: Authority. God had already given me everything I needed. Little by little, my confidence grew in the area of authority. Over time, I began to see God's provision in undeniable ways. Every payment, every opportunity, every connection—it all pointed back to Him.

Today, I continue coaching and providing for my family through the business that began with my own breakthrough and willingness to share. This year, I have even been able to purchase my own home. My understanding of wealth—from when I was that debutante back in 1989—has completely changed.

Wealth is not just about money; it is about identity, stewardship, and trust.

I approach money differently now. I no longer see it through fear or scarcity, but through gratitude and responsibility. Whether I have a little or a lot, I trust that God has given me exactly what I need. If He's done it before, He will do it again.

Stewardship means honoring what God has entrusted to me. It means making intentional decisions, seeking wisdom, and surrounding myself with people who can help me grow. I have a health coach, a financial coach, and a spiritual coach.

Michelle Tascoe has been an incredible resource in this, as she coaches me on healthy finances. She has taught me that I get to tell my money where it goes, which means recognizing that I have authority. That realization was a turning point for me. Money was no longer something happening to me—it became something I was entrusted to manage. I began to see it as a tool for provision, impact, and obedience, not a source of fear.

And I also began to recognize that true wealth isn't just about what we accumulate; true wealth is about what we build, steward, and release. Legacy. It's about alignment with God's purpose and trusting Him not only in lack, but also in increase. Both require faith.

I want to encourage you to break up with the mindset that money is something to hide, fear, or feel ashamed of. Everything belongs to God. We are here on assignment, and money is simply a tool He entrusts to us to carry out that assignment.

Walk in freedom instead of fear. Trust God in both lack and abundance. And use what you've been given to glorify Him. That is kingdom wealth.

Like you, I am still growing, still learning, and still becoming. But I know this: The same God who carried me through struggle, taught me stewardship, and provided for my family—all by way of the biggest thorns in my life, an unlikely calling. He will continue to lead me forward into a glorious future.

He who began a work in you will carry it on to completion
(Philippians 1:6 NIV).

MICHELLE TUFFORD

Michelle Tufford is a kingdom business mentor and founder of No More Dry Ground, a faith and business mastermind and retreat experience for Christian women in business. Based in North Idaho, she is passionate about helping women recognize God's voice and deepen intimacy with Him so they can lead and build from His wisdom rather than pressure, fear, or hustle.

Through her mastermind, retreats, and the Christian Women in Business Networking community, Michelle creates spaces where women slow down, hear the Holy Spirit clearly, and gain aligned strategies for their calling and business. She helps women pair obedience with action, trust God's direction, and steward what He has entrusted to them with confidence and peace.

Michelle believes kingdom impact and provision flow from intimacy with God and faithful response to His leading. Known for her authenticity and compassion, she helps women feel seen, grounded, and encouraged as they grow.

She is a devoted wife, proud mama of two, and loves fitness, travel, and living from the overflow of God's presence.

God of Impossible Math

By Michelle Tufford

I poured myself into building my businesses, chasing financial freedom with everything I had. I worked hard, stayed disciplined, and did what successful people said to do. From the outside, it looked like it was working: I was making more money and hitting milestones I previously only dreamed about—all proof that my effort was paying off.

But inside? It never felt like enough.

I kept telling myself that once I earned a little more, I'd finally feel secure. When I reached the next level, I'd finally be able to relax. After I crossed that invisible line, the pressure would lift, and peace would settle in. But none of those things ever happened.

Every achievement simply revealed another goal waiting behind it. Every increase came with a new weight to carry, a new fear of losing what I had gained. The freedom I was chasing always stayed just out of reach, like a mirage that disappears the closer you get to it. I was doing better on paper, but worse in my soul.

Maybe you've felt that, too—running hard after a financial breakthrough, believing that if you could just get there, you'd finally feel safe. Finally feel fulfilled. Finally, feel free. Only to discover that the finish line keeps moving and the striving never really stops.

That was my Egypt. I was not being held as a slave to failure, but a slave to striving. Lack did not hold me in bondage; instead, I was being held in bondage by the belief that achieving more could make me whole.

In His kindness, God whispered something that interrupted everything I thought I knew: "There's more for you than this. Freedom isn't found in the promise of more. Freedom is found in My presence."

For the Israelites, Egypt was filled with physical chains and forced labor. My Egypt looked different. My chains were invisible—forged from hustle, performance, and the relentless pursuit of more. I wasn't whipped by taskmasters; I was driven by pressure. Pressure to perform. Pressure to maintain. Pressure to keep it all going.

I was constantly on my phone—sending friend requests, commenting on posts, replying to messages. Every in-between moment was consumed by work. Whether standing in line at the store, sitting in waiting rooms, or even lying beside my kids' beds at night, I was scrolling and responding—even when I should have been resting.

I would sneak out for "errands," not because we needed anything, but because it gave me a few quiet minutes alone in the car to work without interruption. I told myself it was temporary, worth it, and just what success required.

But my body told a different story.

I skipped meals, forgot to drink water, pushed past exhaustion, and ignored warning signs. Until one day, my body simply couldn't keep up anymore.

I passed out in the shower.

My husband, Pete, carried me out and checked my pulse to make sure I was alive. When I came to, he told me he was either going to call an ambulance or drive me to the hospital. It terrified him—and it terrified our kids.

My diagnosis was severe dehydration. But the truth went deeper than that. I wasn't just dehydrated physically. I was dehydrated in my soul.

Around that same season, the businesses I had built were providing enough income that we felt comfortable relying on them. It looked like the dream we had worked toward; it was filled with freedom, margin, and opportunity. After prayer and long conversations, Pete and I decided together that he would leave his steady job as a police officer and explore other options.

On the outside, it looked like a victory.

On social media, I was celebrated for "retiring my husband." It was praised as the ultimate success story. The kind people aspire to.

But behind the scenes, it felt like the walls were closing in. What once felt like "extra" now became the only thing holding us afloat. Instead of feeling free, I felt the crushing weight of knowing it was all on me—every bill, every decision, and every unknown future.

And in that pressure, resentment crept in quietly.

Even though we had decided together, even though I had encouraged my husband to quit, I found myself blaming him in my heart. Then I felt guilty for feeling that way. I didn't want to disappoint him. I didn't want to admit how afraid I was. I didn't want to look like a failure after having been celebrated for success. So I stayed silent.

I was telling the world one story—the story of freedom, while secretly living another. And the gap between the two was breaking me from the inside out.

At the height of all this, I sat at a business conference. The room was electric with strategies and formulas for success. People around me scribbled notes, excited to scale and grow. But I sat there with a notebook on my lap and tears welling in my eyes. Everyone else was dreaming bigger. I was barely holding on.

In the quiet of my heart, I whispered, "God, I don't know if I can do this anymore. I don't know if I can keep carrying this weight."

And in the middle of that crowded room, I felt Him speak: "Lay it down."

I resisted. "Lay it down? God, how will we pay the bills? How will this new thing You're stirring provide? The math doesn't work."

Here was the part I hadn't admitted yet: God wasn't just asking me to let go. He was inviting me to build something entirely different. He was stirring within me a kingdom-focused business—one centered on faith, obedience, and serving women deeply. But it would require reach, not high-ticket pricing. Volume, not exclusivity. Presence, not polish.

Everything in me panicked. I had built my businesses around high-ticket offers and even taught that this was the smartest, most efficient way to make money online. And now God was asking me to do the opposite.

This isn't what successful entrepreneurs do, my mind argued. It felt like starting over. It felt inefficient and risky—like a terrible return on investment for my time.

Then came His whisper that pierced my heart. "Why are you so afraid to impact thousands of women for Me?"

God wasn't rebuking me; He was offering me an invitation. I didn't know how it would all work out. But I knew my answer: *Yes, Lord.*

I wish I could say that after I said yes, my uncertainty disappeared and everything turned around instantly—that my obedience immediately produced abundance and our income multiplied overnight. But that's not what happened. Instead of stepping into abundance, I stepped into the wilderness.

Maybe you know that place, too—where everything feels uncertain. Perhaps you, too, have obeyed, but nothing looks like it's working, and you are wondering if you heard God wrong. When you wake up and the bank account is tight and the pressure is still there, all you can do is trust Him for today.

For us, the wilderness looked like bills that were barely getting paid. There was no overflow or cushion. There was just enough. And at first, it felt like failure. I was used to measuring fruit by numbers, growth, and income—by visible success. And by those standards, this season felt painfully quiet.

But slowly, God began to open my eyes to a different kind of fruit. While the financial fruit looked small, spiritual fruit was growing everywhere.

My prayers became more honest. My dependence on God became deeper. Anxiety began to loosen its grip. I noticed my heart softening—toward my husband, my children, and the women God was placing in front of me. I was listening more, striving less, and leading from a place of humility instead of pressure.

I was seeing faith rise in others, too; in women who weren't impressed by polished strategies but were hungry for God's presence, whose questions shifted from "How do I grow faster?" and "How do I make more" to "How do I stay obedient?" and "How do I trust Him here?"

That's when I realized that God wasn't withholding His best from me; He was producing something far more valuable than earthly possessions. It was my manna season.

The Israelites woke up every morning to manna from heaven—bread they had never seen prior to their time in the desert. They were given just enough for the day, not enough to stockpile. This daily provision was a constant reminder to them that God, not their own efforts, was their source.

> *"Yes, he humbled you by letting you go hungry and then feeding you with manna, a food previously unknown to you and your ancestors. He did it to teach you that people do not live by bread alone; rather, we live by every word that comes from the mouth of the Lord"* (Deuteronomy 8:3 NLT).

And that's exactly what God was teaching me.

I didn't live by income alone. Not by business models. And not by performance. I lived by His voice. And there in the wilderness, I was finally learning how to hear it.

One Christmas Eve, my husband and I debated whether we should skip a family tradition we loved. Every year, we'd go out for dinner and leave a $1,000 tip for our waiter or waitress. That year, however, we didn't have the money—logic said to skip it. But I felt God nudging us to do it anyway. So we obeyed.

After our dinner out, we slipped the envelope onto the table and left. But God allowed us to see the look on the waitress's face—the tears in her eyes. And it was worth everything. Our kids saw it too. They saw what it meant to give generously even when it hurt.

A few days later, an unexpected check arrived in the mail. The amount? Just over $1,000. It was like God was smiling and saying, "See? I've got you. Keep trusting Me."

That's manna. Not excess, but always enough. And always on time.

One part that still amazes me is that months before any of this began, God had already planned a lesson I didn't know I'd need. Before my husband quit his job and I let go of my businesses—in other words, before the wilderness, we had donated to *The Chosen*. That gift came with the opportunity to be extras in the filming of the feeding of the 5,000. At the time, it felt like a fun way to support a project we loved. I had no idea it was an appointment written into my story.

By the time filming rolled around, finances were tight. Flights, hotels, and even sewing costumes by hand felt like a stretch. But I knew: We were supposed to be there. The day of filming, we stepped off the buses into a wide open field filled with thousands of people. The air was hot. Dust clung to our feet. Children laughed as they ran between the crowds. "Disciples" moved through the masses with baskets.

And then I saw Him. Not the real Jesus, but the actor portraying Him. Still, in that moment, it felt like we were back in time.

As I watched "Jesus" handing out bread, I found myself wondering what it felt like for the people who had walked miles to see Him, desperate for a word, hungry for a miracle. And right there, I felt God whisper to my heart: "I'm not asking you to feed the 5,000. I'm only asking you to bring Me the loaves and fish you have. I'll take care of the rest."

Tears blurred my eyes. All the pressure I had been carrying—the fear, the striving, and the belief that it was all up to me—began to lift.

I realized I am not the miracle worker. I am simply the girl with loaves and fish. My job is obedience. His job is multiplication. That day, John 6 came alive:

> *"'There's a young boy here with five barley loaves and two fish. But what good is that with this huge crowd?"*
>
> *"Tell everyone to sit down," Jesus said. So they all sat down on the grassy slopes. (The men alone numbered about 5,000.) Then Jesus took the loaves, gave thanks to God, and distributed them to the people. Afterward he did the same with the fish. And they all ate as much as they wanted. After everyone was full, Jesus told his disciples, "Now gather the leftovers, so that nothing is wasted"* (John 6:9-12 NLT).

The boy didn't feed the crowd. He just gave what he had. And Jesus turned it into more than enough. There was plenty of overflow; there were baskets left over. That's impossible math. But that's who God is. And that's what He was teaching me: In God's kingdom, 5 + 2 doesn't equal 7. 5 + 2 equals 5,000, plus leftovers.

When you're in the wilderness, it's tempting to cling to Jeremiah 29:11: *"For*

I know the plans I have for you," says the Lord. "They are plans for good and not for disaster, to give you a future and a hope" (NLT). We quote this verse often. We cling to it tightly, especially when we're tired of waiting, and the wilderness feels longer than we expected. But we sometimes forget where the people were when they first heard those words.

When God shared this message, the people He was speaking to were not standing in abundance; they hadn't arrived. When God's people first heard that promise, they were in exile, displaced, waiting for restoration.

And that promise was followed by an invitation: *"In those days when you pray, I will listen. If you look for me wholeheartedly, you will find me"* (Jeremiah 29:12–13 NLT).

Yes, God has a hope and a future for you. But the real treasure is found when you seek Him *right where you are.*

The promise without His Presence is empty. But His Presence—even in the wilderness—is more than enough.

Standing in that field during the filming of the feeding of the 5,000 and watching the bread being multiplied in the hands of Jesus, something shifted deep inside me. I realized the miracle wasn't just about provision; it was about proximity. It was about people choosing to come close enough to witness what only God could do.

No one there had a guarantee of how the day would end. They just came hungry. And they stayed. Understanding that helped me see my own story differently. The lowest point of that season came when I realized I could no longer keep making money with a message that lacked integrity. I couldn't keep teaching one thing publicly while living something different privately. I had to choose between continuing in what *looked* like success or surrendering to what God was asking of me—even if it meant starting over.

To me, walking away meant looking like a failure—that my husband might need to go back to work, and I would have to release the story people were celebrating online.

It meant laying down my loaves and fish with no guarantee of multiplication. But the moment I truly surrendered, something shifted—not in my circumstances, but in me. I stopped performing for God and started bringing Him my truth. I stopped pretending I was okay and trying to hold everything together by myself. I brought God my fear, disappointment, exhaustion, and questions. And He met me there.

God didn't rush me out of the wilderness, and He didn't shame me for being weary. He pursued me. I began to experience His presence in ways I never had before; He was no longer a concept, but a companion. God was not a promise off in the distance, but daily bread for my soul.

I learned that His love and presence were worth far more than money, milestones, or applause. And I began to hear His voice more clearly, not because I was doing more, but because I was finally quiet enough to listen.

I discovered that God alone was my provider. My source was not my performance, business, income, or ability to make things work.

God's Spirit became living water to my thirsty soul—that's how my joy was restored. Not because everything was fixed, but because I was finally free.

Maybe you're there right now, chasing a breakthrough, striving for more, or believing that if you can just hit that next—number, goal, season—you'll finally feel at peace. But I learned the hard way that even though I made more, it never felt like enough. Because freedom isn't found in the promise of more; it is found in God's presence.

Don't despise the manna. And don't rush the wilderness. That is where God proves Himself faithful, where He teaches you to trust Him one day at a time, and where He shows you that He is enough—maybe even before He shows you His plan.

Don't chase God's promise more than His presence, because without Him, even the promised land will feel empty. Bring Him your loaves and fish. Bring Him what you have—not what you wish you had. And trust Him with the math.

> *"Then you will call on me and come and pray to me, and I will listen to you. You will seek me and find me when you seek me with all your heart"* (Jeremiah 29:12-13 NIV).

Say yes.

Stay close.

Watch the baskets overflow.

And remember, sometimes the richest seasons of your life aren't found in abundance, but in the wilderness, where you discover that God Himself is the reward.

STEWARDSHIP

BREAK DEBT, BUILD DOMINION

When ownership becomes real, you take responsibility for your debt and begin to move out of bondage and into control—stewarding all God has entrusted you. What you take ownership of, you can change.

You were created to live in freedom, but financial bondage can quickly gain a grip on our lives. It often starts with something small that feels harmless, even exciting—a purchase here, a swipe there, a decision made without fully thinking it through. Over time, those small decisions accumulate, and before long, what once felt manageable begins to feel heavy.

I remember the excitement of getting my first credit card. It felt like a step into adulthood, a sign that I had arrived. I did not understand at the time how quickly that small decision could grow into something much bigger, as one purchase turned into many. Minimum payments felt easy in the beginning, but over time, the balance grew, snowballing into something I could not control.

Debt has a way of growing quietly until it becomes overwhelming. Scripture speaks directly to this reality: *The borrower is slave to the lender* (Proverbs 22:7 NIV). Debt limits your options, controls your decisions, and creates pressure that affects every area of life.

You were created with authority. God said, *"Let us make mankind in our image... so that they may rule"* (Genesis 1:26 NIV). You were designed to lead, steward, and walk in dominion. Debt works against that design. It shifts you from leading to reacting, from freedom to obligation.

We each must decide who or what we will serve. Jesus taught, *"No one can serve two masters... You cannot serve both God and money"* (Matthew 6:24 NIV). This teaching is not about whether you should have money; it is about whether money has you. When people begin to examine their relationship with money honestly, they start to recognize where they have placed their trust, focus, and decisions.

Jesus illustrates this in the story of the rich young ruler. This man had wealth, discipline, and a desire to follow God, yet when he was asked to release all he owned, he could not do it. His attachment to money revealed where his heart truly was. We must each have this moment of reflection. Where our money goes often reveals what we value most.

Debt is not only a financial issue; it is a stewardship issue. Debt reflects decisions made over time, often without full awareness or intention. People often enter into debt simply trying to keep up, maintain a lifestyle, or fill an emotional gap. It is a cycle that is difficult to break.

The good news is that cycles can be broken. Awareness is the beginning of freedom. When you begin to see clearly what you owe, how it accumulated, and how it is affecting your life, you move from avoidance to ownership, allowing change to begin.

We are called to be faithful. *It is required of stewards that they be found faithful* (1 Corinthians 4:2). Stewardship means taking responsibility for what has been entrusted to you, including your finances, which allows you to step into a position of leadership.

Paying the minimum on debt keeps people stuck for years. Interest continues to grow, and progress feels slow or nonexistent. Debt becomes a race against time and compounding interest. When you begin to shift your approach and make intentional decisions to reduce and eliminate debt, you begin to regain control. It requires discipline, consistency, and focus to make decisions that may feel uncomfortable but will lead to freedom.

As you commit to this process, you will begin to see progress. It may not happen overnight, but it will happen. Every payment, every decision, and every step forward moves you closer to freedom.

God's desire for you is not bondage; it is freedom. *Owe no one anything, except to love each other* (Romans 13:8 ESV). As you align your actions with this truth, you will begin to experience what it means to live without the weight of debt.

JOURNAL REFLECTION

1. What debt do you currently have? List it out. Be honest and specific about where you are. Stewardship begins when you are willing to see clearly and take responsibility for what is in your hands.
2. Where have you been avoiding looking at your debt? Where have you minimized it or pushed it aside?
3. How would not having debt change your decisions, your peace, and your ability to move forward?
4. Where have you been spending money that is not aligned with what you are building? What needs to shift in your thinking so you can begin to lead your finances instead of reacting to them?
5. Which debt feels the heaviest to you right now? Which one do you feel led to focus on eliminating first? What is one step you can take today toward eliminating it?

Alison K. Daniels

Alison K. Daniels is a woman of faith whose life reflects redemption, resilience, and purpose. After many years battling drug addiction, Alison experienced a life-changing transformation in 2001 when she was saved by Jesus Christ. That moment marked the beginning of a new chapter rooted in healing, faith, and a deep commitment to serve others.

Moved by gratitude for the grace she received, Alison developed a strong passion for service and helping people rebuild their lives. She believes restoration is possible for anyone and that faith, combined with compassion and perseverance, can create lasting change.

Alison is the CEO of Wildwood Properties, Inc., which includes Century 21 Wildwood Real Estate & Property Management and Twain Harte Rentals. Under her leadership, these organizations have grown into trusted, community-focused businesses known for integrity, professionalism, and care.

Married for 21 years, Alison is the proud mother of four wonderful children and one beautiful granddaughter. She considers her greatest accomplishments to be her faith, her family, and her calling to live a life of service and purpose.

Out of the Pit

By Alison K. Daniels

"When you pass through the waters, I will be with you;
And through the rivers, they shall not overflow you.
When you walk through the fire, you shall not be burned,
Nor shall the flame scorch you" (Isaiah 43:2 NKJV).

I do not have many memories of my life before I was 5. I know that a lot of love was given to me—I had a stable home and loving family. When I was 3, my baby sister, Laurel, was born. From the moment my parents brought her home, I loved her so much that I felt that she was mine.

One day, about six months after my sister was born, when my dad picked me up from my preschool, he wasn't his usual playful and happy self, but seemed to be in turmoil. He was driving his GMC frantically as we were going home when he spoke one sentence that is vivid in my memory: "Your mom is leaving me."

Looking back, I know that he was in a whirlwind from whatever news he was given prior to picking me up; he was in a panic as his life was beginning to unravel.

Arriving home that night, my parents went to their room to talk, then my dad came and told me that he was going to go stay with my Uncle Wayne. There was no fighting or screaming; my mom had fallen in love with someone else, and that was that. I begged my dad to take me with him, as I have always been my daddy's girl. He promised he would be back in two weeks; he was back in one.

I went to live with my dad at my uncle's house, while my baby sister stayed with my mom. During that time, my dad poured himself into his Bible, sharing with me all the stories he was reading. My father grew up in a Catholic home on the island of Kauai, and he knew to lean on his faith, especially in the most difficult times. His actions and strength helped instill faith in me, even though I was only 4 years old.

My mom was a broken woman. She was kind and loving but suffered from bipolar, manic depression, and addiction her entire life. She was adopted by a Jewish couple who thought they could not have children; after she was adopted, however, they conceived a little girl, my Aunt Carol. As a result, my mom was always treated like the adopted child. I still don't know the depth of how this fundamentally caused my mother to feel unworthy, unloved, and reckless throughout her life, but I saw her pain. She was a good person with a heart of gold, but as a mother, she was lost.

We did not stay in my uncle's house for too long. We moved into a house, and, in God's perfect planning, my soon-to-be bonus-mom soon moved into the attached in-laws' quarters. We still joke to this day that I picked her to be part of our family. The night she moved in, I heard the smoke alarm coming from her apartment, so I knocked on the door in our kitchen that led to her apartment and invited her to join us for dinner. She came and has been with us since. She is an angel.

My parents and step-parents were amazing at co-parenting. We spent holidays and birthdays together, and they worked out summer vacations so that my sister and I could spend time with each other. Looking back, I am so thankful for their selflessness. We truly had so much love and support.

The home I lived in was much different than the one my sister grew up in. My dad and Donna (my bonus mama) kept a very stable and organized home.

I had chores and responsibilities, and I was sheltered and expected to do well in school. We ate dinner around our kitchen table every night. They poured so much time and love into me and made every little occasion special. Donna was an incredible mother. I thrived in our home, but I was a child, and all I saw was how strict and unfair they were. I was an entitled brat.

My mom's household was the complete opposite. My mom was a lot of fun and liked to take me shopping and do amazing fun things! There was no structure and no rules. During my visits, I saw more than any child should. For example, during Christmas break when I was about 9 years old, my mom and stepdad were gone at work, and I was watching my sister, who was 6. When we decided to look for our Christmas presents, we found cocaine and pornography. My mom liked to party. I know now that she was just trying to numb herself from her lifelong pain,

The summer before high school, I went to visit my mom. It was sooooo much fun! There were no rules, and I got to hang out with older high schoolers. Party! My mom convinced me during that summer that my dad and Donna were way too strict and that it would be so much fun for me to move in with her. I agreed! I broke my dad and Donna's hearts when I told them I was moving in with my mom, but they reluctantly let me go.

Two weeks after I moved in, Mom informed me that we were getting evicted from our home and that we did not have anywhere to go. She proceeded to shut down, so I sprang into action and found a hotel where we could stay. We moved into the Westwind in the flats of Santa Cruz—a very shady, ghetto area—and shared our room with cockroaches and mice. I didn't tell my dad what was going on because I knew he would insist I come home, and I was enjoying my freedom way too much.

When I left my dad's house in the little town of Jamestown, California, in my 8th-grade year, I had been a straight-A student and the president of my school. Things changed drastically as I lived with my mom for three years. Going into my junior year of high school, I only had freshman credits. My mom was so cool that, when I was with her, I didn't have to really go to school—I would skip, and she would call it in. I would go to the beach all day and run around town with my friends. Then, at 16, I got pregnant. When my mom found out, she said I had to get an abortion or move out. My dad told me to come back home, and so I did.

As a teen mom, I was determined not to be just another statistic. I wanted to finish high school and make a good life for my baby and me. I was pretty arrogant and judgmental; I was never going to end up like my mom—in my mind, she was a drug addicted loser! Though I didn't have a relationship with God, my dad was always talking about God and praying and showing faith, but I was in a "but how do you really know there is a God" phase. Still, with the help of so many wonderful people, including my dad, I succeeded in beginning to build a life for me and my son, Aaron. After I finished high school, got my CNA license, and started college, we were living in a cute two-bedroom apartment. I just started my college classes when one night changed my life.

On that one fateful night, while my son was with my parents, I went out with a neighbor girl and some of her friends. Not long into our night out, one of the guys lined up some meth. I kindly declined the first several offers, but as the night progressed, I got curious about what was so enticing, and I snorted my first line. I don't remember a lot now about how it made me feel, but the next morning, while driving to get my son, I cried the whole way, convinced that I had ruined my life and was now the loser I never wanted to be.

For the following eight years, the lying devil told me that I had made my bed and chosen a life of drugs, and that was who I was and all I would ever be—a druggy loser. During those years, I did unspeakable things. I would leave my son, Aaron, with my parents for days on end; he would plead for me not to leave him, but I was convinced he was better off without me and that being with my parents was best for him. I lied, stole, and gave myself away more times than I care to admit. I dated very abusive guys who hit me and cheated on me; because I had no self-worth, I thought I deserved their treatment.

One day, a friend of mine took me to score some weed at her dealer's house. When I walked in, I noticed beautiful young ladies sitting all around the room. Then I met her weed guy, Sean. He was gorgeous and so smooth. He acted like I was the only girl in the room as he showed me pics of his beautiful daughter and told me about himself. He was a true player. Although he was really good-looking, I saw right through his game.

At the time, I had been dating a guy for a while. I am a very loyal person; I've learned I can be loyal to a fault—offering my loyalty to people who are less than deserving of it.

Sean pursued me, and I continued to blow him off. We did, however, become friends; I would get my weed from him. Every once in a while, I would read a story in our local paper about Sean getting arrested for something stupid, and I would think, *Boy, this guy is cute, but he is not very smart.*

I continued down this path, spiraling further and further away from the path that I had so intentionally set, moving toward darkness, pain, and recklessness. For a while, it was fun—staying up all night and driving through the mountains in the snow, spelunking old caverns and living in the fast lane—and then it wasn't.

After eight years of living a life of addiction, I found myself alone, realizing that none of my "friends" were really my friends. My dad, who had always been my biggest fan, wanted nothing to do with the person I had become. I was estranged from my son, and I was homeless. Additionally, I had a no-bail warrant, which meant if I were arrested, no amount of money could get me out, so I was constantly paranoid and running from the law. Then, I discovered that the boyfriend I had been so loyal to had been sleeping with my "best friend" for months. I was devastated. And I was so tired of the lifestyle and the mess that I had created.

Looking back over the years I used drugs, I have clear memories of our

Savior, Jesus, pursuing me and protecting me. I was involved in some pretty dangerous stuff, and girls in my circle were ending up missing and murdered.

One night, while I was at a very dangerous man's house, I was in the back room talking with a guy. As we spoke, I saw his face completely change—he went from being a young man to being an old and scary-looking creature. It was the first time I actually saw a person transform into a demon. I know that sounds a bit crazy, but it is true. But although he was trying to scare and intimidate me, I felt peace. I was actually sorry for the man. In retrospect, it is clear that God was there in that room with me. I am alive only by His grace and mercy.

In addition to protecting me, God was starting to open my eyes to His Word. A friend had introduced me to a guy who, even though he was deep in addiction and the lifestyle, knew Jesus. He would spend hours reading the Bible to me and answering all my questions—I had so many questions. I was seeking something different than the lost journey I was on, and Jesus was pursuing me like a kind and loving gentleman.

One day, I stopped at our local corner gas station, and guess who walked in? Sean, my long-lost friend! He looked so good. We got to chatting; he asked what I was up to, and told him I was single. When I asked him the same question, he told me, very confidently, in his charming fashion, that he had just gotten out of prison and he was "getting my life together." He asked me if I wanted to join him. That was the beginning of my new life. Looking back now, I know that God was offering me a chance to change; all I had to do was take His hand and follow. And I did.

From that moment, at 28 years old, my life path changed as God gave me this gift of a man. When Sean and I met, neither of us was stable enough to nurture a healthy relationship. But we had each grown and now could help rather than hurt each other. I stayed with Sean and his parents, who so graciously opened their home and their hearts to me, giving me a safe, sober place to live.

Since then, I have continued to cling to the robe of Jesus. I have now lived 23 years addiction-free! God has led my life to some incredible places, restored the broken relationships I had carelessly destroyed during my spiral, and blessed me with an amazing bonus child and two more children, who are the joys of my life. I now also have a beautiful granddaughter from my eldest son.

I was able to go to school and finish my bachelor's in Business Administration, which led me to my career in property management and then to real estate, where I've worked for the past 20 years, helping others realize their dream of home ownership and build generational wealth.

Two years ago, God opened the door for me to purchase the company I had been working for, and now I currently act as the Owner/Broker of my own Brokerage! I have 30 agents that I get to pour into daily. We have real estate, property management, and vacation rental management divisions. Every day, I am amazed by how blessed my life is.

Still, life isn't always easy.

In June of 2018, a day before her 70th birthday, I lost my mom after she had struggled with her health for many years. When she passed, although it was very painful, God's presence was so tangible. He carried me through.

The most devastating loss I experienced was losing my little sister. She had struggled with addiction since she was 15 years old and was able to get clean a couple of years after I did, but when my mom was at the end of her life, my sister provided her care in hospice, and it fundamentally broke her. She began using shortly after my mom passed, and then last year, I lost her to a fentanyl overdose.

I had never truly understood the passages in the Bible that describe wailing when someone's life ends, but when I found out my sister had died, I wailed. It hurt so badly. I felt like I had failed to protect her. Like I could have done more to save her. I struggled through my grief, but I know where my help comes from, so I leaned on my Savior, and He provided comfort and peace during the most difficult season of my life. Although I miss my sister every single day, I know where she is—she is with our Lord and Savior. She and my mom only experience joy now; there is no more suffering where they are. That gives my soul so much peace.

Friend, I want to encourage you, no matter how far you have fallen, God is waiting to help you out of the pit! Take His hand, follow Him, ONE... STEP... AT... A... TIME. Let Him show you His glory and mercy. I know far too well how shame can keep you in hiding; let His light shine on you. He loves you. He adores you and wants you to come home to Him. His loving arms are open and ready to embrace you!

When the opportunity arose for me to become the owner of this large brokerage, I experienced imposter syndrome. All the fears that I was not good enough rose again. But then the Lord revealed to me that this is my purpose, and He would use it for His glory. Now, I dedicate my life, my family, and my business to the Lord daily. It is not mine; it is all His.

> *"'I'm sending you off to open the eyes of the outsiders so they can see the difference between dark and light, and choose light, see the difference between Satan and God, and choose God. I'm sending you off to present my offer of sins forgiven, and a place in the family, inviting them into the company of those who begin real living by believing in me'"* (Acts 26: 17-18 MSG).

Mel Mason

Mel Mason is known as The Clutter Expert and has spent the last 12 years helping people clear clutter at its root—inside and out—so it doesn't return. Her work focuses on serving high-achieving believers who love God yet feel weighed down by internal and external clutter that interferes with their intimacy with Jesus and obedience to His call.

Through her signature From the Inside Out approach, Mel helps clients address fear, pride, self-reliance, unresolved pain, limiting beliefs, and physical distraction, so they can walk in spiritual clarity and freedom, and create lasting kingdom impact.

Outside of her work, Mel enjoys rock climbing, running, and hiking—anything that immerses her in God's creation and keeps her grounded in His presence. Her work is rooted in biblical truth, presence, and willingness, paired with practical, step-by-step guidance that leads to sustainable transformation. She is also the author of *Freedom From Clutter: The Guaranteed, Foolproof, Step-by-Step Process to Remove the Stuff That's Weighing You Down.*

Resting Into Kingdom Wealth

By Mel Mason

For years, I lived in a constant state of striving. Eleven years of being in business meant endless cycles of marketing, emailing, making offers, and trying to force things to work. From the outside, it looked like I was doing everything right. But inside, I was anxious and exhausted. There was no consistency in my income, no peace in my spirit, and no freedom in my heart. Every month came with the same haunting questions: *How will I pay the bills? Where will the money come from this time?*

I often believed that I was being punished. I thought maybe I had done something wrong in the eyes of God. If I could just "figure it out," maybe then He would bless me. So I chained myself to my desk, convinced that if I sent enough emails, made enough offers, and hustled hard enough, something would finally break open. But instead of freedom, I found myself in bondage to fear. Instead of joy, I lived under stress. Instead of trusting God as Provider, I leaned entirely on myself—and it was never enough.

This is where so many of us get trapped. The world teaches us that success, wealth, and security are found in how hard we work, how many hours we hustle, and how well we perform. But kingdom wealth does not operate that way. God's economy is not like the world's economy. Where the world says *earn, strive, produce,* the kingdom of God says *rest, trust, receive.*

It took me years of frustration to realize this. I had to come face-to-face with the truth that my striving was not producing fruit because it was rooted in self-reliance, not in faith. *Unless the LORD builds the house, the builders labor in vain* (Psalm 127:1 NIV). I was laboring in vain, trying to build something in my own strength that only God could sustain.

When I reflect on those years, I can see clearly that I was trapped in the very pattern Proverbs 3:5-6 warns against: *Trust in the LORD with all your heart, and lean not on your own understanding; in all your ways submit to Him, and He will make your paths straight* (NIV). My understanding told me that if I didn't hustle, I would fail. My fear told me that if I rested, everything would fall apart. But the truth was that my striving was the very thing keeping me from experiencing God's provision.

The lesson I've learned—and the one I hope to impart to you through my story—is simple but profound: *Kingdom wealth is not earned by relentless doing, but received by resting in the certainty of God's provision.*

When I look back over the first eleven years of running my business, one word rises to the surface: *striving.* Every day felt like an uphill battle. I was doing all the things the business world tells you to do—building email lists, crafting offers, posting on social media, attending networking events. I sent countless messages, built sales funnels, and signed up for marketing programs. On the outside, it seemed like I was doing what a "good entrepreneur" should. But the inside told a different story. There was no consistency in my results. Money never flowed easily. Every win seemed to be followed by a setback, every bit of momentum swallowed by drought.

And the anxiety never left me. I would wake up with that familiar knot in my stomach, wondering, *How am I going to pay the bills this month? What if nothing comes in? What if I can't keep this going?* Fear became my constant companion. Instead of experiencing joy in the work of my hands, I carried stress like a heavy backpack I couldn't put down.

Even worse, I believed God was punishing me. When doors didn't open, I wondered, *What did I do wrong? Why won't God bless me?* Those thoughts kept me locked in shame. If God was punishing me, then maybe my only hope was to work harder, try harder, do more. So I chained myself to my desk, convinced that my breakthrough was always just one more email, one more strategy, one more sleepless night away.

But here's the truth: Striving never leads to kingdom wealth. The more I tried to force outcomes, the more powerless I felt. The harder I pushed, the less progress I seemed to make. My heart longed for peace, but I didn't know how to let go.

What do people get for all the toil and anxious striving with which they labor under the sun? All their days their work is grief and pain; even at night their minds do not rest (Ecclesiastes 2:22-23 NIV). That verse describes my life perfectly. My days were filled with toil, my nights with worry.

Jesus also warned of this trap: *"So do not worry, saying, 'What shall we eat?' or 'What shall we drink?' or 'What shall we wear?' For the pagans run after all these things, and your heavenly Father knows that you need them"* (Matthew 6:31-32 NIV). I was running—after clients, after money, after validation. And every step I took was fueled not by faith, but by fear.

Fear and striving go hand in hand. Fear says, *If I don't do it, it won't happen.* Fear says, *I can't trust anyone else—not even God—to provide for me.* The Lord describes this perfectly in Jeremiah 17:5, *"Cursed is the one who trusts in man, who draws strength from mere flesh and whose heart turns away from the LORD"* (NIV). My strength came only from myself, and it always led me back into the same cycle—work harder, worry more, try again.

Striving is exhausting. It drains not only your energy but also your joy. I remember sitting at my desk one night after pouring hours into a launch that produced little fruit, feeling crushed under the weight of disappointment. I had given everything I had, but the results were so small compared to the effort. In that moment, I thought, *Maybe this is just my lot in life. Maybe I'll always struggle. Maybe God really is punishing me.*

Looking back, I can see that this was the enemy's trap—to keep me so bound in fear and striving that I would never learn how to rest. Striving kept me spinning in circles, never moving forward, never experiencing the true abundance that comes from trusting God's provision.

"Be still, and know that I am God" (Psalm 46:10 ESV). I didn't know how to be still. Being still felt dangerous. If I stopped, the bills would pile up. If I rested, the opportunities would dry up. My entire mindset was built on the lie that my effort was the only thing holding my life together.

This was the prison of striving: constant effort with little fruit, constant anxiety with little peace, constant fear with little faith. I was worn out, burned out, and still empty. And deep inside, I knew something had to change.

In the middle of all my striving, God kept sending me the same message through His people by the prophetic word: *Rest. Trust. Stand still.* At first, I didn't know what to do with that. Rest felt like a luxury I couldn't afford. How could I possibly stop? The bills were real. The responsibilities were real. The fear of lack was real. My mind would whisper, *If you stop, everything will fall apart.* But then came the stronger whisper from the Spirit: "If you don't stop, you'll never see what I can do."

One of the clearest moments came in a prophetic word right before I got baptized this year. God said, "When you're sitting at your computer worrying and stressing about where the money is going to come from, just stop and rest and trust in Me."

That invitation became impossible to ignore.

In May of 2025, I traveled to Costa Rica for what would become a defining moment in my journey. Surrounded by beauty, stillness, and space to breathe, I felt God calling me to make a choice: to step fully into trust. So for nine days, I committed to resting and trusting. I didn't work on my business at all. No emails. No offers. No marketing. Nothing. It was the first time in over a decade that I had completely released control. I chose to rest and trust in Him.

I won't lie—at first, it was uncomfortable. My mind raced with what-ifs. *What if I come back to nothing? What if my business dries up? What if this is irresponsible?* But with each passing day, I felt my spirit settle. For the first time, I was practicing Hebrews 4:10 in real time: *For anyone who enters God's rest also rests from their works, just as God did from His* (NIV).

Nine days of rest. Nine days of no striving. Nine days of surrender.

When I returned home, something miraculous happened. My phone began to ring. Opportunities I hadn't pursued began to show up. People started booking calls on my calendar from out of the woodwork. It was as if God had been waiting for me to get out of the way so He could move.

That was the moment everything shifted for me. I had proof—not just theory, not just a verse on a page, but lived experience—that God is faithful when we trust Him. I didn't have to force outcomes. I didn't have to manipulate circumstances. I didn't have to carry the weight of provision on my own shoulders.

> *"Come to Me, all you who are weary and burdened, and I will give you rest. Take My yoke upon you and learn from Me, for I am gentle and humble in heart, and you will find rest for your souls. For My yoke is easy and My burden is light"* (Matthew 11:28-30 NIV).

I had been yoked to striving, dragging the heavy load of self-reliance, wearing myself out under burdens I was never meant to carry. But when I chose to yoke myself to Jesus, everything became lighter. Not because the bills disappeared, not because life suddenly became easy, but because I was no longer carrying the weight alone.

The turning point was not about learning a better strategy. It wasn't about finding the right program or marketing plan. It was about surrender. It was about finally believing that God is who He says He is—Jehovah Jireh, my Provider.

From that moment forward, I knew I could never go back to the old way of living. Striving had nearly crushed me. Rest had revived me. And I was ready to see what God could do when I finally stopped doing it all on my own.

When I chose to let go of striving and truly rest in God's provision, everything began to change. Not because I suddenly worked harder, or because I finally found the "right" business strategy, but because I stopped trying to be my own source. For the first time in eleven years, I gave God space to show Himself as my Provider—and He did not disappoint.

What happened when I returned from Costa Rica still amazes me. The very first provision came through a simple connection. While in Costa Rica, I had met someone and agreed to a casual follow-up call. I expected it to be nothing more than a friendly conversation, but halfway through the call, he asked me, "Would you be willing to coach me?" Before I even had time to second-guess or strategize, he committed to working with me for three months—and paid me in full up front.

Not long after, another door opened. At the time, I was doing some part-time work for a woman who had seen firsthand the way I showed up and the strength of my work ethic. Because of that, she offered me a full-time contract position—one that gave me the very freedoms I had been striving for when I first launched my business. This role provided time freedom, location freedom, and financial stability, all without the stress of hustling for clients.

Then, just when I thought I couldn't be more surprised, another provision arrived. A woman booked a call with me after hearing a talk I had given that had recently been re-released by the person who interviewed me. The message landed at just the right time in her life, and by the end of our conversation, she committed to working with me for a year—and once again, she paid in full up front.

These three stories happened in rapid succession. And each of them carried the same message: This is what I can do when you stop striving.

And my God will meet all your needs according to the riches of His glory in Christ Jesus (Philippians 4:19 NIV). God was supplying—not according to my effort, not according to my limited understanding, but according to His riches and His perfect timing.

Another verse that came alive for me was Psalm 34:10: *The lions may grow weak and hungry, but those who seek the LORD lack no good thing* (NIV). For years, I felt like a hungry lion, chasing every opportunity, desperate for provision. But when I turned to God instead of the hustle, I lacked nothing.

This shift also opened the door for me to live the lifestyle I had always dreamed of—nomadic and free. For years, I thought freedom would come only when I "arrived" in business, when I had finally hustled my way to consistent success. But God's way was different. When I let go of striving, He opened the exact doors that allowed me to step into that dream. Since June of 2025, home has been wherever God leads me. From Northern California to New Hampshire, Virginia to Montreal, Denver to Miami—and soon back to Costa Rica—every step has been guided by His provision. All because I can work from anywhere with internet and cell service, I'm free to follow His leading wherever He calls. With travel plans already stretching into next spring, I'm living proof that when you trust God fully, He makes possible the life that once felt out of reach.

Now, instead of being chained to my desk in fear, I live with peace. Instead of constantly calculating how to make ends meet, I trust God's provision. Instead of clinging to control, I hold my plans loosely and watch Him lead me.

You will keep in perfect peace those whose minds are steadfast, because they trust in You (Isaiah 26:3 NIV). Peace has replaced panic. Trust has replaced toil.

God has proven Himself faithful over and over again.

Looking back, I see the beauty of God's design. Striving never brought consistency, but rest released abundance. Fear never produced provision, but trust unlocked freedom. My life is a testimony that kingdom wealth does not come from relentless doing—it comes from resting in the certainty of God's provision.

When I look back over this journey, the difference between striving and trusting is night and day. Eleven years of relentless doing produced exhaustion, fear, and inconsistency, yet just a few weeks of surrender produced provision, peace, and freedom beyond what I could have created for myself.

The lesson is unmistakable: *Kingdom wealth is not earned by relentless doing, but received by resting in the certainty of God's provision.*

This truth has changed everything for me. It's not that I no longer work or that I sit idly waiting for blessings to fall from the sky—it's that my work is no longer driven by fear or fueled by striving. My work now flows from a place of trust—trust that God is my Source, that He is faithful, and that His timing is always perfect.

The fruit of that trust is undeniable: Paid-in-full clients. Unexpected contracts. Doors opening without my striving. The ability to live nomadically with the very freedom I dreamed of when I first launched my business. And most importantly, peace in my spirit—peace that can't be bought, manufactured, or hustled into existence.

The blessing of the LORD makes rich, and He adds no sorrow with it (Proverbs 10:22 ESV). That is kingdom wealth. It's not just about money in the bank. It's about abundance without anxiety, provision without panic, wealth without the weight of striving.

And God is able to bless you abundantly, so that in all things at all times, having all that you need, you will abound in every good work (2 Corinthians

9:8 NIV). This is the life God invites us into—one where we are fully resourced, not so we can cling to wealth in fear, but so we can abound in good works, living fully in His calling.

Pause here. Let this search you.

Where are you still striving? Where in your life are you clinging, hustling, or worrying because you believe provision depends on you? What would it look like to lay that striving down, to enter the rest God offers, and to trust Him as your Provider?

> *There remains, then, a Sabbath-rest for the people of God; for anyone who enters God's rest also rests from their works, just as God did from His* (Hebrews 4:9-10 NIV).

Rest is not only possible—it's available to you right now.

My story is just one example of what happens when we take God at His word. When we stop striving and start trusting, the floodgates of kingdom wealth open. And in that place of rest, we find not only provision, but the freedom to live fully the life God has always intended for us.

STRATEGY

MULTIPLY WHAT GOD ENTRUSTED TO YOU

Strategy allows you to shift from maintaining to multiplying. Growth happens when your actions become focused, intentional, and aligned.

God has entrusted you with the ability to make money as a servant, so you do not need to live as a servant to money. You were created to walk in freedom, have dominion, and lead. From the beginning, God designed you to rule and steward what He placed in your hands. When you step into your rightful position and begin to operate in His economy, your relationship with money begins to change: You stop chasing it and begin directing it.

Scripture reminds us, *Do not be deceived: God is not mocked, for whatever one sows, that will he also reap* (Galatians 6:7 ESV). This principle applies directly to your finances. What you sow in effort, discipline, and faithfulness will, in due season, produce a return. This is not complicated, but it does require intention.

People are busier than they have ever been, yet many are not producing meaningful results. Do not mistake activity for productivity. *A slack hand causes poverty, but the hand of the diligent makes rich* (Proverbs 10:4 ESV). Diligence is focused, intentional, and aligned with a clear plan. It produces results.

Negligence looks like scattered effort, constant motion without direction, and exhaustion without progress. This is where many people get stuck—they are working hard, but not working effectively. They may spend their time preparing, researching, and overthinking instead of executing. Or they may move from one task to another without focusing on the actions that actually generate income. Over time, this creates frustration because the effort does not match the outcome.

Diligence is strategic and measured, producing results in real time and refining each step. Diligent people are not driven by appearances or recognition; they are focused on progress, profitability, and long-term sustainability.

My mentor once said, "Weigh your ego with your bank account and see which one weighs more." When ego leads, decisions become reactive and driven by image. When discipline leads, decisions become intentional and grounded in results. Keep your ego in check so you can build something that lasts.

Scripture gives us a clear picture of multiplication through the parable of the servants in Luke 19. Each servant was given resources and instructed to put them to use. The ones who multiplied what they were given were entrusted with more. The one who did nothing lost even what he had. This is a direct reflection of stewardship. What you do with what you have matters. Faithfulness creates increase.

Jesus reinforced this principle again when He said, *"One who is faithful in a very little is also faithful in much"* (Luke 16:10 ESV). Many people overlook small beginnings because they do not look impressive. Scripture records the words of a messenger from the Lord: *"Do not despise these small beginnings, for the Lord rejoices to see the work begin"* (Zechariah 4:10 NLT). Small progress is still progress. It is evidence that something is working, a sign that you are moving in the right direction. When you stay consistent, small results begin to compound.

Multiplication also requires you to put your resources to work. Money that sits idle does not grow. Time that is not used intentionally does not produce. Skills that are not applied do not generate value. Everything you have can be developed, leveraged, and multiplied when you are willing to take action.

Scripture shows us this in the story of the widow and the jar of oil in 2 Kings 4. The widow believed she had nothing, yet God showed her that what she had was enough to begin. As she acted in faith, what seemed small became more than enough to meet her needs. You do not need to have everything figured out to start; just be willing to use what you already have.

As you begin to multiply what God has entrusted to you, generosity becomes a natural extension of your growth. Scripture teaches, *Honor the Lord with your wealth... then your barns will be filled with plenty* (Proverbs 3:9-10 ESV). Generosity expands your capacity. It shifts your focus beyond yourself and aligns your resources with purpose. Money becomes more meaningful when it is used to impact others.

Whoever sows bountifully will also reap bountifully (2 Corinthians 9:6 ESV). As you grow in diligence, faithfulness, and generosity, you position yourself for increase—your effort, stewardship, and giving all work together to create momentum.

Multiplication is not reserved for a few people; it is available to all of us. It begins with what we have, where we are, and the decisions we make today. When you choose diligence over distraction, faithfulness over inconsistency, and generosity over fear, everything begins to shift.

Diligence produces results. What you steward with intention will always multiply.

JOURNAL REFLECTION

1. Where are you currently putting your time and energy? Are your daily actions producing results, or are they keeping you busy without moving you forward? Where do you need to become more focused and intentional?

2. Reflect on your habits. Where have you been consistent? Where have you been distracted? What has been pulling your attention away from what matters most?

3. What skills, resources, or opportunities do you already have in your hands? What would it look like to fully use what you already have?

4. Where are you waiting for something bigger before taking action? What small step can you take right now to begin building momentum?

5. What would it look like to multiply what you have? How can you begin to create more from what is already in your hands?

Deana Kellar La Rosa

Deana Kellar La Rosa is a faith-driven leader, entrepreneur, and the Chief Operating Officer of La Rosa Holdings Corp., a publicly traded real estate organization in Florida. With experience in lending, title services, insurance, coaching, and business development, she has helped build several successful companies alongside her husband, Joe La Rosa.

Raised in Queens and Long Island, New York, Deana learned early the value of grit and perseverance. Her life includes seasons of abundance and adversity, financial hardship, health challenges, blended family dynamics, and significant personal loss. Through each chapter, her unwavering faith in God has been her anchor and guiding strength.

Deana is the founder of Lead Her Forward, a Christ-centered movement empowering women to grow in faith, leadership, and purpose. She also founded the La Rosa Foundation, supporting youth and families through community outreach.

A devoted wife and mother of five, Deana leads with integrity, compassion, and resilience, serving her community with purpose and conviction.

THE BLESSING OF STEWARDSHIP

By Deana Kellar La Rosa

I didn't grow up with wealth, but I grew up with grit and an example of wise stewardship that, when I put into practice, brought me blessings beyond what I could have hoped for.

I am the youngest of seven children, born in Richmond Hill, Queens. Our home was small and full, but it wasn't always loud. My father worked three jobs, and many days, the house had to stay quiet because he was sleeping between shifts. When he made it home between jobs, we would tiptoe through the halls and whisper to each other. Even as children, we understood what sacrifice sounded like.

Sometimes my father didn't come home much at all. There were seasons when he slept in the back seat of his car between his day job and his night job, wrapped in a moving blanket just to get a few hours of rest before starting again.

As children, we didn't fully understand the weight he carried. We just knew that Dad was tired. Dad was working. Dad was providing.

We weren't rich, but we owned our home. In my father's world, ownership meant dignity and stability. It meant we weren't at the mercy of someone else's decisions. Looking back now, I realize something profound: My father wasn't just working; he was stewarding. He was taking what God had given him and managing it to the best of his ability.

God owns everything, yet He is gracious to allow some of what He owns to pass through our hands. It is our responsibility and joy, as His children, to follow His will and wisely steward all He gives us.

When I was a child, we moved to Franklin Square. At times my friends and I would walk through Garden City, a nearby community that felt like a completely different world from where we lived—it was beautiful. The neighborhoods had wide tree-lined streets and large homes with perfectly kept lawns. Everything about it felt peaceful and stable.

One day, as we walked down one of those streets, a friend said something that caught me off guard: "You're going to live here one day."

I laughed. "Me?" I asked. At the time, I didn't feel confident enough to believe that. I was the girl wearing hand-me-down clothes, whose family counted every dollar carefully, and who had watched groceries get put back at the checkout counter because we had gone over budget.

But something inside me quietly responded, *Maybe.* Because even though I didn't yet have confidence, I had something else: Vision. Somewhere deep in my mind, I carried a map of the life I wanted to build. Not a life of luxury for the sake of luxury, but a life of stability. I wanted a life where my children would never have to see groceries being put back at the register because we couldn't afford them, a life where the thermostat didn't have to stay locked because the heating bill might be too high, and a life where I wouldn't lie awake at night wondering how everything would get paid.

Scarcity leaves marks on a child's heart. But sometimes it plants something else too—determination. Even as a young girl, I made a quiet promise to myself: *I will work as hard as I have to so my family will never live under the weight of that kind of financial pressure.*

Looking back now, I realize it was something deeper. God was quietly planting vision in a little girl who had no idea where that path would lead.

MY UNPLANNED LIFE

Working in finance was never my childhood dream, but I knew it could lead to survival. After high school, I took an accounts receivable job simply because I needed to work, but something unexpected happened: I became fascinated by how money moved. I discovered that I loved systems, structure, and seeing how decisions made inside companies affected real families outside those walls.

So I studied, taking college classes at night to earn certifications while working full time. My advancement didn't come from privilege; it came from performance. I climbed because I produced results.

Eventually, I became a financial analyst working on accounting software systems and later stepped into senior software engineering and equities leadership roles. For the first time in my life, I was secure. Or at least I thought I was.

For the first time in my life, I felt like I had outrun the instability I grew up with. I had worked hard, built a career, and created a level of financial security I once only dreamed about. On paper, everything looked solid. But God was about to show me that security is not the same as control. Just when I thought I had finally built a life I could rely on, motherhood became the place where He began reshaping my understanding of trust.

My first daughter, Meghan, was conceived on our honeymoon. I was so excited to become a mother. But early in the pregnancy, things became uncertain. I was diagnosed with placenta previa accreta, a serious condition that made the pregnancy high-risk.

Instead of preparing for a natural delivery, I was told I would need a C-section. Then, during my final trimester, I was placed on bed rest. Eventually, I spent time in the hospital undergoing daily testing while doctors monitored my daughter closely.

When the day of surgery arrived, the doctors explained the risks. There was a fifty percent chance I would need a hysterectomy. I was 29 years old and had always dreamed of having a big family. It felt like everything I had imagined for my future was suddenly hanging in the balance.

Before they rolled me into surgery, I asked to see my mother. I was emotional—overwhelmed and scared. When my mother walked into the room, she was calm, steady, and unwavering. She looked at me and said, "Deana, you and the baby are going to be fine."

At the time, I didn't fully understand what she was doing, but she was refusing to agree with fear. In that moment, she chose to have faith for both of us.

The surgery lasted more than three hours and required blood transfusions, but Meghan and I both came through safely. When I heard my baby cry for the first time, I felt overwhelming gratitude. That moment wasn't just about becoming a mother; it was the beginning of learning what it meant to trust God when outcomes were out of my control.

Not long after Meghan was born, my understanding of security was further shaken in a way I could have never anticipated. I was a young mother working in New York City, building my career, doing everything I believed would create a stable life. Then came September 11th.

The morning started like any other—but as we all know, it didn't stay that way. The city shifted in an instant. Confusion turned into fear, fear turned into chaos, and chaos turned into a reality none of us were prepared for.

I remember the uncertainty—the not knowing what would happen next, and the overwhelming realization that everything we thought was stable could change in a moment.

Above everything else, one thought consumed me: *I need to get home to my baby. My five-month-old daughter.* Nothing else mattered—not my job, my responsibilities, or the life I had built. All that mattered was getting home to her.

When I finally got home and held her in my arms, one thought kept repeating in my mind: *I almost never saw my daughter again.*

That day changed me. Everything I thought was secure... wasn't. Security was not a salary, a job title, or even a city skyline. I knew I needed something deeper to anchor my life.

> *God is our refuge and strength, an ever-present help in trouble* (Psalm 46:1 NIV).

A year later, while pregnant with my second daughter, Emily, my faith was tested again.

I was working in New York City when I received a call from my doctor. The spinal bifida test had come back normal, but the marker for Down syndrome had not. They needed me to come in for further testing. I left work and walked through the city, completely overwhelmed. I called my best friend, crying as I tried to process what I had just been told.

When my husband and I met with the doctors, they explained the risks. Then they recommended something I wasn't prepared to hear: I should consider terminating the pregnancy.

Despite the doctors' recommendation, everything inside me was clear: *No. This is our baby. No matter what.*

We agreed to additional testing, and then we waited... not a few days, but two long weeks. Two weeks of praying and wondering and choosing faith over fear.

> *For we walk by faith, not by sight* (2 Corinthians 5:7 ESV).

When the results finally came back, everything was normal. Our daughter Emily was perfectly healthy.

That season taught me something I would carry for the rest of my life: Faith doesn't mean you don't feel fear; it means you don't let fear make the decision.

TRUSTING GOD'S DIRECTION

When Meghan and Emily were still young, I made one of the hardest decisions of my life. From the outside, our life in New York looked stable: I had a strong career, a steady income, and a clear path forward. It was the closest thing to security I had ever known. But inside my home, things were not as stable as they appeared.

My husband no longer wanted to continue his career with the NYPD. He had always dreamed of living in Florida, near Disney—something that brought him happiness and a sense of escape from the pressures he carried.

So, I was faced with a decision: Stay in the life that felt secure or leave everything I had built in the hope that a new environment might bring peace to our family. I chose to go—not because I was certain it would work but because I believed that if my husband was happier, our marriage might be stronger, and our children might grow up in a more peaceful home.

So I left New York—my career, surroundings, stability, and everything I knew. It was a leap of faith, but not in the way people often think. At the time, I thought I was trusting that a change in environment could fix what was broken. But what I learned is something I carry with me to this day: If someone is not at peace within themselves, no place can create that for them.

> *Trust in the Lord with all your heart and lean not on your own understanding* (Proverbs 3:5 ESV).

That season taught me that true security isn't found in a place, a person, or a plan; true security is found in God.

While in Florida, I experienced two miscarriages. Each one left its own kind of mark—not just physically, but emotionally. I began to question my body and my future. As fear quietly settled in, I began to believe that maybe having more children wasn't part of my story.

And eventually, I found myself walking through divorce. I was in a place I never imagined I would be, one that forced me to stand on my own, figure things out, and carry responsibility. I had to move forward even when I didn't feel ready. But the reality was that I wasn't alone. God was there for every step I took. He was strengthening me, guiding me, and carrying me when I didn't have the strength myself.

Divorce was never part of the life I imagined for myself. I came from a family where you fought to stay together, and for a long time, I wrestled with the shame of feeling like I had failed. But there comes a moment when surrender is not giving up on God's plan; it is accepting that you cannot force peace, healing, or wholeness where it does not exist.

Suddenly, I was no longer just navigating disappointment. I was a mother of two daughters who needed stability, strength, and peace. That season stretched me in every way. I had to make decisions, carry responsibilities, and keep moving forward even when my heart was heavy. But in that place, God began teaching me something I could not have learned any other way: when everything familiar falls apart, He remains steady. He became my provider, my covering, and my confidence.

By the time Joe came into my life, I was not looking for someone to rescue me. God had already begun the work of restoring me. Joe was not an interruption to that healing; he was part of God's redemptive plan. Our marriage and our blended family would require surrender, faith, and stewardship in ways I could not yet imagine, but by then I had already learned that what God brings together must be handled with prayer, humility, and trust.

Joe and I married in 2008, and we began blending our families into one. It was beautiful, but also difficult. There were different dynamics, relationships, and emotions—all coming together under one roof. There were moments of pressure, and some filled with misunderstanding.

There were even moments when it would have been easier to walk away. But we didn't because we knew that God had brought us together. And if He brought us together, He also called us to steward what He had given us—not walk away from it when things became difficult. So we chose to stand, to pray, and to keep God at the center of our marriage and our home.

That season taught me that stewardship isn't just about finances. Stewardship is appreciating and respecting everything God has given you—your talents, treasures, and yes, relationships—and managing them according to His will.

After everything I had walked through with my challenging pregnancies, I had quietly come to believe that adding more children to my family might not be part of God's plan. Then came Ella.

My pregnancy with her was different: It was peaceful, calm, and covered. It was as if God was restoring something in me that had been broken. Ella wasn't just a baby; she was healing. She brought a sense of unity into our family that we didn't even realize we needed.

And because of her, I made a decision I almost didn't make: not to have my tubes tied. Looking back now, I know that wasn't a coincidence; that was God.

Months later, I found out I was pregnant again. My son's name was Joey. Even though that pregnancy was considered high-risk, I had a deep knowing in my spirit: God did not bring this child into my life to take him away.

This pregnancy was not just physically demanding; it was deeply traumatic. Joey had an RH factor issue, which meant my body was essentially fighting against his, while his little body was fighting to stay alive. I was at the doctor's constantly. Appointment after appointment, test after test, concern after concern. It felt like I was living in a cycle of monitoring, waiting, and praying.

There were days I did not just feel weak; I felt completely drained. Emotionally, physically, and spiritually, I was being stretched to the edge. But even in that place, something stronger than fear kept rising up inside of me. I knew in my spirit that God had given me this child, and I believed He would carry us through. That knowing became an anchor for me.

When Joey was born, he was taken to the NICU. Once again, I was reminded how little control I really had. Bringing him home should have felt like the end of the battle, but even then, the faith journey was not over. He came home on a monitor, and every time that machine beeped, fear tried to rush in. Every sound had the power to steal my peace if I let it.

Finally, I reached a moment where I knew I had a choice to make. I could keep living under the torment of fear, or I could trust God completely. The doctors said my baby was going to be okay. At some point, I had to stop letting the machine dictate my peace and start letting my faith do that. I said, "Take him off the machine. We have to trust God."

That moment marked me. It did not mean I was careless, and it did not mean I was without emotion. It meant I understood that true security was never in a machine, a report, or a medical prediction. My security was, and always has been, in God.

> *"Be still, and know that I am God"* (Psalm 46:10 ESV).

Stewarding all God had given me didn't look like control; It looked like surrendering everything to Him.

OBEDIENCE TO GOD LEADS TO SECURITY

There were many seasons in my life when I felt no real sense of security. I learned there is no guarantee in relationships, no certainty in finances, no promise of good health for us or those we love, and no clear path we can completely depend on.

From the outside, it may have looked to others like I was strong, independent, and capable. However, the truth is that I was never strong when I relied on myself, but I was unstoppable when I trusted God. Every time I moved forward, it happened only because I took a step in surrender to Him. What looked like self-reliance was actually wise stewardship of all God had given to me.

> *And we know that in all things God works for the good of those who love Him* (Romans 8:28 NIV).

Kingdom wealth is not built on control; it is built on trust and obedience.

Every one of us has been entrusted with something. Not just money—but influence, relationships, and opportunities. The question is not simply what we build, but how we steward all that God has given us.

Hold all that God has given you, even when it feels scarce or uncertain or not enough, in your outstretched hands, and ask God what He wants you to do with it. Respond in obedience as you steward all He has given you, seeking to walk in His will. Then watch His blessings unfold in ways only He can orchestrate.

> *Now it is required that those who have been given a trust must prove faithful* (1 Corinthians 4:2 NIV).

Julianna Healy

Julianna Healy is a wife of over 31 years, a mother, a grandmother, and a real estate broker and business owner.

As a storyteller, Juli is passionate about sharing her real-life journey of faith and the kind of "true wealth" that can't be measured in dollars. Through life's challenges and moments of deep need, she has experienced firsthand what it means to lean on the Lord and stand on His promises. When the path was not clear, God always made a way for Juli—breaking through her fears and anxieties and leading her and her family as they depended on His Word and walked by faith.

Juli wants to point others toward hope: the kind of hope rooted in faith in Christ, strengthened by love, and carried through generations as a family legacy. Her message is simple: When we trust God with the whole story, He writes a narrative of peace and strength in our present, and a future that's safe in His hand.

More Precious Than Gold

By Julianna Healy

It was the annual Christmas musical, and the air was electric with the buzz of anticipation typical of this joyous event as a small community gathered to honor God and celebrate the amazing gift of His Son. On this snowy night in my tiny hometown in the woods, people from nearby communities gathered for a festive celebration of our Savior's birth and a dynamic presentation displaying passionate devotion to Jesus. After the performance, laughter and Christmas cheer spilled into the fellowship hall for cookies, conversation, and a visit from Santa. This event had been part of many families' holiday traditions for over 50 years.

Although the town was small, the church complex rose from the forest with majestic beauty. There is no doubt that it was the center of a community with believers in action, doing life together and learning to receive and give love to build people and please the Lord with a life that glorifies Him. Most of all, there was a sense of belonging to a family that truly cares.

It was the most wonderful time of the year, and as a young girl in my first year of community college in this small mountain town nestled in the Sierra foothills, the gathering of familiar friends and new faces of the guests was exhilarating. As people entered the foyer, brushing off snow and helping their children remove their coats, they moved forward to accept the program from the smiling greeters who cheerfully welcomed all inside.

Amidst the hustle and bustle, my eyes landed on a man carrying a 3-year-old boy who was clinging tightly to him. The man was the wayward son of a faithful family that had attended the church for as long as I could remember. Walking toward them was the man's father, who had a huge smile on his face as he reached for the little boy. The child shyly peeked out at his grandfather, who was coaxing him with exuberant talk about a visit from Santa. I don't know how I knew, but something told me this father and his young child were all alone in the world, and I felt a pang in my heart.

Fast forward about a year later: I married that once-wayward son, becoming a wife and stepmom to a four-year-old, just months shy of my 20th birthday. Our marriage was the talk of our small town for a hot second. We fumbled a bit as we approached the arrival of our day at the altar, but after some great counseling, repentance, and water baptism to start anew, we became a family of three.

Looking back thirty years later, I know it was divine intervention that caused the crossing of my husband's and my two very different paths. With the support and wise guidance of our loving families, pastor, church leaders, and the undeniable help of the Holy Spirit, we renewed our commitment to God as we started our life together. The success of our family life was greatly impacted by being planted in a church that provided a warm, inclusive environment, sound biblical teaching addressing the issues faced by people of all ages, and accountability that cannot come in isolation. Having many role models and the support of different families helped my husband and me recognize and be encouraged to live Christ-centered lives. Regular family events, prayer support, mentorship from seasoned families, and practical help in everyday life were essential to our growth.

The success in our marriage does not mean we didn't face challenges. Through our union, God healed brokenness in my husband's and stepson's lives and saved me from a path not leading to the ultimate happiness I now know, as He gave me His best plan for my life. When it comes to making major life decisions, it's not always about making the perfect choice; it's about having the perfect One with you on the journey.

Don't get me wrong—there is a path that leads to death: sin. That is, every other way apart from Jesus. Jesus tells us in John 16:33, *"In this world you will have trouble. But take heart! I have overcome the world"* (NIV). During life's storms, God refines our faith and teaches us to focus on Jesus with intentionality.

Although it wasn't my original plan, our family life played out in such a way that I chose to pause further education and career pursuits outside the home. My husband, Andrew, had just obtained his Tile & Stone Contractor's license around the time we married, and we were excited to expand our family. We wanted our children to be close in age so we could create a family dynamic that encouraged friendship and a close bond between the siblings. Starting our family early was the right choice. By the time I gave birth to our first son together, there was a six-year gap between him and our oldest. Three years after our second son was born, we welcomed our daughter, and our family felt complete.

During those years, we lived frugally so I could stay home and care for our children. We were deeply involved in church—volunteering, giving financially, and writing and playing songs. We did the best we could to apply biblical principles to our lives, properly stewarding our relationships with God and others as well as our time, talents, and treasures. My husband and I considered our family—including each other and our three children—among our greatest treasures. We were also blessed to have our parents and some of our siblings close by.

Initially, we lived in an apartment. When I became pregnant with our daughter, dreams of homeownership began to form. The house next door to my parents went up for sale—the location was ideal, but the house needed major work. Andrew, with construction experience and help from family in the trades, believed he could handle the remodel. I was eight months pregnant when we first walked through the home. Three months after our daughter was born, on my mother-in-law's birthday, we closed escrow.

For the next year and a half, Andrew somehow found the monumental strength to carry his booming tile business, the mortgage, apartment rent, and a full remodel. At times, he came home totally spent, with tears in his eyes. But he loved his family so much, and we were encouraged to keep going by the joy that our children brought us and our faith that God was working all things together for our good.

I oversaw the home base—caring for the children, doing household tasks, and paying the bills. We worked together to manage the construction project; I helped with side work, doing some architectural drafting for Andrew's dad, who was an architect, which helped the budget. However, so much of the blood, sweat, and tears it took to build that home came from my husband; he worked so hard to make this dream come true for our family. Two years later, we left the apartment and moved into our home. God truly blessed us with a beautiful place to put our roots down.

Then came 2007. The developers and contractors who regularly used Andrew were experiencing an unusual trend of canceled projects. I handled the bills and could see things tightening. We had many serious conversations and faced the real possibility of losing our home. We leaned hard into God's Word: *Don't worry about anything; instead, pray about everything* (Philippians 4:6 NLT).

> *Trust in the LORD with all your heart, do not depend on your own understanding. Seek his will in all you do, and he will show you which path to take* (Proverbs 3:5-6 NLT).

We discussed a change of jobs for Andrew. Commuting three hours to the San Francisco Bay Area to access more job opportunities that were available in the large city was not uncommon for men in our town. However, such a commute would have been heartbreaking for our family. It would have made for incredibly early mornings and late evenings with minimal quality family time, or might have even required him to stay down there during the week and only be home on the weekends. Andrew especially would have struggled, as he would not have done well being away from us so much.

I was working part-time in a medical office, but we needed something more to make ends meet. I knew I could get that college degree to start a career, but a four-year path wouldn't pay our immediate bills. We needed something faster. We pressed into our faith and into God's Word.

We held tightly to God's promises, trusting in prayer and faith even when our situation felt impossible. With limited options and no clear path forward, we sought something faster to sustain our family while continuing to rely on Scripture for strength. Through this difficult season, I learned to cling to and actively use God's Word like a sharpened sword, growing stronger in faith through the trials we faced.

One Scripture became central in our home. I framed it and spoke it often:

> *May our sons flourish in their youth like well-nurtured plants.*
> *May our daughters be like graceful pillars, carved to beautify a palace*
> *May our barns be filled with crops of every kind.*
> *May the flocks in our fields multiply by the thousands, even tens of thousands, and may our oxen be loaded down with produce.*
> *May there be no enemy breaking through our walls, no going into captivity, no cries of alarm in our town squares.*
> *Yes, joyful are those who live like this! Joyful indeed are those whose God is the LORD.*
> (Psalm 144:12-15 NLT)

Meanwhile, our credit line was creeping upward. We knew we couldn't sustain this. On our knees more than ever, our radar was up, and we spoke to family and friends to get advice.

In the fall of 2007, I began online real estate courses. In spring 2008, I got my license. Then came the crash. The housing market crisis hit a peak in September 2008 with the collapse of major financial institutions. And there I was, a newly licensed real estate agent, hoping that this would help us get through our financial struggles.

I was determined to succeed and viewed my new business like a full-time job, even though few people were buying homes. When my children were in school, I worked at a desk in a small real estate office on the highway in our little town. At the end of their day, the kids would get off the bus at my office; if I had to work later, they would go to my mom's house next to ours. She had retired and was graciously willing to help out.

Because the real estate industry was slow, many agents were forced to leave the business. They could not sustain the extended time without a paycheck. I, on the other hand, did not know anything different coming from a position of a homemaker.

The day my first commission check came in, Andrew looked at me in awe. "You can make money," he said wide-eyed. I had sold a very nice home in a prestigious neighborhood, so even at the lowest commission tier, it was significant. We continued to live by God's promise of provision as we followed His Word.

> *"Therefore I tell you, do not be anxious about your life, what you will eat or what you will drink, nor about your body, what you will put on. Is not life more than food, and the body more than clothing?... But seek first the kingdom of God and his righteousness, and all these things will be added to you"*
> (Matthew 6:25, 33 ESV).

The Lord proved faithful. Even a few sales per year helped. We clipped coupons and cut every unnecessary expense. It was extremely helpful to us that we were not the kind of people to take large risks and go into debt with large purchases that we could not afford.

The market continued to crash, bottoming out in 2013. So many foreclosures filled the newspaper—often names we knew. It was heartbreaking. But it was also a season of new beginnings. Many would become renters and take time to give their credit time to rebound. In this season, I was able to help many friends who had not yet entered the path of homeownership realize the American dream of owning their own home.

Some of my clients had construction experience and were able to flip homes and become very successful. I discovered I loved helping people strategically pursue their real estate dreams. This particular climate of the real estate market caused me to grow into a seasoned agent—pounding the pavement, showing homes, and writing offer after offer in competitive foreclosure situations. I later became a certified short sale foreclosure expert by taking additional education classes. As the chaos of this unprecedented real estate meltdown unfolded, it was clear that my career would be forged in the fires of this recession. What was misfortune for so many was a massive opportunity for others. Sensitivity to the heartbreak of many families was never lost on me. I knew firsthand the miracle of not losing our home.

During this time, I learned a lot about people and how they made real estate decisions. I listened to the heart of why different people buy and sell homes, if they are motivated by the joy of the American dream, having a place to raise their growing family, accomplishing an investment strategy, or navigating a major life change, such as a job transfer, divorce, or even a death. My real estate journey became less about making money and more about caring for people and serving their needs. I stayed grounded in the true motivation behind my hard work—to operate with integrity in everything I do for Christ, seeking His kingdom first and being ready to share His love when opportunities arise.

There is an "emotional rollercoaster" that's a definitive characteristic of the real estate landscape, encompassing a spectrum of feelings from excitement and joy to anxiety, frustration, and even grief. I had to learn not to own the emotions of my clients, yet still walk with them to help them navigate their own path, making the best choices possible with the information that I give them.

When you are advising people on the largest asset they may ever own in their life—which also happens to be a place of safety and happy memories for their family—you begin to understand the magnitude and importance of putting yourself in the shoes of another person. You learn to engage your intelligence, energy, and resources on their behalf to help better their life as best you can. I could not have landed on a better career that utilized my skills, abilities, and desire to serve people.

The best part about this career choice was that I did not have to ignore my priorities: my heart's strong desire to love and serve the Lord and my family. I never missed one of my children's sporting events, and I was able to help in their classrooms when they were young. I have continued to serve at church in various ways and have been able to adjust my schedule to new priorities that have evolved through the years, from caring for aging parents to spending time with my grandchildren. My life has been filled with weddings, baby showers, funerals, and all of the things that pertain to life the way God meant it to be. The type of work God provided for me offered me the freedom of a flexible schedule.

Additionally, when I became a broker and opened my own company, my husband was able to leave the tile trade. He has since worked on our investment properties and been an integral part and support in many aspects of our real estate business.

Above everything, my number one priority remains unchanged: I want to please the Lord and abide in Him daily. I want to know Him, be found in Him, be salt and light in the earth, and make my calling and election sure. The core identity of who I am is deeply rooted in Jesus—who He is to me, for me, in me, and through me. His Spirit continues to transform and sustain my life. I know it is His hand holding the pen that has written my story and made me part of His eternal story, and I hold fast to the promise that He is still working in me a glory yet to be revealed when He returns to the earth. This hope is the anchor for my soul that keeps me from falling into the pitfalls that the love of money can present.

One Scripture has long served as a guardrail in my life: *For the love of money is the root of all kinds of evil* (1 Timothy 6:10 ESV).

And the companion truth: *Yet true godliness with contentment is itself great wealth* (1 Timothy 6:6 NLT).

Financial success is not the true measure of life. If we let God love us, and love Him back by allowing Christ to sit on the throne of our hearts, He will put us on a path where we can steward our resources and our relationships with His guidance as we build a legacy of faith—including a hope that never dies and love that leads the way. That is far more precious than gold.

Cash Flow

Rule Your Money Decisions

Managing cash flow allows you to step into leadership. As people begin earning money, paying bills on time, and keeping everything afloat, they feel like they are doing well financially. But when something unexpected happens, it can feel as if everything falls apart: This can be as simple as a car registration being due, a birthday approaching, or a yearly expense hitting, and suddenly, there is stress. However, these are actually predictable expenses that can become unmanageable when they are not planned for. When there is no foresight, normal life events can feel like financial emergencies.

The simple believes everything, but the prudent gives thought to his steps (Proverbs 14:15 ESV). A lack of financial planning leads to reaction, but wisdom leads to preparation. When you begin to think ahead, you remove pressure and create stability.

Three perspectives shape how you manage your money: hindsight, eyesight, and foresight. Hindsight allows you to understand where your money has been going. It gives you clarity by looking at past spending. Eyesight brings awareness to what is happening in the present. It allows you to build a plan based on your current needs and responsibilities. Foresight prepares you for what is coming next. It allows you to plan for expenses that you know will happen.

When these three work together, your financial decisions become clear and confident. You no longer react to situations as they arise because you anticipate them and prepare for them in advance.

Jesus speaks to this level of planning when He says, "Suppose one of you wants to build a tower. *Won't you first sit down and estimate the cost to see if you have enough to complete it?*" (Luke 14:28-30 NIV). When we plan ahead, we give ourselves the ability to follow through. When we do not, we create unnecessary pressure and frustration.

Don't make large purchases without a plan to support them. Many people move forward based on desire, determining to figure out the consequences later, which often leads to regret, stress, and financial strain. Begin by making decisions based on clarity, not emotion. When you understand your cash flow, you know what you can spend, when you can spend it, and how it will impact your future.

Scripture reinforces this principle again: *The plans of the diligent lead surely to abundance, but everyone who is hasty comes only to poverty* (Proverbs 21:5 ESV). Diligence in planning protects your future. When you slow down long enough to think through your decisions, you position yourself for stability.

Scripture says, *So if the Son sets you free, you will be free indeed* (John 8:36 ESV). Financial freedom is available, and it begins with truth. When you understand your cash flow, you remove confusion. When confusion is removed, confidence begins to grow. When confidence grows, you begin to rule your money decisions.

As you move forward, stay grounded in what you are building. You are not just managing money; you are creating a system that supports your life, your family, and your future. As you continue to apply these principles, you will begin to experience peace where there once was stress, clarity where there once was confusion, and control where there once was uncertainty.

JOURNAL REFLECTION

1. What has your money been doing up to this point? When you look back, where has it been going?
2. Where have you been caught off guard financially? What expenses felt unexpected, but in reality, happen regularly? Where would planning ahead have changed the outcome?
3. Are your financial decisions based on clarity or emotion? Where have you made decisions without fully thinking through the impact? What would it look like to slow down and make decisions with intention?
4. Are you spending everything that comes in each month? Or are you creating margin for what is ahead? Where do you need to become more disciplined in your spending?
5. What upcoming expenses do you already know are coming? Create a plan to prepare for them.

Jesse Jordan

Jesse Jordan is a New Jersey native who relocated to Los Angeles five years ago with a singular vision to make his mark in the entertainment industry. Like many purpose-driven journeys, his path didn't unfold exactly as planned, but it unfolded exactly as needed.

What began as a creative pursuit evolved into a calling in the world of business, marketing, and sales. Through discipline, instinct, and an uncommon ability to connect with people, Jesse pivoted into building and leading high-performing sales initiatives, generating millions in revenue while simultaneously empowering others to elevate their own lives and careers.

Grounded in faith and guided by conviction, Jesse's work lives at the intersection of purpose and performance. He believes success is most meaningful when it's shared, and that true influence isn't measured solely by numbers but by the people you inspire along the way.

His story is one of redirection, resilience, and results, proving that sometimes the detour is the destination.

FUMBLING MY WAY TO VICTORY

By Jesse Jordan

This chapter isn't just about building wealth, handling business deals, or mastering financial strategies. I'm writing today about building legacies, breaking self-destructive pride, gracefully winning, and the brutal honesty it takes to admit you had the world in the palm of your hand, fumbled, and trusted God to get you back up.

The lessons I've learned have left permanent scars that have shaped me into who I am today.

When you're on top, the world calls you brilliant. They crown you with the accolades and titles and sing your praises, but invincibility is the greatest illusion. The higher you climb, the thinner the air and the more fragile the ground beneath your feet becomes. I had to learn that the hard way.

The year 2024 was a season of learning and maturing for me. I had to say my final goodbye to the man who taught me everything about hustle, grit, and going after everything you want in life: my father. He demonstrated for me the art of hustling before I even knew how to spell the word. My father was my professor in the school of grind. Teaching me that success in life isn't just handed to you on a silver platter. You must chase what you desire; you earn it, and you fight for it.

My father showed me how to utilize my persuasiveness and charm to create opportunities when there seemed to be none. His motto was, "You can only depend on you." He believed that a real man didn't wait for doors to open; a real man builds and installs his own doors, and then kicks them open if necessary. I respected that, and I still do.

Dad's lessons shaped me into a class-act hustler, a go-getter, a man who always finds a way of turning a no into a yes, and arguably, one of the greats! But there was one thing my father never taught me, one truth that no hustle, no business strategy, and no late-night grind could ever replace: the power of putting God first in everything, especially in finances.

Ten days after my birthday, my world shattered. My best friend, my father, the man who taught me about hard work and perseverance, closed his eyes for the last time.

Grief is a strange teacher. It strips you down to raw questions and raw truths. As I sat in the car following my father's passing, my painful heart watching the world move slowly around me, a thought hit me: "Maybe my dad is now my angel. Maybe he'll make sure I'm taken care of financially."

Is that strange? Absolutely. But it was real to me.

My father always wanted me to have money, never to struggle. He wanted me to be financially secure, living above lack. And so, in my mind, I imagined him in heaven pulling strings for me. But here is what I later realized: no man, not even my father, could open the kind of financial doors that only God could open. Not an angel. Not an inheritance. Only God. And that's where this journey truly began.

It was a Thursday when I was heading to the airport after cremating my father. All I could think of was the new money-making opportunity I would be starting on Monday. I questioned if that opportunity was my father's way of blessing me. I didn't know, but figured I would soon see.

When Monday arrived, it wasn't just another day; it was a new beginning, a jump into a world of opportunity. I walked into the headquarters of an Inc. 500 company with my chest high and shoulders squared, dressed like I had destiny tucked in my Louie trousers. The energy was electric, that kind of feeling that makes you feel like every move matters. I had just said goodbye to the man who loved me the most, yet something inside me said, "Son, keep going. Don't stop now!" My father had always told me to keep pushing, no matter what. And so, I did. From the moment I stepped into that building, I wasn't just another employee; no, I was the prize horse nobody saw coming. I wasn't there to blend in; I was there to dominate.

With every client, at every meeting, and in every presentation, I spoke like someone who knew failure wasn't an option.

The first deal came in fast. Then the next. And they just kept coming. By the end of nine months, I was a walking headline with 1.2 million dollars in personal production. The top sales leader in the building. Crushing records that stood before me. I wasn't just closing deals; I was rewriting the company's history. And let me be clear, I'm not talking small change. I'm talking 10k weeks, 15k weeks, and 16k weeks. Life was good. No, life was sweet; full of Cartier bracelets, Rolex watches, and 5-star dinners. I'll leave your imagination to wander the rest.

Money came in faster than I could count it. I'd seen money before, but not like this, not at this level of abundance. With every check that hit my account, I told myself, "You did it. You made it."

But then... May 6, 2025...

That morning felt like another winning day as I walked into the office with the confidence of a man on top of the world. My numbers were strong. My reputation was untouchable—a quarter million dollars in equity and growing. The company loved me, or so I thought.

"Jesse, can you step into my office for a minute?"

No warning, no inside tips, just a casual conversation that would change my life in seconds. The glass door closed behind me, and in less time than it takes to check a text, everything I built came crashing down.

"We're going to have to let you go."

Those words hit harder than any punch I'd ever taken. I sat in shock, trying to process what I heard. *Let me go? After everything I've done? After breaking records, making the company millions, and becoming the face of success?*

I felt the ground shift beneath me. My lifestyle—gone. My status and equity—gone. My security—shattered like glass. I walked out of that office numb as a tooth with Novocain; my pride and ego were smashed to pieces.

The parking lot had never felt so BIG! My car never felt so small.

I opened the door of my car and sat behind the wheel. For the first time since my dad's passing, I cried. Not a quiet tear, but the kind of cry that comes from the deep inside of your soul. With my hands gripping the steering wheel, I screamed, "Dad! Dad! Dad, how could you let this happen? What's going on? You were supposed to protect me! Why now?"

The silence that followed was louder than my screams.

I drove home in silence, like a man who lost everything at the casino. My mind was racing and my heart sinking. Every mile felt like a funeral procession for my dreams.

When I got home, I didn't pour a drink, and I didn't confide in a friend. I dropped to my knees and prayed. "God, why?"

In that moment, something stirred in me. A thought so clear I couldn't ignore it. "YOU TRUSTED YOUR HUSTLE, NOT ME. "

It hit me like a lightning bolt. During all the success, all the hustle, and all the influence. I never put God first. I tithed nothing. I gave nothing back. I was completely disobedient.

I could almost see my father in heaven pleading with God. "Give my boy another chance. He'll get it right this time." And in that moment, I realized something powerful. God didn't take something from me to punish me; He took something away to prepare me.

What I thought was good, God knew wasn't great.

That same day, yes, the very day I lost everything, I opened my laptop, determined to find something that could keep me in my lifestyle. I wasn't thinking about purpose; I was thinking about bills. I started searching, scrolling, dialing numbers like a man possessed. And then it happened. I called a company, expecting to get a receptionist, maybe a voicemail. Instead, the CEO himself answered the phone. I gave him my introduction elevator pitch right on the spot, voice steady, heart racing. And do you know what he said? "Can you meet at 1:30?"

By 1:30 that day, we were standing in front of each other at a coffee shop, sizing each other up like two cowboys in a standoff. Our eyes locked, and with a confidence only God can give, he looked at me, smiled, and said words that still echo in my head: "I'm impressed. How about we do this 50/50 partnership, you and me?"

Just like that. There was no probation, no training, and no begging for a seat at the table. God didn't just give me a chair; He gave me half the table. That day, God took me from worker to owner. From paycheck to partnership. From asking for permission to writing my own rules.

And here's what I knew: It wasn't my hustle that did it, it wasn't my skill, and it wasn't my connections; it was God. And that revelation changed everything.

I made a vow that day—God gets His 10% first. Every business decision goes through Him, and every dollar is under His direction. Because the truth is, the blessing of the Lord brings wealth and adds no sorrow (Proverbs 10:22).

Let me make this clear: You can hustle without God and get rich, but you can't hustle without God and keep peace.

You can grind and make millions, but if God's not in it, you'll always live with holes in your pocket and emptiness in your soul.

The world says to secure the bag, sleep when you're dead, and chase the paper.

The kingdom says to seek first the kingdom and all things will be added (Matthew 6:33), and to honor the Lord with your wealth and your barns will overflow (Proverbs 3:9-10). One path leaves you empty, the other fills you beyond measure.

Then there is the law of the tithe. When I didn't tithe, I was living under a closed heaven. My money was flowing, but it wasn't growing. I was making it rain, but I was also sowing seeds of disobedience.

Malachi 3:10 records the Lord's words: *"Bring the whole tithe into the storehouse... and see if I will not open the floodgates of heaven and pour out so much blessing that there will not be room enough to store it"* (NIV). God isn't after our money. He's after our trust. Giving a tithe proves that money doesn't control us and that our hope is in God, not the hustle.

When I lost that job, I thought I had lost everything. But the truth is, I lost nothing; I gained alignment. God took what I thought was good and gave me what He knew was great: ownership. Now, everything I touch begins with Him. Every deal starts with a prayer. Every dollar begins with a tithe.

Our culture can make the hustle look appealing, like the holy grail. But if we want true wealth, wealth that lasts, brings peace, and builds legacies, we must do it God's way. Here are some practical steps to achieving kingdom wealth.

1. *Commit to tithing*—giving 10% of your income to God's work.
   Don't wait until you're rich to start. Tithe on what you have now.

2. *Pray over your finances daily.* Invite God into every transaction.

3. *Steward what you have well.* Don't live like a king if your wallet says servant.
4. *Be generous.* Beyond the tithe, give to others. Generosity breaks greed.
5. *Think legacy, not lifestyle.* Build something that outlives you.

As I look back, I thank God for the storm. Because without it, I would've kept trusting the hustle instead of trusting Him. That's why I wrote this chapter for you, the generation of kingdom builders. Don't just make money, make an impact. Make history. Build wealth that honors God and blesses people. Because when you do, the world will know, this is what His kingdom looks like.

We live in a culture that glorifies the self-made story. Instagram is flooded with people posing in front of luxury cars, holding stacks of cash, preaching the gospel of "hustle" like it's the eleventh commandment. Hustle hard, sleep when you're dead. Secure the bag at all costs. But here's the truth that the world doesn't tell you: If God is not in it, your wealth, if it does last, will never be fulfilling.

Proverbs 10:22 (NKJV) states, *The blessing of the Lord makes one rich, And He adds no sorrow with it. Read that again.*

The blessings of the Lord make us rich, not the blessings of our hustle, our connections, or our genius idea. And here's the best part: God does not add sorrow. That means we don't have to sell our souls for success. We don't have to sacrifice our peace, integrity, or walk with Christ to build wealth. The kingdom way is different.

The kingdom way says:

> *Seek first the kingdom of God and His righteousness, and all these things will be added to you* (Matthew 6:33 NKJV).

Honor the Lord with your possessions, and with the firstfruits of all your increase; So your barns will be filled with plenty, and your vats will overflow with new wine
(Proverbs 3:9-10 NKJV).

I learned that God doesn't just want us to be saved; He wants us to be secure. He doesn't just want you holy; He wants you whole spiritually, emotionally, and yes, financially. But God can't bless what we don't surrender.

Storms will come, but when we listen to God, those storms can redirect us instead of destroying us. My storm stripped away the illusions of invincibility, the false crowns, and applause of men, until all that remained was raw faith and a heart that had no choice but to depend on God. And in that silence, in that surrender, I finally found what my father had been preparing me for all along. See, my dad taught me the hustle. He showed me the art of persuasion, the rhythm of the grind, the power of never taking "no" as the final word. He raised me to be a fighter in a world that doesn't hand out free passes. But what I didn't understand until I lost it all was that his lessons were never meant to stand alone; they were meant to be paired with the wisdom of heaven.

My father's voice echoed resilience, but God's voice echoes grace. My father gave me the blueprint of survival, but God gives us the blueprint of legacy. Together, they formed the kingdom formula that saved my life.

When I close my eyes, I can still see my dad standing with that confident smirk he always carried, like a man who knew he could bend the world with nothing but his will. And I imagine him now, looking down, watching me finally connect the dots, taking his earthly lessons and fusing them with divine truth. Watching me turn failure into foundation, scars into symbols, hustle into holy purpose. I know what he would say. I can almost hear his voice saying, "Son, I'm proud of you."

I know my dad is not just proud that I've closed million-dollar deals, flexed the presidential Rolex, or worn the tailored suits that make strangers stare. No, he'd be proud that I became a man who could lose everything and still rise stronger. A man who discovered that true wealth isn't counted in zeros, but in obedience. A man who finally understood that success without God is nothing more than a decorated coffin that is good to look at, but empty inside.

The movie of my life doesn't play like a tale of a hustler; it's the story of a son who walked through fire and learned how to dance in the flames. A man who discovered that broken crowns still shine when God places them back on your head. A man who carries his father's lessons not as a heavy weight, but as wings.

Every boardroom I enter now, every deal I structure, and every check I write is not done by me alone. I've learned to submit to God as I carry my father in my heart. My father's legacy is alive in my grind, his voice lives in my decisions, and his spirit smiles every time I put God first in what I do.

If you take nothing else from this chapter, take this: Don't just build wealth, build alignment. Don't just chase paper, chase purpose. Don't just hustle for applause, hustle for eternity. Because money will fade, markets will shift, and empires will crumble, but the man who honors God and carries the lessons of his father walks in a wealth that no recession, no pink slip, and no betrayal can ever take away.

I am that man. Scarred, but stronger. Humbled, but lifted. Broken, but built into something greater. And I know without a question that somewhere beyond the veil of this life, my father is grinning with pride. Not because I became rich. Not because I became great. But because I became the man he always knew I could be—the one who took his lessons, added God's truth, and turned them into a kingdom's legacy.

That, my friend, is what real wealth looks like.

Elisabeth Gilliatt

Elisabeth Gilliatt is a woman rooted in faith, a devoted wife, and a joyful new mama stepping into the beauty of motherhood with grace and wonder. Alongside her husband, Eric, she lives with open hands and a willing heart—passionate about loving people well, serving her local community, supporting small businesses, uplifting nonprofits, and faithfully sowing into their church, Word of Life Fellowship.

With a life anchored in worship, Elisabeth serves in many areas of ministry—from the worship team to volunteer coordination, cleanup, coffee, and dance—showing up with a willing heart, carrying joy and intention into each place she's called to serve. She finds her deepest fulfillment in marriage, motherhood, and living fully present within the body of Christ.

In her professional life, she serves as a personal assistant to Michelle Tascoe, striving to serve with excellence, care, and integrity in all she does. Elisabeth shares her journey to encourage women to live with faith-filled purpose, embracing each season with love, intention, and a heart surrendered to God.

BUILDING GOD'S KINGDOM

By Elisabeth Gilliatt

Throughout my life, I have always been provided for. Even in uncertain seasons, there was somewhere to turn, and I was given good tools to forge my own path. My grandparents taught me steadfastness, consistency, and healthy habits—and showed me the stability that comes with following these practices. My parents taught me to embrace refinement—to admit when you're wrong and get back up when you fall. They showed me that strength isn't just about what you start with, but about showing up and allowing God to transform you. These examples laid the groundwork for my life.

I grew up in Stockton, California, from 2000 to 2013. My city and my family demonstrated both visible strain and resilience. Stockton was shaped by the hard work of agriculture and the steady movement of goods through the Port of Stockton. However, many households, including ours, were sustained paycheck to paycheck. Some families were just getting by, while others were building slowly and steadily.

The Great Recession brought a shift. Even though, as a child, I didn't understand all the economics, I felt the effects in the atmosphere as I witnessed tense conversations about money and sensed an underlying uncertainty.

Although I didn't understand the national weight, by the time Stockton filed for bankruptcy in 2012, I was already living in the ripple effects. You could feel it in everyday life—in the strained systems and worn-down resources.

Crime was also part of the backdrop. It was not always visible, but it was present enough to shape my awareness of it. Being told which neighborhoods to avoid, hearing sirens often enough that they blended into the background, and practicing safety drills at school all became part of my early education in vigilance.

And yet, life was just life. Kids played outside until the streetlights came on. Families gathered. There was laughter, warmth, tradition, and a normalcy that existed alongside everything else.

School reflected that same reality. Many classrooms were full and under-resourced, filled with kids from all kinds of home lives. I sat among a wide range of stories—some similar to mine, many not. Yet I had teachers who cared deeply, even when they themselves were stretched thin. Though my teachers' time, encouragement, and attention weren't guaranteed, when they were offered, they were treasured.

Stability wasn't assumed, but it was appreciated because it had to be earned. People leaned on each other. Families stayed close. And often, they extended that care outward. Even while navigating our own challenges, my family opened our home to other kids, often my friends, whom my mom would call "non-biologicals." We gave them a safe place to land, simply, as an option, and there were just as many times when I was also invited into the homes of my friends, which offered that same sense of belonging.

During my childhood, I developed grit. Although there was hardship, seeing the people around me persevere through difficulties taught me that no matter how hard things may become, things go better if we keep showing up. I learned I could try to build something meaningful with my life, even when the ground doesn't always feel secure.

Still, many times, I cried out to God to remove me from my circumstances. Things often felt unstable and uncertain, and I wrestled with fear and anxiety.

Looking back today, I can see the keeping hand of God on my life. Despite seeing what life looked like on the impoverished side of town and witnessing many who had their childhood stolen, I was kept from the harshest of realities that others dealt with.

> *"For I know the plans I have for you," says the Lord. "They are plans for good and not for disaster, to give you a future and a hope. In those days when you pray, I will listen. If you look for me wholeheartedly, you will find me. I will be found by you"* (Jeremiah 29:11-14 NLT).

My name, Elisabeth, means *consecrated to God—God is my abundance.* Looking back, I can see how that has marked my life. God has always kept me and set me apart for Himself, not only in the way I've been protected and guided, but in the reality that so many prayers I once prayed, I am now living in. What I once asked God for in hope, I am now seeing the fruit of with my own eyes.

I've always viewed the Lord as my Father. I didn't have the greatest relationship with my earthly father, but God showed up for me in a way that met all of my needs. Still, I battled with an internal conflict: I reached out to God when I needed Him, but I struggled to ask boldly, wondering if it was wrong to ask for more, especially given all that He had already blessed me with.

Now, I know the truth: God invites us to ask Him and walk with Him in honest conversation. He wants us to abide in Him—staying attuned to His heart, partnering with Him, and aligning our lives with His will.

> *"And when you pray, do not heap up empty phrases... for your Father knows what you need before you ask him. Pray then like this: Our Father in heaven, hallowed be your name. Your kingdom come, your will be done, on earth as it is in heaven"* (Matthew 6:7-10 ESV).

I didn't realize that withholding my desires from God wasn't humility, but distance. I was afraid that asking for abundance or even for the desires of my heart would be ungrateful or selfish, which led me to hold God at arm's length. Eventually, I was faced with questions: Do I truly believe that God is not only good, but abundant? Do I believe that He came so that I could have life in Him fully? Jesus teaches:

> *"I am the door. If anyone enters by me, he will be saved and will go in and out and find pasture. The thief comes only to steal and kill and destroy. I came that they may have life and have it abundantly. I am the good shepherd. The good shepherd lays down his life for the sheep"* (John 10:9-11 ESV).

If this is true, it means that I, a daughter of the King, have access to His abundance. Not *partial* access or *conditional* access, but *full* access.

Although I had seen God provide for me in ways that were far beyond anything I could have imagined, a part of me still believed it was circumstantial—that somehow I had just *ended up* on the receiving end of provision. But it wasn't happenstance; it was God's heart. God loved me and desired to bless me, and I had to learn how to receive that without shrinking back or questioning if it was "too much."

When I first stepped into independence, everything felt new all at once.

Managing money, working consistently, making decisions about my future, learning how to steward what I had—it was a lot. It created pressure. While I trusted God, I also felt responsible for making it all work. Without realizing it, my mindset became focused on striving. I began to chase an image of what I thought adulthood was supposed to look like rather than seeking where God was actually leading me.

I was still operating from a place of survival—hustling, pushing, and trying to hold everything together in my own strength. At first, it didn't feel like this was a problem as I entered a completely new season of life. I was engaged, living on my own for the first time, and trying to prepare for everything that would come next. I wanted to do it right. I wanted to be responsible, to feel stable, and to know that I was building something secure before stepping into marriage.

I sat down one day with a notebook, writing out what I made and what I planned to spend. I mapped out months ahead—wedding expenses, future home ideas, bills, savings. It gave me a sense of control. I thought that if I could just plan well enough, then I could create stability for myself.

Then the unexpected happened.

By early 2020, the world began to change. What started as uncertainty quickly turned into something none of us could have planned for. By March, everything had shut down. And by April, I was out of a job.

Everything I had planned no longer applied. My paycheck, what I thought would bring security, was gone. Yet I still had bills to pay and a wedding ahead of me. So I kept going.

I started my own house cleaning business and took on staging homes on the side. While between jobs, I remember looking at my account and seeing I had something like 20 cents to my name. All I could do was laugh. I was humbled, dumbfounded.

Even in that season, God sustained me. I hardly had time to market my housecleaning business—yet through word of mouth, I kept getting clients. God carried me through that season in a way that I can now only describe as His provision.

Looking back, I can see that God was teaching me something I hadn't fully learned yet—that my security was never in my planning, but in Him.

By the following year, the world slowly began to find a new rhythm. I stepped into a new job, feeling like I was breathing fresh air. I loved what I did. My job drew out my creativity and built confidence in areas I hadn't explored before. For the first time in a while, I felt steady. I was making good money and felt capable, like I was thriving.

Yet somewhere along the way, my heart began to shift. After enduring a season of lack, I didn't know how to handle abundance.

Instead of stewarding what I had, I used money to reward myself, to cope, and to fill spaces I didn't know how to sit in. What once felt like survival slowly turned into indulgence, and my gratitude faded into carelessness. I stopped being intentional and inviting God in and began simply consuming.

A couple of years into our marriage, after what had felt like a long and steady season, everything shifted again. The job I had come to love—the one I had poured so much of my time, energy, and creativity into—was suddenly gone. What had once felt stable quickly unraveled as the economy shifted again after COVID, and I found myself among many who were let go.

This loss hit hard. I had built a sense of security, and when it was taken away, it seemed everything I had been working toward was slipping through my hands. I felt like I had failed—not just myself, but my husband, Eric, and the life we were working so hard to build together. The plans we had talked about suddenly felt uncertain again. I was left standing in a familiar tension I thought I had outgrown.

But God, in His faithfulness, was not absent in that moment—He was inviting me deeper. He was showing me, again, that anything I build apart from Him—no matter how good it looks, no matter how secure it feels—is still temporary. Placing my hope in provision instead of the Provider would always leave me grasping.

I had spent years relying on my own strength and ability to figure things out, to build, to sustain. But God was beckoning me back, to dependence and trust. I had to lay down my own control and repent.

Through trusted counsel, I began to see that I didn't fully understand God's heart. I knew all the right things—that He saved me, gave His Son for me, and I could talk to Him about anything. But deep down, I related to His love as *tough love,* as if He stayed with me despite my flaws, guiding me forward when I fell short. I believed that was enough. I didn't yet realize there was so much more to His love than just being carried through my mistakes. I learned, in a deeper way than before, what it truly meant to rely on Him.

From that place, God began to rebuild me. He wasn't just restoring what I had lost. He was reshaping how I operated and how I saw Him. I began understanding that vision wasn't something I had to force—it was something God planted in me. He began to draw things out of me that I didn't even realize were there: desire, vision, and hope for greater things. He reminded me of who He was calling me to be, and was teaching me how I was to live.

> *Where there is no vision, the people perish:*
> *but he that keepeth the law, happy is he*
> (Proverbs 29:18 KJV).

God was preparing me, expanding me, and growing my capacity for more.

If I'm honest, the thought of "more" scared me, because the last time I had experienced it, I hadn't stewarded it well. I was afraid that if God entrusted me with more again, I would fall into the same patterns—wasting it, mishandling it, and ending up in that same place of disappointment and shame.

One night during this season, I had a dream. I was walking into our backyard behind my husband and a few friends. There was a gate we passed through, and for some reason, a small body of water had formed in the yard. They all made their way ahead of me, eventually going inside through the sliding glass door.

I followed behind, but as I stepped forward, I saw a tree trunk submerged just beneath the surface of the water. It was one of those moments where you feel yourself about to slip—and then you do.

I fell in.

I remember the panic, even the pain I felt when my leg slipped. I tried to catch my breath and call out for help. I could see my husband inside, but he couldn't hear me. I was drowning, desperate to be seen.

And then I cried out to God.

In that moment, Jesus—Himself—reached down, took hold of me, and pulled me out of the water.

And I woke up.

That dream has stayed with me because it felt like a promise.

> *When you go through deep waters, I will be with you. When you go through rivers of difficulty, you will not drown* (Isaiah 43:2 NLT).

God promises us—not that we will live a life free from challenge, but if we rely on Him, we will have a life anchored in the assurance that we will not be overtaken.

I've seen His blessing unfold in ways that reflect that truth. My husband and I were able to purchase our home and begin building our family. Ministry responsibilities were growing, and leadership opportunities were expanding. Eric stepped into a completely new season—leaving behind years in construction to pursue his contractor's license, and eventually stepping into a role as Facilities Director at our church.

Then, through prayer, wise counsel, and seeking the Lord together, I stepped into a new opportunity as well—working as a personal assistant to Michelle Tascoe.

What began as a simple role has grown into something far more meaningful over time. In His grace, God didn't leave me, forcing me to figure it out on my own. He remained with me, giving me guidance, structure, and people—like Michelle—to walk alongside me. I learned how to build by changing the way I see myself and operate from.

My understanding of *kingdom wealth* began to take root. God didn't just teach me how to get through seasons passively; He taught me how to be an active member of my life, to be a good steward, and to build with Him. He dispelled the lies I had believed about my abilities and the authority I had been trusted with. I discovered that God, in His grace, wants to use me for more. And I can, with assurance, share that God wants to use you to build His kingdom, too.

In this current season, my husband and I were given the opportunity to receive financial coaching from Michelle Tascoe. As our lives began to expand—our home, our family, and our responsibilities—my husband and I recognized we needed more than good intentions. We needed structure. What we established was a framework to live within—one that keeps us grounded, aligned, and intentional.

Utilizing this framework reminds me of learning to bowl with bumpers. At first, the bumpers are necessary to keep us from falling into the gutter and give us room to learn. But over time, something shifts. We begin to understand the rhythm, the release, and the consistency. Eventually, we no longer rely on the bumpers because we've developed the discipline to stay in the lane.

I still don't have everything figured out, and my husband and I are not perfect. But we're learning not to operate from a place of fear, pressure, or performance, but from a place of abundance—rooted in God. Living life His way is not about being perfect; it's about being obedient and consistently showing up. God asks us to have a heart that remains yielded—willing to be led, to be corrected, and to grow.

Ultimately, I want to be a part of God's plan to build His kingdom here on earth and to be a willing and able vessel to steward it. Everything my husband and I are building now—our home, our family, the life we are creating for our son—flows from the desire to help build His kingdom. Not based on what we have, but in how we live with what we've been given. Through stewardship that reflects trust, obedience that builds legacy, and living in a way that multiplies—not just for our lives, but for the kingdom of God.

Kingdom wealth is a life built on trust—trust in a God whose love has no limits and whose power knows no end. Being anchored in a love too vast to measure and a God who does far more than we could ever imagine. It is a life fully yielded, fully supplied, and fully poured out for His glory. And when we live from that place, we become vessels through which He accomplishes far more than we could ever ask or imagine, all for His glory.

SUSTAINABILITY

BUILD WEALTH THAT LASTS

What you build must be sustained. Consistency allows your progress to hold over time as you exercise your faith each step of the way.

God's economy is grounded in faith, and as your faith grows, the fruit in your life expands. Finances are one expression of that fruit, but what God is building in you goes far beyond money; it touches your marriage, family, business, communication, health, and influence. When you begin to operate in His economy, you begin to experience a fuller expression of what it means to live abundantly.

God created you to be a steward, *to make known the riches of his glory for vessels of mercy* (Romans 9:23 ESV). You are one of those vessels. What you carry is meant to reflect both the natural and supernatural provision of God. Stewardship becomes the connection point between your faith and your finances. As you apply what you have learned, you begin to build a life that reflects both obedience and wisdom.

Jesus affirms this when He says, *"Well done, good and faithful servant. You have been faithful over a little; I will set you over much"* (Matthew 25:23 ESV). Faithfulness unlocks increase. As you steward what is in your hands well, your capacity begins to grow—in business, service opportunities, and relationships.

Stability and sustainability build on each other, and together they create a secure foundation that lasts.

Financial stability is the ability to maintain your income and cover your living expenses without falling into debt. Stability brings peace because it removes the constant pressure of trying to keep up. It is built through consistency that includes intentional spending, avoiding unnecessary debt, and creating a plan that aligns with your income.

Scripture reminds us, *He who loves money will not be satisfied with money* (Ecclesiastes 5:10 ESV). Remembering that money is a tool instead of a master and using it with intention helps create stability.

Sustainability is the ability to maintain your financial life over time without falling off track, which happens through consistent discipline—showing up repeatedly, making aligned decisions, and staying committed to the process.

Scripture says, *Those who hope in the Lord will renew their strength... they will run and not grow weary* (Isaiah 40:31 NIV). Sustainability is built when we rely on God while continuing to do our part. It requires accountability, structure, and a willingness to stay the course even when progress feels slow.

Scripture warns about the pursuit of wealth without wisdom. *Those who desire to get rich fall into temptation... into many senseless and harmful desires* (1 Timothy 6:9 ESV). Being unwise can cause people to lose what they have built. The desire for more, without discipline or alignment, can lead to decisions that create instability. There is nothing wrong with growth, but it must be grounded in wisdom and faith.

Contentment plays a key role in this process. *Godliness with contentment is great gain* (1 Timothy 6:6 ESV). Being content in who you are as God's chosen allows you to build from a place of peace rather than pressure as you keep your focus on what matters, which prevents you from chasing things that ultimately do not satisfy.

At the same time, being prepared for real life is wise. There will be challenges, unexpected situations, and moments that test what you have built. Scripture teaches us to *Count it all joy... when you meet trials... the testing of your faith produces steadfastness* (James 1:2-4 ESV). Trials reveal the strength of your foundation. When you have structure and stewardship in place, you are better equipped to navigate those seasons.

You have a choice: You can continue building on what you have learned in diligence, or you can ease up and return to old patterns. If you work consistently, you will continue to see growth. Your habits will compound, your confidence will increase, and your financial life will reflect the decisions you are making today.

A faithful man will abound with blessings (Proverbs 28:20 ESV). Financial sustainability can be gained when we are faithful with all God has given us. It is not about perfection; it is about consistency, obedience, and a willingness to keep going.

Journal Reflection

1. Looking at your finances, do you feel stable? Are your current income and expenses aligned in a way that feels consistent?
2. Breaking it down, where have you been disciplined? Where have you been inconsistent? What tends to cause you to fall off track?
3. What would it look like for you to maintain a steady financial life over time? What needs to change for that to become your reality? Do you need more structure or accountability?
4. Are your financial decisions grounded in peace or pressure? Urgency or alignment? Do you have a buffer to handle unexpected situations? How can you slow down and build with intention?
5. Have you been relying on your own financial understanding instead of trusting God? Are you looking to Him and godly sources for wisdom? What is one change you can make that will strengthen your foundation?

Jonathan A. Foley

Pastor Jonathan A. Foley carries a deep passion for serving people and solving problems. His life was transformed when God awakened his faith at 18 years old, when he was on a soccer mission trip in Europe. Since then, he has built his life on serving God wholeheartedly and pursuing His purpose.

Jonathan's journey includes both biblical training and secular education through the California State University system, earning a Bachelor of Arts in Economics and a Master of Public Administration with a nonprofit emphasis. Jonathan uses his skills to help individuals rise above challenges and pursue success within God's will. He served as Executive Pastor of Word of Life Fellowship from 2017 to 2023 and now serves as Lead Pastor alongside his wife, Shelly, loving the community through service, moral conviction, and faith.

Jonathan believes lasting community impact begins when people encounter God. His mission is to follow God faithfully and trust Him to reveal Himself to those he is called to reach.

Content to Trust

By Jonathan A. Foley

Early rays of sunshine started breaking through the glass of our family room windows as I took up my normal Sunday morning pleasures with hours of free time to play and relax. On this particular morning, I had taken a set of my favorite Legos downstairs to play out an epic battle saga with Robin Hood and the evil Prince John, complete with knights and a castle. This activity was something I found to be very enjoyable during this early adolescent period of life. For the Foley household, this was a typical start to our Sunday mornings before going to our 12 pm church service.

What wasn't normal was the break of calm on this morning as I entertained myself alone downstairs while my brothers and sisters were still confined in their bedrooms, either sleeping or playing their morning away. What began as a mere thought of the abnormal escalated to worry when a loud, harsh, and somewhat frightening argument between my parents, whose room was just above my forest and castle battlefield, spread across the living room floor. Shouts and accusations pierced my ears as I tried to ignore what was happening, but I was absorbing the intense argument that was released into that early morning of play.

As the arguing continued, I was doing all I could not to let it affect my intentions of battle play, but that really consisted of me just staring at the pieces in front of me while listening to my parents' own battle over finances and home stresses play out. Though this wasn't the first time I had experienced my parents arguing, this instance carried an edge of intensity that I had not heard before. When it finally ended, the threat of divorce was released, and the morning had been invaded with worry and division.

Fortunately, the feelings from that argument were resolved, and my parents did not get divorced, but sadly, that would not be the last argument I would witness. The fact that the argument was driven by the pressure of finances began to set a desire in me to find financial stability for my life. I figured to someday have a family of my own, and I hoped to avoid painful clashing dialogue in my future world.

Financial stress is a common struggle and has been cited as one of the leading causes of divorce. News articles, websites, and personal experiences all reinforce the fact that finances are capable of bringing peace or storms to a relationship; I wanted peace. Arguments between my parents instilled in me a desire to do all I could to prevent that kind of turbulence in my life. My challenge, however, was not being motivated to acquire peace and stability for my own family, but figuring out how I would arrive there.

I would need to make many decisions to go from those unpleasant adolescent experiences to the actual attainment of financial freedom. That freedom ended up coming from a path I didn't predict—a path that carried me through not only financial decisions, but also through varying difficult and disappointing life challenges. That path came from a simple discovery: Following God, trusting Him with all my heart, and serving Him would lead me to a life of financial freedom. This discovery has been directed and amplified by a particular banner Scripture in my life, Proverbs 3:5 (NLT), which says, *Trust in the Lord with all your heart; do not depend on your own understanding. Seek his will in all you do, and he will show you which path to take.*

Fast forward to today—I have arrived at a place where I own one home and am paying off a second. I have two cars, my kids are adults in college, and my wife and I are preparing for our retirement through the work we do and the investments we make. All of this is the result of following God and discovering how to trust Him with all our hearts.

The journey of faith will provide a unique path for every follower of Jesus, but each will have a similarity: learning to rely on God as we witness Him work in miraculous ways. That is the essence of this book, and that is how I had to overcome the worry I took on after witnessing my parents fight through incredible challenges of poverty and uncertainty in their financial struggle.

To trust in the Lord with all your heart requires finding peace in knowing and doing the will of God. With that mindset, we can discover a path that God has prepared for us and a path connected to the promises He gives to those who settle into this place of discovery. Trusting in God requires releasing our worries, fears, and agendas. Within that attitude and those actions, there comes financial freedom. Ironically, financial freedom doesn't begin with a focus on finances, but as the result of a life given to following Jesus and trusting Him with all our hearts.

I learned this lesson to be true and reliable, even though it did not always appear to be something I could count on.

Allow me to pick up my story again and go to the time in my life when I received an acceptance letter to a university that I felt God had positioned me for. I did not know clearly what I was supposed to do with my life, but I did know that I didn't want to have the financial struggle my parents endured, and a good next step in my mind was attending college.

Getting a college degree was something my grandparents wanted, my mom wanted, and all my high school teachers endorsed. It also made sense to me as all the important voices in my life said that college was my path to financial freedom. I had completed my college selection process, and I had peace about attending California State University Stanislaus, where I supposed I would step onto the path of financial freedom.

Before this time, God was not a major voice in my world, but He began to prod my heart and get my attention. And just weeks prior to the beginning of my college years, He revealed Himself to me in such a personal and powerful way. In fact, He showed up and made Himself known to me with such absolute clarity that I was determined to give my all and follow Him wherever He led me. I carried this passion through the next three years of college, reading my Bible every day, memorizing verses, and watching God bless my effort in classes, in relationships, and in life. My life was better than I could have ever imagined for myself.

Now, you are probably guessing that this is about to change, and you are right. God had a plan for me, and that plan was to teach me how to put my life, worries, fears, and agendas in His hands. He would soon teach me how to trust Him in all my ways.

God's path for me became clear, but it was undesirable to me in many ways. It was clear because He was directing my steps; it was undesirable because I didn't like all He was asking of me, and the painful situations that would later unfold.

My banner Scripture was put to the test of faith. Should I allow God to walk me through difficult, uncharted waters, or should I take the reins of my life and make a path of my choosing?

I did choose to let God lead me, and that path looked ugly for a time—weak and illogical in light of my goals and desires. But I chose to believe that following God would bring the best path for my life, and life soon challenged my soul.

With three years of college under my belt, God directed me to drop out. Without going into too much detail, God gave me a clear lead that this was His path for me, and I decided I needed to follow it. Certainly, this was not easy. Remember, I loved my life at this moment in time, and further, God was now asking me to step away from my planned path toward financial freedom. He would use everything about the next season to accomplish one of the most important lessons of all time: Following God will always yield the best results.

My results of financial stability started there in that season of letting God be the leader of my life. His leadership did not look promising at first, but ultimately, His direction led me to find work, build a family, and serve my church. I spent the bulk of my time in those areas over the next ten years. I took on a minimum wage job at my church just days after dropping out of college, and continued serving as an all-in volunteer with my church and my community, giving myself away on the path where God had placed me.

My life began to take on the wisdom of Proverbs 3; I believed life would be best lived in obedience to this Scripture.

> *Don't be impressed with your own wisdom. Instead, fear the Lord and turn away from evil. Then you will have healing for your body and strength for your bones. Honor the Lord with your wealth and with the best part of everything you produce. Then He will fill your barns with grain, and your vats will overflow with good wine* (Proverbs 3:7-10 NLT).

This Scripture carried a weight and clarity for my life as I strived to apply it with every decision and activity. For instance, I would not lean on my wisdom and reject a minimum wage job if that job was where God wanted me to be. Further, I made decisions to turn away from evil by committing myself to doing God's work and finding other ways to live that were healthy and good. In addition, I aimed to honor the Lord with my wealth by tithing and giving generously from the best of what I produced in my life.

Many people will read God's Word without ever really considering the possibility that it will unlock wealth for our lives. It is true that the Scripture literally says, *Then He will fill your barns with grain, and your vats will overflow with good wine* (Proverbs 3:10 NLT); however, connecting the concept of wealth with trusting God with all your heart by finding His wisdom, turning from evil, and being generous is not normal. These are atypical ideas for the journey of wealth creation, but they are the essence of real wealth.

God had to teach me these principles for me to generate and—more importantly—hold on to real wealth. Life is a sequence of scenarios; many controlled and many uncontrolled. Our path to financial freedom in life has no guarantee unless we understand who holds the real wealth of life. Proverbs give us this clue as to how we can acquire real wealth in an uncertain world.

If I could have one more opportunity to bring you back into my story, I want to reveal some uncertainties and disappointments in my journey that greatly impacted my world. First was my decision to work a minimum wage job out of college and stick with that job for 25 years, despite there being no evidence or guarantee that it would help get me to where I now stand. The time of working in a low-paying job required me to learn contentment and draw from the Scripture that *godliness with contentment is great gain* (1 Timothy 6:6 NKJV). Following God was my focus, and He brought me this important revelation, which became a place of strength, health, and financial peace.

Included in the journey of learning to trust God were experiences of significant pain. Shortly after dropping out of college, I lost my mother to a car accident. That uncontrollable event disrupted my life, my family, and my faith. However, the outcome and effect hinged upon whether I would trust God and stay the course He had set me on. The tragic loss was enormous for our family of seven, and with the main stabilizing voice of our home now gone, we all experienced a major void.

Everyone in my family reacted differently to this disastrous incident, and each one of us has a story of what brought us through it, but mine involved grabbing hold, with unrelenting faith, to the iconic set of Scriptures contained in Proverbs. Believing God's promises of health, strength, and real wealth, I decided I was going to trust Him rather than set a course of my own making.

Following God required me to stay in that minimum wage job, working 50-60 hours a week to make ends meet. Things were tight—far from what I had hoped for, but God was teaching me that He could meet every need if I could live in contentment. Trusting Him through this time required me to not focus on becoming rich, as 1 Timothy 1:9 warns us when it says, *those who desire to be rich fall into temptation and a snare* (NKJV), but instead, learn to lean upon the wisdom of God and His plan for my life.

Added to this season of God training, I learned humility. Often, I had to deal with emotions of embarrassment or ego checks when people asked me where I worked. Outside of my church family, this job was not valued or respected, which meant it was not an opportunity for confidence building, but it was an opportunity for trust building. I learned to trust God in this career path even though it showed no promise of financial freedom or noteworthy praise.

Financial freedom was no longer a focus in my Jesus-following journey; more importantly, my journey continued as God's path for me grew me how He knew I needed to grow. My generosity blossomed as I practiced giving my time and money. Since I started college until today, I have given a minimum of 10% of my income continually. Never once did I skip tithing to my church, even when I could not see how I would pay all our bills. Further, I never stopped giving my time away, volunteering every week of my life since college. As a result, I've found myself living a life of giving that has brought me incredible rewards.

Finally, my journey in following Jesus challenged me to turn away from evil. This instruction carries both an enabling and preserving quality. Make no mistake, I have failed to turn away from sin on many occasions, but those mistakes always cost me peace, stability, and promise. On the contrary, choosing properly and turning away from evil in many other moments have added to the place I stand today.

My life is in God's hands in such a way that I know He will bless me beyond what I could ask or think.

God's faithfulness to teach me how to walk His path has enabled me to enjoy the promises of Proverbs 3:5-10.

> *Trust in the Lord with all your heart,*
> *And lean not on your own understanding;*
> *In all your ways acknowledge Him,*
> *And He shall direct your paths.*
> *Do not be wise in your own eyes;*
> *Fear the Lord and depart from evil.*
> *It will be health to your flesh,*
> *And strength to your bones.*
> *Honor the Lord with your possessions,*
> *And with the firstfruits of all your increase;*
> *So your barns will be filled with plenty,*
> *And your vats will overflow with new wine.*
> (Proverbs 3:5-10 NKJV)

Real wealth, good health, and God's voice of leading have become distinguishing markers for my life. I live according to His instructions and find His blessing in all that I produce, whether in my career or my ministries.

Life is more glorious than we could imagine when we are content to trust God with all our hearts.

Allison Pope Bramlett

Pastor Allison Pope Bramlett is a dynamic communicator, author, and podcast host with a passion for helping people live and lead with love. As Executive Pastor of Covenant Church in Douglas, Georgia, she teaches practical faith and leadership principles that empower others to walk in purpose, build strong families, and lead with integrity.

Through her podcast and her book, *Don't Take It Personally,* Allison encourages others to find freedom, grow in spiritual maturity, and lead from a place of authenticity and grace. Married to her husband, Jeff Bramlett, for over 30 years, Allison treasures her family and the legacy of faith they are building together. Her life and message remind us that no matter the season, love never fails.

Living in Heaven's Overflow

By Allison Pope Bramlett

I am Allison Pope Bramlett—a wife, mother, daughter, grandmother, and pastor. My life has been shaped by faith, family, and the legacy of generosity passed down through the generations before me. I grew up watching my parents serve Jesus and give sacrificially, and now I have had the privilege of carrying that same heart into ministry and leadership.

My husband Jeff and I have walked through seasons of plenty and seasons of lack, but in every season, we have seen the faithfulness of our generous FATHER. My testimony is that generosity has not only transformed our lives, but it has built a foundation for our children and grandchildren to walk in blessing.

Proverbs 11:24 says, *The world of the generous gets larger and larger; the world of the stingy gets smaller and smaller* (MSG). What a promise! I have found this to be true time and time again; when you live generously, your life expands in ways you can not even imagine. GOD loves us into loving, and He gives to us into giving. If you ever find yourself getting addicted to giving, don't worry, FATHER GOD will support your habit.

Generosity is not just about finances; it is about living with an open heart and open hand, trusting that GOD is your source. Our giving is a direct reflection of our revelation of WHO He is. When we give in partnership with heaven, we receive heavenly returns that are not just for us but for future generations.

GOD is a generational god—the GOD of Abraham, Isaac, and Jacob. His blessings are designed to flow through family lines, multiplying from one generation to the next. When we live generously, we align ourselves with His eternal pattern of legacy and inheritance. Generosity is not just a personal act; it is a generational investment. It is the key that unlocks heaven's overflow, transforming your life and generations to come. When you trust GOD as your source and live with open hands, you step into His eternal cycle of blessing, provision, and legacy.

My great-grandmother was a faithful giver. She sowed seed into ministry; long after she went to heaven, the fruit of her generosity continued to bloom. My mother inherited that same spirit of generosity. I watched her and my father sow in faith when it didn't make sense in the natural, which taught me that GOD'S kingdom operates on a different economy—one not based on fear or scarcity, but on trust in Him as the source. As a young woman growing up on the farm, I remember my grandmother and mom canning the vegetables my dad brought in after harvesting the crops; those cans fed us as well as missionaries, pastors, and families in the area. This offering represented many hours of toil and prayers and was a beautiful example of the giving of first fruits.

Psalm 112:1-3 declares, *Blessed is the man who fears the LORD, who delights greatly in His commandments. His descendants will be mighty on earth; the generation of the upright will be blessed. Wealth and riches will be in his house, and his righteousness endures forever* (NKJV). That Scripture is more than ink on a page; it has been the story of my family line.

Generosity blesses generations. It doesn't stay buried in the soil, but it multiplies through time, traveling forward, preparing blessings for your children, grandchildren, and generations to follow. Your seed is your voice in the future, declaring that GOD is faithful from one generation to the next.

It is important to put your trust in GOD and know that He gives seed to the sower. Money is a terrible master and an unreliable source of security, but it is a tool we can use. 1 Timothy 6:17 reminds us to *not trust in uncertain riches, but in the living GOD, WHO gives us richly all things to enjoy* (NKJV). And Jesus told us, *"For where your treasure is, there your heart will be also"* (Matthew 6:21 NKJV). What we value shows up in how we spend our money.

When I read the Word, I take it personally. The LORD says to be a cheerful giver and to be extravagant in our generosity, and I want in on His giving plan. That's where the big GOD-adventure begins.

Isaiah 32:8 says, *But a generous man devises generous things, and by generosity he shall stand* (NKJV). Giving is foundational to the kingdom. God honors the law of sowing and reaping. He doesn't forget our sacrifice, prayers, time, tears, or giving. Even though we may feel unseen, heaven sees our investment, and the payday always comes. Your seed knows your return address.

Even Cornelius in Acts 10 got GOD'S attention through his generosity, and he was not even a believer yet. His giving rose as a memorial before GOD! That shows us that generosity transcends culture, religion, and even background. GOD always notices the heart that is willing to give.

In Mark 12, JESUS stood and watched as people gave their offerings. Many gave out of their abundance, but one widow gave only two small coins. From a natural standpoint, her gift was almost nothing. But JESUS declared her gift greater than all the other gifts, not because of the amount, but because of the cost. Others gave what they would not miss; she gave what she could not afford to lose.

For GOD, it's about the heart. The measure of generosity is not in the number written on the check, but in the faith, love, and obedience behind it.

Think of King David, who said in 2 Samuel 24:24 that he would not offer to the LORD *"that which costs me nothing"* (NKJV). David understood that true generosity always carries a cost, but it is a holy cost and produces eternal reward. The soil of the kingdom responds to sacrificial seed, not casual giving.

Perhaps Abraham was the greatest example of generosity. GOD asked Abraham for his son, Isaac—the promised child he had waited, prayed, and believed for. Abraham's willingness to lay his son on the altar revealed that his trust was not in the gift but in the Giver. Genesis 22:12 records the moment when GOD stopped Abraham from taking Isaac's life: *"Now I know that you fear GOD, since you have not withheld your son, your only son, from Me"* (NKJV).

That act of faith opened the door for generational blessing. GOD declared over Abraham, *"Blessing I will bless you, and multiplying I will multiply your descendants as the stars of the heaven and as the sand which is on the seashore"* (Genesis 22:17 NKJV). Abraham's costly obedience didn't just impact him; it secured a covenant for Isaac, Jacob, and generations beyond.

Sacrificial giving releases generational blessing. When we hold nothing back from GOD, He holds nothing back from us. Abraham's altar moment became the foundation for Israel's future, and ultimately pointed to the greatest gift of all—when GOD Himself did not withhold His SON, but gave JESUS as the seed for our salvation.

So when you give, do not measure your generosity by the size of your wallet, but by the posture of your heart. GOD is still the GOD of Abraham, Isaac, and Jacob. HE is a generational GOD, and your seed today has the power to release blessings far beyond your lifetime.

There are times that we must sow in famine and trust GOD in lack. Think of Isaac in Genesis 26:12. Scripture says, *Then Isaac sowed in that land, and reaped in the same year a hundredfold; and the LORD blessed him* (NKJV). The land Isaac sowed in was experiencing famine. Everyone else was holding back, storing up, and protecting what little they had, but Isaac sowed anyway, and GOD brought increase. The ground was dry, the economy was collapsing, and fear was everywhere. Common sense said, “Hold back. Save what little you have. Don’t risk it.” Yet Isaac chose to sow. His obedience made no sense in the natural, but it positioned him for the supernatural.

Isaac’s harvest reaped a hundredfold that year. While others were experiencing loss, he experienced multiplication. While others were shrinking back, Isaac’s world was expanding. His obedience in a hard season turned into a testimony of GOD’S covenant faithfulness.

That’s been Jeff’s and my story, too. We’ve sown when it didn’t make sense. We have given when we didn’t know how we’d make ends meet. There were times when what we held in our hands looked too small for the need in front of us. And yet somehow, FATHER GOD stretched what we had, and a bill got paid. A check showed up. The pantry did not run out.

One time early in our marriage, when we were struggling financially but remaining faithful in our giving and serving, a young man showed up on our doorstep with a check for almost the exact amount of our electric bill. This young man had been coming to our home for Bible study, and the LORD had laid it on his heart to sow a financial seed into our family. In that moment, I realized that the LORD was very aware of all of our needs, and the little we had been faithfully giving became much in His hands.

Every time we have sown in a “famine” season, we have watched GOD bring a harvest greater than what we could have produced on our own. GOD has always proved faithful. Just like Isaac, we’ve seen Him turn our famine seasons into seasons of unexpected harvest.

The truth is, famine doesn’t cancel the law of seedtime and harvest, but it proves it. Anyone can give when times are good, but faith shines brightest in times of lack. When you sow in famine, you are declaring, “My source is not this economy, not my paycheck, not my circumstances. My source is GOD ALMIGHTY.”

Just as He did for Isaac, He can do for you. The same GOD who multiplied in the midst of famine is the GOD who multiplies today.

Famine will bring out our spiritual integrity and can be a barometer for our generosity. Spiritual integrity is the ability to take an honest inventory of ourselves before the LORD. If we do not intentionally choose giving, then we will naturally default to selfishness. Selfishness always leads to justifying and excusing our behavior; trusting GOD leads to our transformation.

Generosity is not just about money; it is about the condition of our hearts. When we are humble and trust GOD, we permit Him to dig up the rocks in our identity—to remove the hidden lies and deceptions buried deep that keep us in endless cycles of defeat. Transformation requires humility and obedience.

JESUS always goes to the root. He never settles for surface change, but He brings inner healing if we will allow Him to. JESUS reminds us, *"In the world you will have tribulation; but be of good cheer, I have overcome the world"* (John 16:33 NKJV). When we hold on to joy, we stay strong even when we face trials and tribulations.

Generosity is one of the HOLY SPIRIT'S greatest tools for transformation. Every time you give, you declare, "GOD, I trust You more than I trust myself." Every time you sow, you align with heaven's economy. Pray daily, "HOLY SPIRIT, show me ways to be more generous." You'll be amazed at the opportunities He puts in front of you: an opportunity to sow a kind word, a financial gift, a prayer, or even an act of service.

When you partner with heaven, you don't just sow seed; you also receive heavenly dividends. And those dividends are not just money in your pocket, they are joy in your spirit, healing in your soul, and a legacy for your children.

When you give to the kingdom, you are not donating to GOD; you are making an investment. Earthly investments may rise and fall, but a kingdom investment carries eternal return. In GOD'S economy, giving is never subtraction; it is multiplication. I've learned that when I put my seed in

GOD'S hands, it always grows beyond what I could do with it myself. That is the difference between spending and sowing—one empties your account, the other fills your future. Giving is always a gain.

Second Corinthians 9:7 teaches, *Every man according as he purposeth in his heart, so let him give; not grudgingly, or of necessity: for God loveth a cheerful giver* (KJV). Often, we are not cheerful givers because we give with a consciousness of our sacrifice instead of a consciousness of GOD'S generosity. We must shift our thinking to realize that giving is not subtraction; it is investment.

Heaven will always multiply what we sow. Give with the promises of GOD in your mind, sow with joy, knowing who our GOD is.

In Philippians 4:19, Paul tells the Philippian church that GOD will supply all their needs according to His riches in glory. Why? Because they had sown into kingdom work, and their giving had drawn heaven's attention, opening a flow of divine provision.

Growing up in a farming family, I understand seedtime and harvest. Farmers know the power of the seed. In fact, many will borrow money to buy good seed, because the seed determines the harvest. Genesis 1:12 records that everything produces its own kind—this is GOD'S design!

The most important machine on a farm isn't the tractor; it is the planter. If there is no seed in the ground, there will be no crop. So, if you are experiencing a lack, let me ask you: Have you checked your seed? Are you sowing intentionally, or just hoping for a harvest without planting anything?

Ecclesiastes 11:1 says, *Cast your bread upon the waters, For you will find it after many days* (NKJV). Sometimes the hardest part of sowing is waiting. Getting to the harvest takes time. But do not let that discourage you. GOD is working under the soil even when you cannot see Him. The cycle of blessing gives your faith a good workout!

When you put GOD'S agenda before your own, you invite Him to move on your behalf, and life becomes a GOD-adventure. You'll begin to live with divine appointments, surprising blessings, and miraculous interventions.

Moses once cried out, *"Show me your glory!"* (Exodus 33:18 NKJV). GOD responded by showing His nature: *"The LORD, the LORD God, merciful and gracious, long-suffering, and abounding in goodness and truth"* (Exodus 34:6 NKJV). His glory is His goodness. He is a good, generous Father.

I wake up every morning and remind myself that I am on assignment for the kingdom and for King JESUS. Whether I am going to the grocery store, the motocross race, or the church building, I expect to be a vessel of blessing. When you start your day with that mindset, your ordinary days become extraordinary.

Jeff and I made a decision to allow increase to stretch us outward—that was a playful faith adventure. Jeff would come home excited about an opportunity to give, and we would make a plan to sow, sharing ideas to bless someone, to which the other normally would say, "I was already thinking the same thing." We are continually learning how to listen to the nudge of HOLY SPIRIT and respond quickly, joyfully, and without hesitation.

One season, a young mother crossed our path during one of the lowest points of her life. She was worn down, overwhelmed, and unsure how she would make it. She loved her child deeply, but life had taken more than it had given, and she did not have the strength or resources to climb out on her own. We did not have a grand plan, but we did feel the LORD saying, "Help her." Our generosity looked very practical, but more than that, it let her know that she was not alone or forgotten. Slowly, something beautiful began to happen; seeds began to grow. She found her footing, and hope began to rise. Today, she is a thriving wife and a devoted mother. This all came from our simple yes to GOD.

Generosity begins with an attitude. We bless people first with love, then with giving. We can bring the fragrance of heaven everywhere we go. When love leads the way, generosity follows. And when generosity flows, the world of the generous gets larger and larger.

Everything hangs on love. Galatians 5:6 says, *Faith worketh by love* (KJV). The fear that stops us from giving, trusting, and sowing is cast out by love (1 John 4:18). Love fuels our faith, generosity, and boldness.

So whatever you sow—whether time, encouragement, finances, or prayer—sow it in love. That is how the law of blessing works, not through obligation or pressure, but through love.

These are divine principles. King JESUS did not give us suggestions; He gave us instructions. When you obey, you position yourself for overflow.

Are you ready to live in overflow? Are you ready to move beyond comfort and into the throne zone, with your faith anchored in a generous GOD?

Generosity expands your life. The world of the generous truly does get larger and larger.

Generosity builds legacy. Your seed outlives you, blessing your children and grandchildren.

Generosity requires trust. You cannot cling to GOD and money at the same time—you must choose HIM as your source.

Generosity transforms you. It keeps your heart tender, your faith strong, and your eyes on JESUS.

Generosity releases heaven. Every act of giving unlocks divine provision and miraculous intervention.

You don't need to be rich to be a giver. You just need to trust the source and say yes.

Let the abundant life begin to flow to you and through you. Because when heaven sees a generous heart, it has to respond. You were made for this. Live generously, on purpose, every day, and watch what GOD will do.

Income

Increase Your Earning Power

When it comes to increasing your earning power, there are so many tactics and approaches, which often change and revolve around what you do to generate income. But even with all that variety, we can examine three essential biblical truths that span the vast array of jobs and skillsets. These earning enhancements, which I refer to as "practical power-ups," allow you to take what you're already doing and add a few simple ingredients to energize your earnings.

Before we jump into these power-ups, let's shore up our understanding of a few essential biblical income principles that are foundational truths for every kingdom citizen to stand on and operate from.

The Bible speaks about money a lot. It's a prominent topic that even the Lord Jesus Christ spoke many times about, including earning it, managing it, investing it, and giving it away. At the core of all the money scriptures are a few principal pillars that undergird everything for us as stewards of everything that God provides.

Principle Pillar 1: God owns it all. Everything is His.

Your money, your time, your body, and your life all belong to the Lord. King David knew this well. The book of 1 Chronicles records one of David's prayers expressing that everything in heaven and earth is His; *Wealth and honor come from you; you are the ruler of all things* (1 Chronicles 29:12 NIV). If God owns it all, then everything we have from Him has been lent to us as stewards. Understanding this will keep us in the right posture before Him and set us up for increase.

Principle Pillar 2: Stewardship is the foundation of increase.

Stewardship is all about growing in wisdom, being faithful, and remaining diligent with all God has entrusted into your hands. Practically speaking, good stewardship is about living within the resources God has provided; not racking up unwise debt, but earning, managing, saving, and investing. The Lord will give more to those who prove to Him that they can care for what He gives. It's not so much about the amount, it's about the attitude and action one takes with whatever amount God has given.

Principle Pillar 3: If you sow little, you'll reap little. If you sow much, you'll reap much.

There are rewards for action taken and consequences for action not taken. The more we take generous action—giving of our time and resources—the more abundantly we will reap. When we sow God's way, He supernaturally increases the return by multiplying it. If we sow in laziness, we will reap poverty. This principle is essential to know, as it will guide our motivation.

Now onto those power-ups!

Practical Power-Up #1: ASK.

If you have a boss, ask for a raise. As simple as that sounds, many people don't ask. It's simply in your best interest to ask, and it may be the quickest way to increase. Asking obviously doesn't guarantee you will get a raise, but what it does do is create an opportunity for a goal to be proposed and give you a target to aim for. Then, by standing on the three pillars and engaging with purpose, you can earn additional income. If you ask and don't get the raise, take the additional time to ask what more you could do, or what additional attributes or skills you can develop, so that you can earn that next increase!

Practical Power-Up #2: GROW.

We all need to have a growth mindset. Growing even just a little every day adds up to huge benefits down the road. An increase in earnings comes from an increase in skill. The more valuable you make yourself, the more value you bring to your place of employment. There are, of course, the job or task-specific skills that one should always endeavor to increase in competency, but there's also a special skill of working with people that often opens up promotions. Being good with people is an essential skill that many people leave on the table. Get creative, look for the gaping needs in your place of work, and begin to grow into filling them. Go the extra mile to show your heart, and your work will be rewarded.

Practical Power-Up #3: SAVE AND INVEST.

One of the simplest increases we can achieve is to pay ourselves. I often share a simple framework for money management that will help you build a habit of increase: 10/10/80. Tithe 10%, save 10% (high-yield savings), live on 80% (bills and essential expenses). This simple concept is exactly how I was able to pay off over 30k in debt in less than two years and simultaneously grow a savings account without an increase to my income. You can adjust the percentages to make room to invest, for example: 10/10/10/70. Tithe 10%, save 10%, invest 10%, and live on 70%. The overall goal over time is to reduce how much you need to live on. As that percentage begins to drop, allocate earnings into these other buckets that will drastically increase your earning power.

JOURNAL REFLECTIONS

1. Are you willing to ask for a raise?
2. Do you trust God that He will bring increase?
3. What's one area you can start stewarding better today?
4. What skill can you begin to develop that will increase your value to your employer?
5. How could you increase how much you save each month?

MEGAN LIS FELIX

Megan Lis Felix is a certified Life Mentor on a mission to empower women to heal and become the best version of themselves. She is a licensed real estate professional and investor, as well as an entrepreneur who was recently awarded an Honorary Doctorate in Business Administration.

Megan is a wife and mother, as well as the proud author of a life-changing book, UNLOVED, in which she shares her own inspiring journey from abuse to abundance, and gives you her life lessons and the blueprint she used to go from poverty to prosperity.

With extensive experience in life coaching and hands-on life experiences, Megan has mastered the essential lessons required to overcome internal struggles and shift the attraction process.

Megan possesses the tools, understanding, and knowledge necessary to guide clients in creating the life they know exists but are uncertain they can attain. Megan is here to show you that not only is this life attainable, but you are worthy of receiving it.

https://msha.ke/creatingyourdreamlife

I Will Build a Table for You

By Megan Lis Felix

I will build a table for you.

Those words jumped out at me during my time with the Lord as I was trying to make sense of the mess my life was in. I came from nothing and never wanted my children to feel the way I did as a child, so I made a promise to myself that my kids would never have to go through even half of the things that I did, and I meant that with every fiber of my being.

I hated not having money and hearing the words "We can't afford that" so much that I started working and trying to save money as early as I could in life. My mom was a single mother who was fighting her own demons, if you will, and was never good with money. When she saw that I had a job, she told me that I had to start purchasing the things that I wanted and needed. At that time, it did not seem fair to me that I had to start buying my own shoes and clothes at such a young age, but as I look back, I know it was all part of the plan. God knew I was going to be on my own before I turned 17 and would have to pay all of my own bills, so He was teaching me how to be responsible.

Our financial struggles, along with the emotional, physical, and sexual abuse that I was subjected to growing up, forced me to mature a lot faster than most. I often say that my story has stories, BUT GOD! He likes to turn the tables and take the last and make them first.

> *"So those who are last now will be first then, and those who are first will be last"* (Matthew 20:16 NLT).

God has allowed me to go through a tremendous amount of pain throughout my life, and I have learned many valuable and life-changing lessons. Thankfully, He loves us enough not to leave us in places we do not belong, and He knows how to get our attention. When God wants us to move, He will allow us to get shaken from the inside out. Have you ever heard the saying "He wrecked my life in the most beautiful way"? That is exactly what He did for me, but the wrecking part was anything but beautiful.

God alone can take us from being broken and living in poverty to being blessed and living in prosperity, but we must be willing to heal and truly surrender our hearts to Him, and sometimes He asks us to do things that seem crazy. He asked me to leave everything and everyone I had ever known and move nine hours away to South Carolina with my 3-year-old daughter. It was the scariest thing I have ever done, but I was tired of "just surviving," and I wanted what God wanted for me.

In a twist, I ended up being in South Carolina for only a few days. After sending us off, my daughter's dad filed papers forcing us to return to Delaware. None of it made any sense at the time, but, looking back, God had a plan.

After returning to Delaware with my daughter, I had to fly back to South Carolina to nullify the lease I had signed. While traveling, I met a man who was standing behind me in line at the airport and then "just so happened" to be sitting next to me on the plane. His name was Eric. We had an instant connection, talked the entire length of the flight, and exchanged numbers.

A few days later, Eric invited me to lunch—and brought me tulips. We had a great time and continued to talk frequently. While we were out together one day, he asked if he could stop by his house to drop something off. When we pulled up to the gate, I couldn't believe my eyes. I had never seen anything so beautiful. At the top of the hill sat a 23,000 sq ft architectural masterpiece. A lot of women, after seeing that, would have tried to start a relationship with him for all the wrong reasons. Don't be that kind of woman.

Despite our connection, I was not in a good place internally, and I knew I needed to heal. I also still believed that my worth was intertwined with the amount of money I had, and having lost everything when I left my ex, I didn't have much. I needed to build myself back up, so I told Eric that I needed time; I trusted that if it was meant to be, then it would be.

During that time alone, I committed to learning and growing in every possible way. I read the Bible, and I read the book *Think and Grow Rich* by Napoleon Hill. This practice began to change my life and my way of thinking as I strived to live with integrity, work hard, remain teachable, write things down, and do the right thing when no one was looking. I even went to conferences and got up early to give God my first in the mornings.

Not long after, I was presented with an amazing opportunity. My doctor wanted to build a home health care company and needed someone to start it. I said yes, even though I had no medical background. I knew that I could learn, and I was willing to do whatever I needed to do to be successful. I would figure it out—I had run a business before and knew what it took.

The company went from having zero patients to doing over a million dollars in revenue in the first year. I made more money than I ever had before, bought my dream car, and built back my confidence and self-worth. I was happy internally, but I still longed for a husband. After not seeing him for about a year, I reached out to Eric. Before I knew it, we were meeting for dinner. The timing was right for both of us, and we decided to give our relationship a try.

Eric wanted to fly me down to Florida to visit him so we could really spend some time with each other to determine if we should be together. He booked my flight and was at the airport waiting for me as I walked off the plane. We had the best time together that weekend, and I knew in my heart that he was my person.

For the first time in my life, I felt safe. I had never felt that way with anyone before. He was everything I had prayed for and more. He was stern but soft, and strong but gentle. I soon realized that we both had needed that time apart—God had been preparing each of us to be what the other person needed. That showed me how important it is to trust God's timing.

The Lord is good to those who depend on him, to those who search for him (Lamentations 3:25 NLT).

The next few months were amazing; Eric and I fell in love with each other more and more every day. We introduced our children to each other and started spending all our time together. It was truly like a Hallmark movie. Before I knew it, we were talking about marriage. A few months later, on our dock in Florida during the Fourth of July fireworks, he proposed to me. I loved that so much that we decided to get married the following year on the same day.

I did not want the stress of a huge wedding, so we decided to spend a week in Jamaica with just our children and those closest to us. We rented a villa and got married on the water behind it. The wedding coordinator took care of everything—it was amazing. All I had to do was plan what I wanted people to wear and what options we wanted for the food and cake. We had a chef and butler the entire time we were there and didn't have to worry about anything. There was an ease and a flow with no confusion.

For God is not a God of disorder but of peace, as in all the meetings of God's holy people (1 Corinthians 14:33 NLT).

God knew I wouldn't willingly quit my job and let my husband completely provide for me, so He allowed something to happen that was out of my control. A woman we hired to be our director did not like me. Due to the licensing requirements, the position required an RN with at least five years of administrative experience, so it was not an easy position to fill. The new director had a big ego and gave the owner an ultimatum: She wouldn't work with me; if the owner wanted her to stay, then I had to go.

When I found out, I felt so betrayed. I was devastated. Fear crept in, and I found myself afraid my husband wouldn't look at me the same. That was when I realized that I still believed my value was tied to the amount of money I made, which was not God's wisdom, but a lie from the enemy.

> *For wisdom is more profitable than silver, and her wages are better than gold. Wisdom is more precious than rubies; nothing you desire can compare with her* (Proverbs 3:14-15 NLT).

Thankfully, my husband is good at being a voice of reason, and he is a stand-up man who wants to be the protector and provider. He reminded me that I didn't have to make money to be of great value; he said I brought him something that money could not buy—peace! He told me that my job was to be a good wife and mother, and his job was to "make the money," which he happened to be very good at. He wanted me to be able to travel and be the best wife and mother I could be. Eric is such a blessing in my life and has given me an opportunity to shift out of "doing" and find the power in "being."

Through this life change, I was given an opportunity to serve God, and I did not want to become complacent. My purpose is to help women heal and turn their pain into power, so it was time to focus on that. I had made a promise to God during my pruning season: "I promise when You get me to where You are taking me, I will turn around and help everyone else get there, too." I knew that was what I needed to do.

About the same time that I made that promise to God, He told me to "write the book." I knew that He wanted me to share all my experiences, lessons, and wisdom with the world, so that is where I started. I became a published author, writing *Unloved,* which tells my story of turning pain into power, and I focused on becoming a better leader.

When you are willing to give God your yes, He will take care of the rest.

Since then, I have hosted in-person and online events, spoken on other people's stages and podcasts, and traveled the world—and I know that I am just getting started. When we focus on being and becoming better, God has a way of positioning everything and everyone around us. No matter where you are in life, it is so important to continue to learn and grow.

Of all the things I have done in life, one that I am most proud of is what I was able to help my daughter do. When she was 9 years old, she went through a difficult season and got grounded for a few days. In her mind, "her world was coming to an end" because she hated having to stay in her room. I told her to learn something from the experience and look for the good in it, because there is good in everything if we look hard enough. I told her to use that time and make something creative.

I reminded my daughter that she was good at being creative, and I told her that I wish I had a few days in my room because I would finish my book. I unwittingly told her to go "write a book or something," and to my surprise, she did! The very next day, she said, "Mommy, I wrote a book!" When she read it to me, I cried and knew that we had to get it published. It was so good. I knew God was speaking through her to help thousands of children all around the world. Her book is *You Are Loved,* by Mia'Bella "Lovie" Baylson. Not only has God blessed me by giving me more than I could ever ask or think, but He has also changed the trajectory of my family lineage. My childhood story is titled Unloved, and the book my daughter wrote at just 9 years old is titled *You Are Loved.* That alone is priceless.

When we surrender to God and focus on being and doing what pleases Him, He blows our minds in the best possible way. The life I have now is better than I could have ever imagined. Although God has taken care of us financially, the most valuable thing He has given us is freedom. The enemy wants us to think that we must hustle and wear ourselves out to be successful; that is such a lie. Yes, God desires that we be disciplined and work faithfully, but He also shows us that there is power in the pause. True power comes from our intimate time with God and the Holy Spirit. We can accomplish more in one moment of allowing God to move in and through us than we ever could on our own.

One moment of surrender to God is more powerful than a lifetime of struggle. When we are truly aligned with Him and are doing the best that we can to live righteously, we don't have to chase wealth—because He is our provider. When we seek Him wholeheartedly, we find our identity as a byproduct, discovering our worthiness.

You must believe it before you receive it and be it before you become it. Trust God that you are worthy in His sight just as you are. Then claim the gifts He has given you, nurture them, and use them for the good of His kingdom. Trust the dream He has put in your heart and act on it. If you want to be a loving wife, start doing things that a loving wife does. If you want to be financially free, develop the habits of those who have found financial freedom and stability. God doesn't bless us based on what we say we will do, but He has a way of blessing us beyond what we can imagine when we seek and follow His will for us.

> *To those who use well what they are given, even more will be given, and they will have an abundance. But from those who do nothing, even what little they have will be taken away* (Matthew 25:29 NLT).

The best advice I can give you is to ask God in every situation what He wants you to learn from the experience and if He is testing you somehow, pass the test. God will test our hearts and our character to see if He can trust us and to see how we will respond in certain situations. If He can trust us with a little, He will give us a lot. God's plans for you are so good—seek His wisdom, trust Him, and respond in obedience.

> *"For I know the plans I have for you," says the Lord. "They are plans for good and not for disaster, to give you a future and a hope"* (Jeremiah 29:11 NLT).

True kingdom wealth has little to do with money. It has more to do with our heart posture and our way of being, which is why it is imperative for us to cling to God and allow Him to help us heal from our past. If we don't, we can find ourselves in relationships that are unhealthy and distract us from being the people God intended us to be.

Look at everything you can as if it were a test. God wants to know if He can trust us and if we will obey Him. I remember asking God why I had to go all the way to South Carolina to meet my husband when he only lived a few minutes from me, and His response was, "I wanted to see if you would obey me." I didn't know it at the time, but that was a big test for me. There were also a bunch of smaller tests, too. For example, not being charged for something and going back to a store to pay for it.

Our God is an extravagant provider, and His heart is that we give our hearts to Him. He built a table for me, and He is longing to build one for you. Give Him your heart, and trust Him with the outcome.

I pray that you allow the lessons written in this chapter to take root in your heart. I pray that you take the time to build an intimate relationship with our Father and allow Him to complete His good work in you, and as He builds a table for you, I pray that you extend it for the kingdom.

Now all glory to God, who is able, through His mighty power at work within us, to accomplish infinitely more than we might ask or think (Ephesians 3:14-20 NLT).

MICHELLE TASCOE

Michelle Tascoe is a financial life coach based in Los Angeles. She has appeared on *Dr. Phil* as well as Chelsea Handler's show as a guest financial expert.

Her 15-year coaching track record has earned her the privilege of working with noteworthy coaching clients, including executives at Victoria's Secret, Capitol Records, Honest Company, Disney, Warner Brothers, and Netflix, New York Times best-selling authors, a former Miss New York, and a US Senator.

Michelle has helped her clients pay off tens of thousands of dollars in debt, get 5-figure raises, double and triple their money in their bank account, buy their first house, buy their first investment property, and ultimately become debt-free.

Her approach is hands-on and practical. It's not what you make but what you keep that matters most!

At home, Michelle is a loving wife and mom of four children. She loves ministering with her husband, Jeribai, and attends Word of Life Fellowship Church in Northern California, where she is the head of the dance ministry.

FROM DEBT TO DESTINY

By Michelle Tascoe

Growing up, I knew my parents loved me. They came to the United States from the Philippines to give us a better life, and they worked hard to do so. They shared one car, and my mom worked the night shift so she could be home with my sisters and me during the day. Dad drove Mom to work in the evening, then he would pick her up early in the morning on the way to dropping my two sisters and me off at school. We didn't have the newest clothes and never wore anything name brand, but we were always provided for. Before each school year, we shopped at the sales rack, and a few times, we were given hand-me-down clothes from my mom's co-worker; it was exciting to try them on.

When I went to high school, I began noticing that we lived differently; other families made more money. Many girls wore put-together outfits with matching accessories. Still, I never felt like I did not have enough. I was happy.

I knew that my parents did their best; they did not overspend, were mindful of every dollar, and made intentional decisions that allowed me to do extra activities like joining the school band and the dance team. When I graduated from high school, I was surprised that they bought me a new car, an emerald green Honda Accord. Their sacrifices enabled them to always provide for me.

Unfortunately, as I entered adulthood, I was not as intentional as they were with money.

After high school, I decided to put my University of Southern California acceptance off for two years to save money by going to community college for general education classes. That was a good financial start, but then I got my first credit card offer in the mail. I used it to buy a 12-for-1 CD offer from BMG Music and found how easy it was to buy things like new clothing and lunch out with friends.

I was a hard worker and had a few jobs right out of high school. I worked at a movie theater where I became a manager, at a clothing store, and as a bank teller. I made decent money, but it never seemed to be enough. I got caught up paying for an expensive social life, dressing well, and buying nice things. When I got my own apartment, my income increased from my new job in sales, but so did my expenses. Pretty soon, my lifestyle surpassed my ability to pay for it.

When I finally went to USC for my junior year, I earned a presidential scholarship for my good grades, which covered 1/2 my tuition, and the Cal Grant at the time covered another 10K. Unfortunately, I had racked up $18,000 in credit card debt, so I took out a student loan to cover that debt, and I didn't learn my lesson. My debt was absorbed by another form of debt, simply disguising my problem.

When I graduated from USC with my bachelor's degree in business administration, I was proud of myself for making it across the finish line, but my debt story was just beginning. It felt like a snowball that turned into an avalanche. Living on my own in Los Angeles was expensive. I had roommates, but what I saved on rent, I spent on eating out every day, shopping, getting my nails and hair done, and getting massages.

My car was another story. I let my roommate drive my Honda, and I upgraded to a Mercedes C-Class, which set me back $800 a month plus another $200 on insurance. As a 25-year-old, I had no business driving that level of car, not to mention paying that much for a car payment and insurance. A friend who had high taste but no income had convinced me to buy the car; my ego got the best of me.

I actually ended up covering things for that friend, including a 3-bedroom apartment in a fancy gated complex. That was a common story for me: I was always giving gifts to friends and treating them to meals. It wasn't a problem—because I just put it on a credit card. Although my minimum payments kept increasing, I never actually looked at my credit card balances until I was forced to... when I maxed my cards out. That was when I had a very sobering moment: After all that time of avoidance and focusing on the good times, I was shocked to discover that I was $68,000 in credit card debt.

My resume looked great: I worked as an assistant to both the president of Guess clothing and to a real estate mogul who owned and managed hotels and multi-family complexes nationwide, and, impressively, drove an Aston Martin. For a time, I was also an executive assistant to a celebrity photographer, and later an executive assistant to a celebrity interior designer. Looking back, I think being in Hollywood really jaded my perspective about money. Although my resume was impressive, my bank account showed that I was drowning in debt.

My ego weighed more than my bank account, and soon, I could not keep up anymore. I had to make it all stop; I was drowning just trying to keep up with the minimum payments. But what do you do when there is not enough money even to pay the minimum on your credit cards, and you still have to cover the basics of rent, utilities, phone payments, and food?

I finally learned my lesson and stopped eating out, paying for everyone else, getting my nails done, getting massages, and taking trips that I really could not afford. It was a sobering season of my life. Still, I ended up deciding to stop paying my credit cards and let them all go into collections. I even stopped paying for my car, surrendering it to the dealer as it was about to get repossessed. I went back to driving the Honda my parents had given me. It was humbling, but also very eye-opening. I actually moved back home for a time. My parents, with their humble way of life, gladly allowed me to come home to get back on my feet. It was then that I began to heal.

After my season of hard lessons with debt, I started to look for ways to make extra money. I was invited to join a network marketing company in the travel industry. Get paid to travel? Yes, sign me up. I never did much with it, but it exposed me to training and the world of personal development. I loved to learn. I typically did well in school. Personal development? This was genuinely exciting. I learned, "Work harder on yourself than you do at your job, and you will be unusually successful!"

My friends in the network marketing company suggested I go to one particular training seminar called First Steps to Success. I bought my ticket and flew to Denver in hopes that I would learn something that would turn my finances around. The event literally changed my life. The speaker said, "I am going to teach you the truth about money. I am going to teach you the truth about life, and I will teach you about sales and communication and building relationships."

The morning session was not what I expected. The whole room was led through an exercise in forgiveness. Reluctantly, I started to forgive people who had hurt, betrayed, used, and abused me. And then I proceeded to forgive myself. I forgave myself for many things—for trying to impress people with what I had and wore, and for trying to win friendships and please people by giving them gifts and covering their meals. I forgave myself for overvaluing other people's opinions and trying to keep up with a lifestyle that, at the end of the day, wasn't really me. The tears started rolling off my cheeks until all I could do was to cry out in pain and sadness, and then surrender it all. Finally, the weight of it all broke off. I forgave myself for all the credit card debt and the car repossession. At that moment, I experienced my heart turn around.

I had my "never-again moment."

What is a never-again moment? It is the moment you say, "No more. Never again." The moment you focus forward with everything in you and never look back.

I remember someone once saying that you can't drive a parked car. Well, my "car" was parked, with the gas on empty and the windshield covered in dust. My never-again moment gave me a spark on the inside that warmed my heart, and I felt hope for the first time in a long time as I listened to the training on what it takes to be successful in life and in business. Later that weekend, all the attendees were invited to an extra event called Spiritual Equipping. I had no idea what this session was about, but I was curious and open. I had already learned so much from the first forgiveness exercise, and my heart was open and willing to make a change for the better.

"Everything I have been teaching you this weekend about success, business, communication, and marketing is in this book!" the speaker said as she held up the Bible. *Wait, what!?! The Bible is the best success book ever written!?! I never learned this in Catholic school. How can this be?*

As the presenter began to share her testimony and her message from the Bible, it all started to make sense, although I had never had the Bible explained to me that way. The hope that was ignited at the beginning of this event began to illuminate deep inside of me, and I started to have a vision for my future. I had lost that vision for a long time as I was drowning in debt.

As her message was wrapping up, I heard loud and clear, "If you want to know the God that I know, come up to the front, and I want to pray with you."

Yes, I want to know that God that she knows! I couldn't get to the front of the room fast enough. She led us all in prayer to accept Jesus as our Lord and Savior. I thought I knew of God because I attended church on Sundays, but what she was unpacking was different: it was to know Him personally. She specifically asked, "Do you want to know the God that I know?" The shift in me was immense. She knew God herself. She had a personal relationship with God, and she was inviting me to also know God personally, to have my own personal relationship with Him. I didn't know what it all really meant, but I knew that something within me wanted what she was sharing, and I gave my life to God at the end of that event.

At first, life didn't seem any different. I stopped using credit cards because I had let them all go into collections. It was actually strange not to use my debit card—real money. I recognized that if I couldn't pay for it in full, I couldn't swipe my card. This exposed my buying habits, forcing me to change my impulsive spending and instant-gratification shopping. I also realized how reactive I was with money.

I decided to attend the personal development event again since it was offered in Los Angeles. Do you know how, when you watch a movie the second time, it feels like a whole new movie because there are parts of it you hear that you didn't hear the first time? That is what happened to me at the event. One line the presenter said continues to resonate for me: Excuses are well-planned lies. This thought uncovered all the excuses I'd made over the years that had kept me stuck. When I stopped living by my excuses and started to see who God really created me to be, I learned to live by the financial principles of the Bible. I learned how to manage money with stewardship, ownership, and eventually leadership.

I met my husband at that event in Los Angeles. He worked for the speaker and greeted me at the door. Looking back, God had aligned our paths at a critical time.

> *The blessing of the Lord makes a person rich,*
> *and he adds no sorrow with it*
> (Proverbs 10:22 NLT).

This was the Scripture that was spoken over my husband and me on our wedding day. It has anchored our financial journey since. Neither of us was great with money, and as we dated long-distance, we learned the power of honesty and transparency regarding all the moments in our lives when we struggled and were in survival mode. We vowed never to make those mistakes again.

Scripture says that when you are faithful with a little, you will be ruler over much (Luke 16:10). I took the skills I learned from the training seminar about sales, business, and communication, and generated $42000 in the first six months of starting my own direct sales business.

Life was great, and my husband and I were looking to buy our first house. However, my past collections were standing in the way. I knew I needed to stop running away from my past and face it head-on. I courageously called each creditor and negotiated a settlement. By the grace of God, I was able to clear the $68,000 that went into collections for only $22,000, which was about 32 cents on the dollar. Thank You, God. My life was turning around!

Faithfulness is an indicator that you can be trusted with more. After our first home purchase, we started to learn about real estate investing and began to not only work to earn a paycheck but to put our money to work for us, creating additional streams of income. We learned to invest in houses, flip houses, rent houses, and sell houses. My husband became a realtor since we were our best clients. Fifteen years later, we have bought, flipped, sold, and rented ten houses. Each of our three kids has a paid-off house with a renter in it, and we have begun to build wealth.

At the same time, at the beginning of our marriage, I picked up a book called *Leadership Coaching: The Disciplines, Skills, and Heart of a Christian Coach*. By the time I finished reading the book, every page was highlighted and underlined because so much of it spoke to my spirit, and I decided I was to be a coach. Living a life of financial freedom can only be defined by understanding that you are meant for more, and I realized that God had more for me. He had a plan and purpose for my life beyond what I could hope for or imagine.

I started coaching for free at first. Then, one of my first clients said I was helping her so much that she wanted to start paying me. She asked if $25 per session was okay. That was the first time I saw another lesson from the training seminar show up in real life: "The marketplace pays for value." If you increase your value to the marketplace, then you will be paid more. This is exactly what happened. I learned to take what I learned from the coaching book and applied it to give value to people. As a result, someone was getting so much value that she wanted to pay me. This is the truth about business that the speaker was talking about.

At the time, I was only looking to make an extra $2000 a month. We just had our first baby, and we were buying our first home. I still remember my husband saying to me, "Sweetheart, this is a million-dollar business." I looked at him funny and kept on making dinner. Days later, because I had my own personal relationship with God, I talked with Him and said, "God, I love coaching, and I want to help more people. Please, God, if You could just put a line of people in front of me that I can help, I will coach my heart out! I will coach 27 hours a day and help as many people with their finances as I can." God was so faithful.

Today, I am so grateful for the opportunity to coach clients worldwide. I've been coaching clients all over the world for almost 17 years, giving anywhere from 800 to 1000 coaching sessions each year. God continues to amaze me. Last year, my coaching business reached 4 million in total revenue. My husband saw it in the very beginning and has always been by my side, encouraging me to go to God with my vision for the future and the legacy that I hoped to create.

God is my greatest marketing plan. He knows who needs me, and He guides them to me with the leverage of the internet.

The speaker at that training event taught me that facts tell, but stories sell. She was implying that stories are testimonies that help people believe the impossible to be possible. The impossible happened for me. When I was 25 years old with four credit cards in collections and a car that was repossessed, I never thought that one day I would be 45, married, with four paid off houses, and coaching clients all around the world, helping them get out of debt and create a budget that actually works to live a life of financial freedom.

This is my chosen profession, but it is also my ministry and a way to pay it forward. If I can do it, with God's help, so can you. God had a wonderful destiny in store for me, and He has one for you, too.

GENEROSITY

UNLOCK THE KINGDOM ECONOMY

When it comes to generosity, some people seem to think they can only be generous once they are wealthy, as if giving a lot of money is the only way to be generous. I definitely thought this way; I planned to focus on earning money, and eventually, someday, when I had amassed enough for myself, maybe then I could break off a crumb for someone else.

While money is one way to express generosity, the Word of God conveys to us a myriad of ways to express generosity, no matter what our bank account says. When we learn that the kingdom of God is expressed more so in who we are than in what we possess, our lives will truly transform and bring godly kingdom impact to a world starving for His goodness.

Generosity is supernatural, and it applies to both the giving of material things and immaterial things. Let's dive into understanding both of these, but first, let's get a clear picture of what biblical generosity is. God is the ultimate expression of generosity. He's the Creator of all things and gives freely. He gives life, He gives breath, He gives restoration, He gave His Son to redeem us. He gave the Holy Spirit. He gives and gives and gives because it's His nature.

He who did not spare his own Son but gave him up for us all, how will he not also with him graciously give us all things? (Romans 8:32 ESV). God didn't just give a little. He didn't break off a tiny portion; He gave His everything to everyone, even though many have unfortunately chosen not to receive it. His divine power has given to us all things that pertain to life and godliness

(2 Peter 1:3 NKJV). *Every good gift and every perfect gift is from above, and comes down from the Father of lights* (James 1:17 NKJV). Wow—what a Father, what a King, what a God we serve!

Generosity is rooted in nobility. It is the ultimate expression of royalty, not from a high-brow place of wealthy arrogance, but rather a secure position of humble abundance. There is so much security to be found in generosity. The immaterial essence of generosity is a heart that trusts the Lord, a heart that is willing, a heart that cheerfully gives, but interestingly, generosity actually starts in your spirit. When you received Jesus as your Savior and Lord, He gave you a new spirit. You are born of a new nature, a royal and noble nature. Second Peter 1 says we are now partakers, a covenant spiritual shareholder, in His divine nature!

Generosity is grasping the reality that you are God's royal son or daughter. Your new reality is within His kingdom, and as a spiritual shareholder, you have a vested interest in the kingdom of God spreading and expanding. Again, this starts in your new spirit, but must pour into the doors of our hearts. This is why it's supernatural. It's inspired by our Father in heaven who freely has given, so we must also freely give. This giving is not just emotional philanthropy or a mere mechanical transaction; it's the deepest expression of our new nature, and in conjunction with a willing, cheerful, giving heart, begins to unlock blessings and abundance from the treasuries of heaven that God's children are meant to distribute throughout the earth.

Practically speaking, generosity is the unselfish giving of one's time, energy, or resources. Many Christians today think generosity is just in giving some money to the church or a worthy cause; that's truly wonderful, but my dear friends, being generous involves so much more. God didn't give 10% of Himself; He gave all of Himself, freely. There's a wonderful account about a widow in Mark 12:41-44 who gave her last two mites. The Lord Jesus says that *"She out of her poverty put in all that she had, her whole livelihood"* (Mark 12:44 NKJV). That's the security of generosity. God provides. God supplies. God is worthy. And God will take care of His children.

See, generosity is operating as a noble son or daughter and giving freely while drawing on heaven's trust fund by faith. It doesn't mean we give everything away or squander what we've been given, as stewardship is also an essential component of Christian living. Generosity is positioning our heart to align with heaven's divine design and letting the kingdom of God express its power and abundance to everything and everyone we touch.

As you step into your abundant life, remember that generosity is within you. It's who you are. God owns everything and is looking for His royal children to humbly and cheerfully give like royals should. Be like your heavenly Father and be generous. *But a generous man devises generous things, And by generosity he shall stand* (Isaiah 32:8 NKJV).

JOURNAL REFLECTIONS

1. What's one area you can grow in trusting the Lord more?
2. How can you be more generous with your time?
3. How can you be more generous with your energy?
4. How can you be more generous with your resources?
5. What's one area where you are holding back or holding on?

PHOEBE WILSON

Phoebe Wilson is a mortgage and real estate broker, entrepreneur, and investor dedicated to helping individuals and families build lasting wealth through real estate, strategic financing, and financial education.

Raised in Twain Harte, a small mountain town in Northern California, Phoebe learned early the values of faith and hard work. After earning a full-ride softball scholarship to Cal State Stanislaus and majoring in mathematics, Phoebe entered the mortgage industry, where she quickly experienced success at a young age. When the financial market crash forced her to rebuild her life from the ground up, it ignited a calling to help others navigate credit, financing, and real estate opportunities while teaching them how to create and steward generational wealth.

Phoebe helps clients secure financing for homeownership and real estate investments while navigating both traditional and creative lending solutions. Known for her analytical skills and problem-solving mindset, she frequently collaborates with financial advisors and CPAs to help clients structure their finances in ways that position them for successful loan approval.

Phoebe lives in Southern California with her husband, Joshua, and their daughter, Nahla.

Building to Withstand the Storm

By Phoebe Wilson

I am the third of seven children, raised in a small mountain town in Northern California. Although my childhood wasn't marked by financial abundance, it was rich in something far more valuable: faith, family, and resilience.

With six children and a seventh on the way, my parents received the news that we had 30 days to move out of our house. The landlord was selling our home. Suddenly, my parents faced the reality of having nowhere for their growing family to live.

In an act of grace, the Cuellars, another family from our church, invited us all to stay with them. For months, we slept on their floors as my parents searched for a home. My father was an alpha male who believed deeply in his responsibility to provide for his family. The weight of finding a career and putting a roof over our heads was enormous. Through it all, my parents never spoke in fear, but in faith—reminding us that God is our provider, and He always makes a way where there seems to be none. And He did.

My father began working with the United States Postal Service after being chosen out of more than 2,000 applicants. Soon after, a local real estate agent recommended my dad check into his VA benefits to see if he qualified to buy a home, and he did. My parents chose a small cabin house in town. My dad stood in the driveway, looked around the property, and said, "There's a big yard for the kids to play in, and a place to cut and stack our firewood. We'll take it."

My mom asked, "Don't you want to see the inside first?"

My dad shook his head and said, "Nope. This is the one."

That little outdated cabin, with three bedrooms, two bathrooms, thin walls, and no insulation, became the home that would hold our family for years. At times, 14 people lived under that roof.

Money was always tight, but love and the lessons of work ethic were never in short supply. In our home, if you needed a place to stay, you had one. If you needed a meal, there was always room at the table. We may not have had square footage, but we had togetherness. We didn't have luxury, but we had loyalty. My father taught us that family means showing up for one another. And if you couldn't make it to an event or a moment that mattered, someone else from the family would show up to *represent* you.

It was his version of *Ohana*—the belief that family means nobody stands alone.

Long before I understood business, wealth, or success, my parents were already teaching us the principles of kingdom living.

> *Train up a child in the way he should go, and when he is old he will not depart from it* (Proverbs 22:6 NKJV).

We may not have grown up wealthy in dollars, but we were rich in values. And those values would eventually become the foundation for everything God would build in my life.

THE GIFT OF OPPORTUNITY

"Show me your five closest friends, and I will show you your future." Looking back, I see how true this is.

Growing up as the third of seven children, it was easy to get lost in the mix. With so much going on in a crowded, busy household, there were times when I carved out space for myself elsewhere. One of those places was at my neighbor Molly O'Brien's house.

Molly and I had known each other since kindergarten. I spent many evenings at her kitchen table doing homework or working on school projects. She was always a step ahead when it came to thinking about college and opportunity. She and other friends encouraged me to sign up for honors and college prep classes. Molly pushed me to think bigger than I naturally would have on my own, even signing us both up for campus tours at the University of California and Cal State colleges.

I didn't realize that Molly wasn't just being a good student; she was expanding my vision. She was helping me to see possibilities that I couldn't see on my own.

Another close friend was Deborah Flores, who became a spiritual sister to me. Deborah had a different kind of influence on my life. Where Molly pushed me academically, Deborah held me accountable spiritually.

Deborah wasn't afraid to speak her truth. In high school, she informed me she wouldn't be able to continue our friendship if I started to go to parties. It wasn't said with judgment; it was said with conviction. She cared deeply about the direction of her life and the company she kept, and she expected the same from the people around her. That kind of accountability might have felt strict to some people, but looking back, I recognize it as one of the greatest blessings God has given me.

> *Walk with the wise and become wise, for a companion of fools suffers harm* (Proverbs 13:20 NIV).

Molly helped me think bigger. Deborah helped me live better. Together, they became the kind of friends every young person needs: people who push you toward opportunity while also anchoring you in faith.

Their influence taught me that you become who you surround yourself with.

To become successful, spend time around people who are building something meaningful with their lives. To grow spiritually, surround yourself with people who encourage you to walk closer with God.

I still remember the day my parents sat me down on the couch, looked at me with a mixture of pride and concern, and said, "We want to see you go to college. We just don't know how we're going to pay for it or how we're going to get you there." My parents believed in my future; they simply didn't have the financial means to make my dream of college happen. That moment stayed with me; they weren't discouraging me, they were being honest. As a result, I knew I needed to work for opportunities that could change the direction of my life.

With the encouragement of friends and family who believed in my potential, I earned a full-ride scholarship for softball to attend college and major in mathematics. That scholarship was nothing short of a miracle, and it felt like confirmation that God was already making a way where we couldn't previously see one.

> *"For I know the plans I have for you," declares the Lord, "plans to prosper you and not to harm you, plans to give you hope and a future"* (Jeremiah 29:11 NIV).

At the time, I thought I was taking the next step in my education. I didn't realize that God was already directing the path that would eventually lead me into business and a life that I could have never imagined growing up in our little mountain town.

After college, I made a decision that forever changed the trajectory of my life: I packed my bags and moved to Southern California.

THE ILLUSION OF SECURITY

In Southern California, the pace was faster, the energy was bigger, and the opportunities seemed endless. Coming from a quiet mountain town surrounded by pine trees and winding roads, Southern California felt like a place where dreams moved at highway speed.

I began searching for my place in the world. I was willing to work hard and loved solving problems and connecting with people, but I didn't know exactly where those gifts would lead me.

That's when I was introduced to the mortgage industry through a multilevel marketing company. It was electric and full of driven people who believed that life could be bigger than what most people settled for. I learned a simple and powerful truth: *In life, it's not just what you know, it's who you know.* Relationships mattered. Networking mattered. Showing up with confidence and belief in what you were building mattered.

It was a perfect fit for me.

Almost overnight, everything began to take off. I started closing loans, then more loans. My team grew, and the momentum built quickly. The income came faster than anything I had ever experienced before. By the age of 24, I was making incredible money, driving a Porsche, traveling first class, and sitting in rooms with successful entrepreneurs and powerful business leaders—people who seemed to operate at a completely different level than anything I had ever seen growing up.

I bought two properties and was living the dream. From the outside looking in, it appeared as if I had figured life out early. Success had arrived quickly, and it was exciting to watch everything rise. Every escrow felt like another tower being built. Every closed loan felt like another brick added to what I believed was the kingdom I was creating for myself. Money was flowing in waves, and with that success came a sense of confidence that things would only continue to grow.

I wasn't thinking about storms, market cycles, or economic downturns. I wasn't thinking about the possibility that industries can change overnight. I simply believed that the success I was experiencing would continue indefinitely. I spent money with the assumption that more would always be coming.

Success had arrived faster than wisdom.

I had ambition, work ethic, and drive, but I had not yet learned the deeper kingdom principles of stewardship and preparation. I had learned how to generate income, but I had not yet learned how to protect it or multiply it with wisdom.

There is nothing wrong with success; God often blesses His people with opportunity and provision. But when our identity becomes tied to our success, we've built our lives on something that can shift.

Jesus spoke about this principle in the parable of the wise and foolish builders:

> *"The rain came down, the streams rose, and the winds blew and beat against that house; yet it did not fall, because it had its foundation on the rock"*
> (Matthew 7:25 NIV).

THE STORM'S ARRIVAL

My kingdom was growing, and I loved watching it rise. But kingdoms built on sand don't survive storms. When the market crashed, it wasn't just a financial collapse—my pride crumbled with it.

The emails began showing up in my inbox early in the morning: "If your loan is not funded today, you will need to find another lender. We are closing our doors." At first, the emails trickled in slowly. Then it began to downpour; banks collapsed as the mortgage industry unraveled faster than anyone expected.

The pillars I had leaned on fell. Deals died in my hands. Savings evaporated. One of my homes had to be short-sold, and I had to bring $15,000 to the closing table just to get out from under it. The bank would not accept the short-sale terms for my second property, and the home eventually went into foreclosure.

My pride shattered.

I, the girl who once stood on grand stages at corporate conventions speaking to thousands, was now wondering how I was going to put gas in my car.

By the time I was 30, I was no longer a business owner, but packing my car and moving in with a friend, praying the gas in my car would take me that far. And so I started over—not as a business owner, not as a loan officer star—but as a server at The Cheesecake Factory.

I tied my apron. My feet hurt. My pride hurt even worse.

Despite these challenges, I showed up every day, determined not to quit on myself and to do whatever it took to get back to where I had once been.

And that's where my kingdom began to rebuild—quietly, unexpectedly, in the most humbling place.

THE PARKING LOT SEASON

Starting over is never easy, especially when you remember what life used to look like.

After my financial fall, something inside of me shifted. I made a decision that no matter how humbling the work was, I would show up and give it my best. My goal was simple: to become 1% better every day until I rebuilt what had once been.

One night, I borrowed $20 to put gas in my car to drive to work. I needed that shift. I needed the tips. Every dollar mattered. About 30 minutes after I arrived, the manager said, "Phoebe, it's slow tonight. You can go home." Inside, my heart sank. I had driven over an hour to get there, and I had borrowed money to make the trip. I took a deep breath and didn't complain. I asked if I could stay for anyone else, but they all needed the money too. So, I left. Instead of driving all the way home, I pulled into the parking lot of a nearby Holiday Inn and sat in my car. I didn't have the gas to keep driving back and forth, so I decided I would wait until morning. That night, I slept in my car. The next morning, I went to a nearby 24-Hour Fitness, took a shower, put on my makeup, and went right back to work.

That season could have filled my heart with bitterness. Instead, it taught me gratitude.

> *"Do not despise these small beginnings, for the Lord rejoices to see the work begin"* (Zechariah 4:10 NLT).

What I thought was the lowest point of my life was actually the place where God was rebuilding my foundation. And slowly, my kingdom began to rise again—because that's where I met my husband.

A man who saw me—not the money I used to have or the business I once ran, but the woman standing in front of him in a white uniform and name tag, carrying hope the size of a mustard seed.

Together, we worked, prayed, saved, dreamed, and rebuilt—not out of desperation, but with intention.

REBUILDING THE MIND & KINGDOM

Losing everything has a way of changing how you see the world.

When I began rebuilding my life, I didn't just focus on rebuilding my career. I focused on rebuilding my mind, I realized something that changed my life forever and became the key to my success: Our mind is our greatest asset.

Scripture says that we were created in God's image and likeness (Genesis 1:27). If that is true, then our thinking must begin to reflect His nature; we must choose faith instead of fear, gratitude instead of complaint, and hope instead of doubt.

I stopped focusing on what I had lost and, with gratitude, started focusing on all God had already given me.

I began thanking God every morning for the opportunities in front of me. I thanked Him for my health, my work, the roof over my head, and the food He provided. I thanked Him for the people He was placing in my life and for giving me the chance to rebuild.

Gratitude shifts your perspective. The more I thanked God, the more I saw His favor in my life. Opportunities started appearing again; favor flowed in ways I hadn't experienced before.

I left The Cheesecake Factory for Mercedes Grill, where I could earn in five days what used to take me six days at The Cheesecake Factory. The following year, I moved to work at The Whaler, where I could make the same income in just two to three days. Now I had something even more valuable—time.

This shift gave me the opportunity to return to the mortgage industry part-time while also earning my real estate license.

By 2013, just two weeks before I got married, I left the restaurant industry completely. That same month, I started my own mortgage and real estate business.

And then came our miracle baby. Holding my precious daughter gave me a new definition of wealth. It wasn't square footage anymore. It wasn't deposits, cars, status, or business cards. My kingdom shifted from what I built to who I was building it with.

Brick by brick, I was rebuilding my kingdom better than it ever was.

My business grew again; this time, I approached success very differently. I learned from one of my pastors the importance of building multiple streams of income. I decided that I could never again rely on just one industry. I built wisely: a mortgage company, a real estate company, investment properties, stocks, bonds, and other investments—multiple streams of income.

The first time I made money, I spent it as if it would always keep coming. The second time, I understood something far more valuable: Wealth must be stewarded.

True kingdom wealth is not just about making money. It is about managing it wisely and teaching the next generation how to build, protect, and multiply what God has entrusted to them.

> *A good person leaves an inheritance for their children's children* (Proverbs 13:22 NIV).

Inheritance isn't just financial. It is spiritual. It is the mindset that teaches your family how to build, protect, and multiply what God has entrusted to them.

Now, my desire is to build something that impacts generations—to teach my children and their children's children how to build and steward their money with faith, gratitude, discipline, and wisdom so the legacy we build is preserved for generations.

When God is your foundation, storms may come, but your kingdom will stand.

THE FOUNDATION THAT NEVER FAILS

If my story teaches anything, it is this: Success can come and go, but the foundation we build our life on will determine whether our kingdom stands.

Jesus reminds us in Matthew 7 that the house built on the rock will withstand the storms, while the house built on sand will fall. I learned that lesson the hard way.

But I also learned that God is not finished with us when we fall. In many ways, the storms in our lives are simply opportunities for Him to rebuild our foundation stronger than it was before. And that rebuilding doesn't just happen in our circumstances—it begins in our minds.

When we choose faith over fear, gratitude over complaint, and discipline over pride, we begin to think the way God created us to think. Our mindset becomes the soil where everything else in our lives grows.

Today, I understand that true kingdom wealth is not measured only in dollars. It is measured in faith, gratitude, relationships, and the legacy we leave behind.

And when God is the foundation—and our minds are aligned with Him—the kingdom we build will stand.

Let the abundant life begin to flow to you and through you. Because when heaven sees a generous heart, it has to respond. You were made for this. Live generously, on purpose, every day, and watch what GOD will do.

Vaishali R. Nair

Vaishali R. Nair is a distinguished pharmaceutical scientist with 31 years of leadership experience across research, technology transfer, and project management. Having held senior leadership roles in the pharmaceutical industry, she combines scientific rigour with strategic vision and people-centric leadership.

Vaishali is the Founder and CEO of Enduring Genesis, a purpose-driven platform anchored in the philosophy "Creating Skills, Building Strengths." What began as a pharmaceutical R&D consultancy has evolved into a dynamic ecosystem offering pharma consulting, leadership mentoring, life coaching, and corporate training, with a strong emphasis on leadership excellence and soft skills development.

An International Author and Amazon USA No.1 Bestseller, Vaishali is also a certified mentor and life coach committed to empowering over 100,000 women by 2027.

A dedicated Rotarian and Inner Wheel leader, she serves as Secretary (2025–26) of RCMB and IWCMB, President-Elect (IWCMB 2026–27), and President-Nominee (RCMB 2027–28). Her leadership reflects discipline, service, and an unwavering commitment to community impact.

WEALTH BEGINS AT HIS FEET

By Vaishali R. Nair

The world defines wealth by possessions, positions, and power. People may often say wealth begins with education, a good job, a thriving business, or wise investments. But kingdom wealth begins somewhere unexpected. It begins at the feet of Jesus.

At His feet, we learn that God—not our careers, our skills, or our investments—is the true source of provision. At His feet, we exchange striving for surrender, fear for faith, and ownership for stewardship.

> *The blessing of the Lord brings wealth, without painful toil for it* (Proverbs 10:22 NIV).

Early in my career, I saw my salary as my security. I worked hard, climbed the ladder, and thought, *This is where my provision comes from.*

After nearly three decades as a scientist and leader in the pharmaceutical industry, I discovered that true wealth—the kind that endures and multiplies for God's kingdom—does not flow from my effort alone. It begins in moments of kneeling before Him, trusting Him with my resources, and honouring Him with what He places in my hands.

One turning point came while leading a high-stakes technology transfer project in a giant pharma multinational corporation, where I was heading the project management. Deadlines were unrealistic, resources scarce, and pressure immense as the next step was a timely product launch in the market. Logically, it seemed destined for failure. But during my prayers in the early hours, I laid it before God every single day, saying, "Lord, You are my source, not this company. Help me steward this well."

The project not only succeeded but also earned recognition that opened new doors for both the team and me. That season taught me that my pay cheque was only a channel—God was the true source.

> *And my God will meet all your needs according to the riches of his glory in Christ Jesus* (Philippians 4:19 NIV).

At His feet, I stopped seeing my job as my provider and began to rest in the truth that God is my unfailing source.

GOD IS THE OWNER; WE ARE THE STEWARDS

As a scientist and project leader, I was used to being in control. But God began teaching me that resources in my hands were not "mine"—they were entrusted to me for His purposes.

One year, I received a significant bonus. My first instinct was to use it for personal plans. But in prayer, I felt God whisper: "This is not just for you. Sow it." It was a struggle. I had already earmarked that money for something I wanted. Yet, I obeyed and supported the education initiative of two orphan girls.

Months later, unexpected opportunities opened in my career, far surpassing what I had given. I learned firsthand that when we release ownership and embrace stewardship, God multiplies resources.

> *The earth is the Lord's, and everything in it, the world, and all who live in it* (Psalm 24:1 NIV).

At His feet, ownership turned into stewardship, and stewardship brought multiplication.

TRUST GOD; HE WILL PROVIDE

The year 2022 marked a turning point in my life. The world was still reeling from the aftershocks of the deadly COVID wave, and so was I. For years, I had known the comfort of structure, stability, and success in my pharmaceutical leadership roles. Yet, deep within, a new calling was stirring—one that whispered about coaching, mentoring, and empowering others.

It wasn't an easy leap. Leaving behind a well-defined career to step into the unknown felt like walking without a map. The questions wouldn't stop swirling: *Will this really work? Will I have enough? What if I fail?*

There were nights when these doubts became louder than my dreams. But in those quiet, anxious moments, I found myself drawn to surrender—to kneel at His feet and simply pray, "Lord, if this is truly Your calling, then provision will follow."

And, slowly, it did. Opportunities began to unfold in ways I couldn't have planned. Clients arrived exactly when I needed them. Partnerships blossomed without strain or struggle. My consultancy evolved into a steady stream of work—not just work that sustained me, but work that fulfilled me.

What touched me most deeply was seeing how my journey was beginning to impact others—especially women in leadership roles who were standing at the crossroads of their own big decisions. Watching them choose courage over fear and purpose over pressure reminded me of the grace that had carried me, too.

At His feet, I learned that provision isn't a product of human certainty; it's a reflection of divine faithfulness.

> *But seek first the kingdom of God and his righteousness, and all these things will be added to you* (Matthew 6:33 ESV).

The scarcity mindset I once carried so tightly began to dissolve. In its place grew something far more powerful: a quiet, unwavering trust that where God leads, He provides.

WORSHIP GOD WITH YOUR GIVING

One of the most powerful lessons I've learned about kingdom wealth is this: Giving is worship.

Before God entrusts us with greater riches—financial, relational, or positional—He purifies our motives. This isn't about loss; it's about alignment. God detoxes our spirit so that our giving can become worship.

> *Therefore, rid yourselves of all malice and deceit, hypocrisy, envy, and slander of every kind. Like newborn babies, crave pure spiritual milk* (1 Peter 2:1-2 NIV).

That Scripture has become so real to me over the years. Malice, deceit, hypocrisy, envy, and slander aren't just character flaws; they're spiritual blockages that prevent divine flow. God blesses clean hands because clean hands can hold blessings without corrupting them.

Over the years, I've learned that true giving isn't a transaction, but an act of worship. When I give—whether it's feeding the hungry, supporting orphans, helping the physically or visually challenged, empowering women to be self-reliant, or building prayer towers—I'm not just giving resources; I'm giving from a place of surrender. It's my way of saying, "Lord, everything I have is Yours." In those moments, I don't see myself as a donor, but as a steward—carrying what belongs to Him.

Just as newborns crave milk to grow, kingdom builders crave truth and wisdom to steward well. The more I grow in grace, the more I understand that wealth is not meant to be stored, but sown. Every act of generosity dismantles greed and magnifies gratitude, transforming resources into revelation. Every gift becomes an altar of worship.

Once you've tasted the goodness of God, your definition of wealth changes. You stop asking, "How much can I keep?" And you start asking, "How much can I give to reveal His goodness?" Generosity becomes your lifestyle. Wealth becomes your witness. And giving becomes your purest form of worship.

This is what I like to call "The Kingdom Wealth Equation": Purity + Generosity + Gratitude = Worship that Attracts Wealth.

God doesn't just want your offering; He wants the heart behind it. Because when your heart is purified, your giving becomes powerful, and your wealth becomes worship.

One of the deepest joys of my journey is giving to God by empowering women. When I invest time, skills, and finances into their growth, I see ripple effects in families and communities. I once hosted a workshop for working professionals. Some women arrived unsure of themselves, weighed down by responsibilities. As I poured into them—sharing knowledge and sponsoring resources for a few—they blossomed. Weeks later, they returned with testimonies: promotions, new ventures, restored confidence.

One measure of kingdom wealth is in the lives we touch, and even help transform.

She opens her arms to the poor and extends her hands to the needy (Proverbs 31:20 NIV).

GOD BLESSES THE GIVER

There was a season in my life when I quietly experienced the pain of losing people I once believed would always remain close to me. Relationships that once felt secure began to shift. Some people distanced themselves, while others gradually disappeared from my daily life. At first, it felt deeply personal, almost as if a chapter of belonging had unexpectedly closed.

Moments like these force us to pause and reflect on many things—our relationships, our identity, and sometimes even our purpose. For a period of time, I carried that silent weight within me. Yet today, when I look back with greater clarity, I recognize that what once felt like loss was actually a divine redirection.

During that time of emotional transition, God gently opened new doors for me—doors that led me into a larger world of service and leadership through Rotary International and the Inner Wheel clubs within my community. What began as simple participation slowly evolved into deeper involvement. I started contributing my time, ideas, and energy to initiatives aimed at uplifting others. Gradually, service stopped feeling like an obligation and began to feel like a calling.

The Bible reminds us in Proverbs 3:5-6 (NIV), *Trust in the Lord with all your heart and lean not on your own understanding; in all your ways submit to Him, and He will make your paths straight.*

At the time, I did not fully understand the direction my life was taking. Yet step by step, the path became clearer.

I had the privilege of serving as the Vocational Director for Rotary during the year 2024-25, focusing on promoting professional ethics, leadership, and meaningful community engagement. The role connected me with individuals who believed that their professional skills could be used to benefit society. Currently, I serve as the Club Secretary for both Rotary and the Inner Wheel Club in my locality, a responsibility that has given me deeper insight into collective leadership. Behind every successful community initiative lies teamwork, commitment, and a shared vision of service. Leadership within such organizations is never about personal recognition. Instead, it is about creating platforms where service can flourish.

The journey continues to unfold in ways I never anticipated. I have been entrusted with the opportunity to serve as President of the Inner Wheel Club for the year 2026-27, while also taking on responsibilities as Vocational Director for Rotary during the same year. In the coming years, I will also have the privilege of serving as President of my local Rotary International Club for the year 2027-28.

Each of these roles represents far more than a title. They represent trust, responsibility, and the opportunity to contribute meaningfully to society. Through these experiences, I began to recognize something profound: God was not only opening doors for leadership; He was shaping my character through service.

While working on community initiatives, I encountered individuals facing hardships far greater than my own. There were children yearning for educational opportunities, families striving for stability, and women courageously rebuilding their lives despite difficult circumstances. Their stories touched my heart deeply.

Gradually, I realized something remarkable: The pain I once carried began to dissolve when I focused on serving others. Giving time, compassion, and effort to uplift someone else has a powerful way of healing our own hearts. Service became my therapy. Every smile I witnessed and every grateful expression reminded me that life's true richness lies not in what we accumulate, but in what we contribute.

Proverbs 11:25 (NIV) beautifully expresses this truth: *A generous person will prosper; whoever refreshes others will be refreshed.*

The more I served, the more peace and fulfillment I experienced. Through this journey, I began to understand what I now call kingdom wealth. Kingdom wealth is not measured by financial success alone. It is the abundance that grows through compassion, generosity, purpose, and service.

And through service, I discovered healing.

OUR POSTURE AT THE CROSS

Over time, I realised that wealth in the kingdom is deeply connected to posture—not posture of the body, but posture of the heart. When we kneel before God, we acknowledge that everything we have and everything we hope to become flows from Him.

In my years in the pharmaceutical world, strategy, analysis, and planning were essential. Those skills still serve me well today. But there is a wisdom far greater than strategy—the wisdom that comes from surrender. When the heart bows before God, clarity begins to emerge where confusion once lived.

There were moments when decisions about finances, investments, or new initiatives felt overwhelming. Yet each time I paused to pray and wait quietly for guidance, peace followed. That peace became my compass. It reminded me that kingdom wealth is never built merely on human intelligence; it is built on divine alignment.

I have also learned that humility attracts grace. When we approach God with open hands rather than clenched fists, He entrusts us with more—not simply for personal comfort, but for greater responsibility.

> *But he gives us more grace. That is why Scripture says: "God opposes the proud but shows favor to the humble"* (James 4:6 NIV).

At Jesus' feet, pride dissolves and purpose awakens. And in that sacred place, wealth becomes more than resources; it becomes a tool to reveal God's goodness in the world. And kingdom wealth does not simply accumulate—it flows. Just as rivers remain fresh when water keeps moving, the blessings God gives us are meant to move through us to bless others.

There were seasons when I wondered whether I had enough to give—enough time, enough resources, enough strength. Yet every time I chose obedience over hesitation, I witnessed something remarkable: God always replenished what I released. Sometimes the return came through unexpected opportunities. Other times, it came through new relationships, fresh wisdom, or the quiet assurance that I was walking in alignment with His purpose.

Obedience is one of the most powerful currencies in the kingdom of God. When we obey His prompting—whether it is to give, to serve, to lead, or to step into a new calling—we step into a divine flow where provision follows purpose.

The Bible reminds us in Deuteronomy 28:2 (NIV): *All these blessings will come on you and accompany you if you obey the Lord your God.*

At His feet, obedience transforms ordinary resources into extraordinary impact. And when our lives begin to reflect that obedience, wealth is no longer something we chase; it becomes something that follows a life surrendered to God.

PRACTICAL APPLICATIONS

Kingdom wealth is more than having a mindset—it's action-filled living.

Over the years, the following practices have grounded me and opened my spirit to hear God's calling to walk in His will. I invite you to join me.

1. Begin with prayer.

   Commit to the Lord whatever you do, and he will establish your plans (Proverbs 16:3 NIV).

   Every decision, whether about investing, giving, or starting a new venture, begins in prayer. Seek the Lord's will by asking, "Lord, what would You have me do?" Before launching my women's empowerment programs, I prayed for wisdom. God not only provided resources but also sent the right people to partner with me.

2. Pay off debt.

   The borrower is slave to the lender (Proverbs 22:7 NIV).

   Debt is a burden that limits impact. Clearing financial obligations gives us the freedom to sow generously. Each debt I paid felt like a chain broken, freeing me to be used in God's kingdom.

3. Save and invest wisely.

   "Suppose one of you wants to build a tower. Won't you first sit down and estimate the cost to see if you have enough money to complete it?" (Luke 14:28 NIV).

   Stewardship includes prudence. I maintain savings and invest strategically (such as in index funds and utilizing long-term instruments), not just for personal security but to multiply resources for greater impact.

4. Create multiple streams of revenue.

   Sow your seed in the morning, and at evening let your hands not be idle, for you do not know which will succeed (Ecclesiastes 11:6 NIV).

God gives each of us many gifts and talents. Don't be afraid to use them. God used both my pharma consultancy and coaching business as avenues of provision. Diversifying income gave me greater capacity to serve and give.

5. Prioritize giving.

   "Bring the whole tithe into the storehouse... Test me in this," says the Lord Almighty, "and see if I will not throw open the floodgates of heaven" (Malachi 3:10 NIV).

   We are made in God's image; as He gives to us, we are to give to others. Tithing—giving 10% of what you receive to the Lord—became my declaration that God is my source. Beyond tithing, I set aside funds for kingdom initiatives.

6. Build generational wealth.

   A good person leaves an inheritance for their children's children (Proverbs 13:22 NIV).

   Wealth is not just about having money; it is a mindset. Teach your children and those God has entrusted to you these godly principles—teach them to start at the feet of Jesus. I work with mentees and other women as they learn to steward resources faithfully.

AT HIS FEET

The world taught me that wealth was about possession. Jesus taught me that wealth is about surrender.

At His feet, I discovered that God is the source.

At His feet, I learned that stewardship is more powerful than ownership.

At His feet, I saw that giving is worship.

At His feet, fear of lack turned into faith in His provision.

If you ask me today, "Where does wealth begin?" my answer is simple: Wealth does not begin in a bank, in a salary, or in a business plan. Wealth begins where Mary knelt, where I had to come, where you, too, are invited: at Jesus' feet.

> *Cast your bread upon the waters, for you will find it after many days* (Ecclesiastes 11:1 ESV).

LEGACY

LEAVING A LEGACY OF FREEDOM

Everything you've been building leads here. What you build today is shaping what will extend beyond you for future generations. A good man leaves an inheritance to his children's children, but the wealth of the sinner is stored up for the righteous (Proverbs 13:22 NKJV).

Leaving an inheritance is a beautiful and godly practice. God, our heavenly Father, has given each of His children access to an inheritance through our Lord Jesus Christ. We are heirs with Christ! We are God's legacy on the earth today. I know this sounds so ethereal and spiritual, but we must grasp the reality of who we truly are and what God has in store for us. This is the whole idea of leaving a legacy.

While we're here on the earth, the Bible teaches us to do business until He comes (Luke 19:13)—to remain engaged, faithfully trusting the Lord to provide, walking by faith and not just by sight, stewarding all He has entrusted into our hands, and investing for a future. We are not to live just for the moment and fleeting material goods, but rather we should be working to not only take care of our current needs, but also be looking ahead to the future needs of our kids. This can be as simple as stewarding monthly finances well and eventually paying off a home, or laying up a fund for your children's schooling or professional development. Everything we can do to train up and lay up for our children is a wonderful kingdom legacy.

Leaving a legacy of material wealth is very good. I would say any amount of assets without major debts is a really good thing, but it's not the only thing. The greatest inheritance we get to leave with our children is a personal relationship with Jesus Christ and the access granted to the kingdom of God. This inheritance is priceless. It's eternal life. Jesus prioritized laying up treasure in heaven, where no corruption can touch it, no market can crash it, and no thief can steal it. Jesus further instructed us in Luke 12:15 (ESV) to *"Take care, and be on your guard against all covetousness, for one's life does not consist in the abundance of his possessions."* What an essential truth to pass on to our children's children. Do business till He comes, steward well, store up on earth what you can. But the greater is storing up treasure in heaven, walking in fellowship with God, and displaying His kingdom wealth to everyone you can.

Wisdom is one of the greatest legacies a parent could leave to a child. As Psalm 78:4 teaches, telling our children about the Lord's might and all His glorious deeds and wonders is leaving a legacy. Think of a legacy free from excessive fears, poor attitudes, and a lazy work ethic; a legacy of faithful stewardship, hope and promise, and a life of faith and accomplishments. What a wonderful legacy that would be.

Our legacy is so much more than material things that will naturally come with faithful stewardship. Galatians 5:1 says, *For freedom Christ has set us free; stand firm therefore, and do not submit again to a yoke of slavery* (ESV). Our legacy of freedom cost our heavenly Father much. It cost Him His Son. Galatians 5:13 goes on to say, *For you were called to freedom, brothers. Only do not use your freedom as an opportunity for the flesh, but through love serve one another* (ESV). This beautiful legacy from our heavenly Father is one of serving others—leading them into freedom and keeping ourselves free from the burdensome yoke of this present evil age.

Kingdom wealth includes both natural resources and spiritual resources.

Stewardship of the natural opens doors to the greater resources of the spiritual. It all matters to God. Everything we do, we are to do heartily as unto the Lord and not unto men. We're working, stewarding, and building for His glory, not our own. What a legacy to leave to our children's children. Every natural decision today can lead to our spiritual dynasty in Christ. Every well-managed material thing will qualify us for managing supernatural kingdom matters. This is our future, our inheritance as joint heirs with Christ!

Freedom isn't just a financial endeavor; it's the spiritual family business. God will bless and increase us with material goods as we increase in our trust in Him. A legacy of trust, faithfulness, and stewardship is ours for the taking, building, and passing on. Truth is what sets us free and keeps us free. No matter how much one makes or stores up or passes on, the real freedom is in the rich inheritance of the truth. *"And you will know the truth and the truth will set you free"* (John 8:32 ESV).

Until the Lord returns, we are to be diligent, watchful, hopeful, and prayerful, faithfully stewarding all He has given us. We should all desire to hear those glorious words, *"Well done, good and faithful servant"* (Matthew 25:23 ESV). We are not to be obsessed with earthly wealth, caught up in the grind of striving while neglecting the things that actually matter most in life. Focus on your relationship with God and fellowship with others as you look forward to the Lord's return.

Father, let Your kingdom come and Your will be done as it is in heaven.

JOURNAL REFLECTIONS

1. What are you storing up in heaven today?
2. What opportunities do you have to help others?
3. What would you like to leave as an inheritance?
4. Do you trust God to provide for all your current and future needs?
5. What do you want your legacy to be?

AFTERWORD

Congratulations! You've reached the end of this book, but this is not the end of your journey. Now it's your turn to build kingdom wealth—something that is far above and beyond financial success. Kingdom wealth is established by aligning your heart, mind, and money with God's truth; it is about who you are becoming.

As you've read each testimony in this book, you've seen what it looks like to surrender to our heavenly Father, claim your identity in Christ, and trust God's healing. You've witnessed the importance of building on God's foundation, following His direction, and stewarding all He has given you. We pray the teachings have caused you to reflect on your own path and helped you better understand how discipline, challenges, and humility have shaped you to this point, and that you now recognize that only aligning with God can lead you to purpose and legacy.

Building kingdom wealth is something we are called to live out every day by making consistent decisions, developing God-honoring habits, and responding with His wisdom—even when things don't go as planned. As you begin to apply all you've learned, you will see growth in your finances, but even more than that, you will see growth in your spiritual life. Jesus taught us, *"He who is faithful in what is least is faithful also in much"* (Matthew 16:10 NKJV). That faithfulness begins in the small, unseen moments.

We will all experience seasons when everything feels clear and steady. However, there will be other seasons when we feel stretched and uncomfortable—that does not mean something is wrong, but that something is happening. God shapes and refines us; He prepares us for what is to come.

Count it all joy when you fall into various trials, knowing that the testing of your faith produces patience (James 1:3 NKJV).

As you put this book down, know that what you do next matters. It's easy to read something like this, feel encouraged, and then slowly drift back into old habits, old thinking, and old patterns. We've all been there. Consistent growth requires making a daily decision to live differently. Scripture reminds us to be doers, not just hearers, and now is when that becomes real.

You can't unknow what you've learned as you have read. You now understand how surrender and identity shape everything. You recognize the role of discipline, stewardship, and alignment in your life. That awareness carries responsibility, not in a heavy way, but in a purposeful one. God is not just interested in what you build; He cares deeply about how you build it.

Be intentional. We live either by default or by design. Purposefully manage your time, handle your finances, and choose your thoughts and responses. Kingdom wealth is not established in one big moment; it is built over time through consistent obedience that is often unseen by the rest of the world. But God sees.

It can be tempting to rush the process or take shortcuts. As you go forward, return often to what you've learned. Stay grounded and aligned. Remind yourself that what is built the right way will last. Scripture says, *The integrity of the upright will guide them* (Proverbs 11:3 NKJV); integrity will keep you steady when everything else feels uncertain.

As you continue forward, think beyond yourself. What you are building is not only for you—it impacts your family and the people connected to your life. Your legacy is being shaped right now in the decisions you make today. You are not walking alone; God is with you every step. He is guiding you, providing for you, and continuing to develop you as you walk this out.

The steps of a good man are ordered by the Lord
(Proverbs 37:23 NKJV).

Stay consistent. Walk in obedience. Be willing to grow. Build something that lasts. Stay grounded in truth and aligned with God. Most importantly, keep going, even when it feels slow and challenging.

It's your turn now to take what you've learned and apply it, to move with intention, and to trust God more deeply. It's your turn to build kingdom wealth.

Where you are today is not your final destination. God is still working. He is still building. And as you stay faithful in this process, you will begin to see the fruit of it in ways you may not even expect.

Now, go build kingdom wealth!

MORE WPP ANTHOLOGIES!

God placed something valuable inside you, something meant to influence and impact the world. *Kingdom LeadHERship: Stepping Joyfully Into God's Calling* is a collection of voices of women who have said yes to God in various seasons and circumstances, which will encourage and propel you into your calling.

Like the mighty bison that charge directly into approaching storms, true leaders do something extraordinary—they run toward the chaos. The stories in *Unstoppable Leaders* feature faithful men who discovered that God's strength is perfected in weakness. And how ordinary challenges become extraordinary breakthroughs when faced with Biblical courage.

Faith Unchained: Climbing to Freedom by God's Grace is more than a book; it's a lifeline for weary hearts ready to rise. On these pages, you'll discover powerful testimonies from women who have walked through fire and found freedom. The words within don't present a quick fix; they offer hope and healing.

The stories and teachings in *Restoration* will fill you with hope as you witness God's steady and sure hand at work. Although we may feel like we've lost everything, we can stand strong, knowing God will bring beauty from the ashes of our lives. There is no need to despair—God's restoration will begin the moment you give your heart and circumstances to Him.

Men, families, communities, and countries must be on guard as courageous and battle-ready warriors. Men of God are each commissioned to be vigilant conquerors, prepared to lead the fight to overcome evil. The valiant authors in *Fit 2 Fight* share how they have overcome using the weapons that ensure victory no matter what we face.

God longs for you to have ferocious faith grounded in His unwavering love. Get ready to be encouraged as you open the pages of *Unshakable: God Will Sustain You.* Through true stories written by faithful and resilient women, you will witness God's sustaining power available to those who rely on Him.

The authors of *Unseen: You Are Not Alone* share their struggles of feeling isolated and unnoticed and detail how our awesome God helped them overcome every obstacle to find what truly matters: Him. These stories and devotional teachings shed light on the truth of your significance and value. You are never alone!

Despite all the adversities we face throughout our lives, God is the source of our hope. As you read the pages of this book, you will see how God brings *Hope Alive* to every person who is yearning for a reason to go on. Like a broken tree in a dark place is primed for new growth, God can use the rich soil of your dark place to prepare new life to sprout in you.

The authors of *Miracle Mindset: Finding Hope in the Chaos,* have experienced the wonders of God's provision, protection, and guidance. These stories and teachings will ignite a spark within you, propelling you to encounter the marvel of God's miracles, even in the chaos.

Life is full of storms and rough waters. The stories in *Navigating Your Storm: By United Men* of Honor will give you the ability to see the light of God and navigate your storm victoriously.

With *Joy Unspeakable: Regardless of Your Circumstances,* you will learn how joy and sorrow can dance together during adversity. The words in this book will encourage, inspire, motivate, and give you hope, joy, and peace.

Surrendered: Yielded With Purpose will help you recognize with awe that surrendering to God is far more effective than striving alone. When we let go of our own attempts to earn God's favor and rely on Jesus Christ, we receive a deeper intimacy with Him and a greater power to serve Him.

United Men of Honor: Overcoming Adversity Through Faith will help you armor up, become fit to fight, and move forward with what it takes to be an honorable leader. Over twenty authors in this book share their accounts of God's provision, care, and power as they proclaim His Word.

Embrace the Journey: Your Path to Spiritual Growth will strengthen and empower you to step boldly in faith. These stories, along with expertly placed expositional teachings will remind you that no matter what we encounter, we can always look to God, trusting HIS provision, strength, and direction.

Victories: Claiming Freedom in Christ presents expository teaching coupled with individual stories that testify to battles conquered victoriously through the power of Jesus Christ. The words in this book will motivate and inspire you and give you hope as God awakens you to your victory!

WPP's Mission

World Publishing and Productions was birthed in obedience to God's call. Our mission is to empower writers to walk in their God-given purpose as they share their God story with the world. We offer one-on-one coaching and a complete publishing experience. To find out more about how we can help you become a published author or to purchase books written to share God's glory, please visit: worldpublishingandproductions.com

More than ever, the church needs believers to step into the God-ordained servant roles Jesus has called and commissioned us to fill. *Feeding Jesus' Sheep* will empower readers to step out in faith, overcome hesitations and fears, and dance in victory.

Don't Let Misunderstanding Win empowers you to transform the interactions in all your relationships, shifting them from adversarial to win/win partnerships. Stop being driven by a scarcity mindset, and begin living from a place of abundance.

From the award-winning, bestselling *I'm Sober... So Now What?* series, comes *Unity in Recovery*—a powerful next step for anyone seeking deeper healing after addiction. This book goes beyond staying sober and explores what it means to live in true connection—with ourselves and with others.

Who Is Able? The Dana Louise Cryer Story is an incredible journey of tremendous pain, pierced by tumultuous circumstances and filled with twists and turns. God's incredible love transforms this true-life survival account into a miraculous outcome of total freedom. This book will leave you breathless and in tears at what only God can do.

At seventeen, Audrey Marie experienced a sudden and relentless excruciating firestorm of pain. *Chronically Unstoppable* tells of her true-life journey as she faced pain, developed strength, and battled forward with hope.

The world has become a place where we don't have a millisecond to think for ourselves, often leaving us feeling lost or overwhelmed. That is why Max Gold wrote *Planestorming!*—a straightforward guide to help you evaluate and change your life for the better. It's time to get to work and make the rest of your life the BEST of your life.

Riley Rossey is not your everyday bullied student, but one who discovers how to utilize his talents to assist other shy and picked-on individuals. Journey with Riley as he meets bullying head-on and becomes a God-given blessing to so many in *The Bullied Student Who Changed All the Rules* by Robert M. Fishbein.

www.ingramcontent.com/pod-product-compliance
Lightning Source LLC
LaVergne TN
LVHW052227200926
848481LV00001B/232